St. Mary's Church, V

(formerly The Church of the Blessed Virg

St. Mary's - October 1909 (fig.1).

900 Years of Noble History

Cyril F. Hearn

Leslie G. Dingley

Book Vault Publishing

St. Mary's Church, Whaplode. 900 Years of Noble History

ISBN: 9781804678077
Perfect Bound

First published in 2024 by bookvault Publishing, Peterborough, United Kingdom.

An Environmentally friendly book printed and bound in England by bookvault, powered by printondemand-worldwide

Foreword

By the Rt. Hon. Sir John Hayes CBE MP

Member of Parliament for South Holland and the Deepings

Lincolnshire boasts some of the nation's most splendid churches. Indeed, in England's Thousand Best Churches, Simon Jenkins concludes that our county betters others in enjoying many of the finest of them, with the Church of the Blessed Virgin St. Mary, Whaplode standing proudly amongst those listed.

Much more than a place of worship, important thought that is, each church represents a local community's expression of Christian faith in local life. Yet village churches stand and speak of still more; being pillars of communities, points of reference, hope and meaning which, by their very age and status, symbolise the particularity of places. As all around it changes, the church at the heart of Whaplode remains a steadying presence, mitigating what alters.

From its proud tower to the rounded pillars in the west end of the Nave, to the complete pre-Reformation Altar Stone and the splendid Irby Tomb, St. Mary's Whaplode is a gem. Whilst the essence of the building we know now dates from the 12th century, a church has been situated in Whaplode since the Anglo Saxons gathered for the Wapentake.

What lies in the pages of this 'Noble History' is a record of a place, enjoyed and endeared by countless generations of local people, lovingly and meticulously compiled by former Churchwarden Cyril Hearn. I have long been proud to know and admire this splendid church, which is a blessed expression of faith, devotion, and community. Our church is treasured in the way which I hope this lovely book will be too.

Preface

By Cyril F. Hearn - Local Historian

Myself in the Norman Nave of the Church (fig.2).

I hail from Liverpool, and spent ten years in the RAF, and thereafter worked in the motor industry for Ford. I moved to Whaplode in the late 1990's, and having already developed a keen interest in history, one day I walked into St. Mary's Church, and just fell in love with this historic building, its history and that of Whaplode. I served as Churchwarden for 4/5 years and for the last 20 years I have researched the village, and its noble church which, in its Norman form, is now nearing 900 years old.

My research has involved trawling through many academic documents and historical books, consulting with Cambridge, Oxford and Durham Universities, The British Library and figures such as Professor McNcil from York University, 'one of the most prolific historians in ancient and medieval church history', and in the course of so doing gaining support and encouragement from local enthusiasts in the development of the history of not only the Church, but also Whaplode, itself, through the auspices of the Whaplode Local History Group.

When you walk into St. Mary's you get a wow factor – the immense pillars (supporting the grand arches inside the building) belong in a cathedral. They do not belong in a village church of Medieval times, and yet here they are. Back then, Whaplode was a town with a larger population than Spalding or Holbeach, and it housed a harbour that traded with the continent long before Boston. It was one of three islands within a great fen, the others being Crowland and Thorney. Thorney has an Abbey, Crowland has an Abbey, and it is very plausible that the original plan was to build an abbey here at Whaplode. It is believed that there was once a Saxon church built on the site of the current building. The stone used to build the present church is said to have been brought from Barnack by barge and transported down the Fen rivers and causeways.

Aside from the overall architectural magnificence, inside the church are two stone $12^{th} - 13^{th}$ century coffins that were discovered when part of the floor of the south aisle collapsed in the 1850s. The coffins each contained a priest, which is known because of the chalice and paten (small dish used to hold bread during the Eucharist) on the breast, and I challenge anyone to locate another one that has such an elaborately decorated coffin cover atop such as can be seen on one of them - since even Westminster Abbey does not have one of such design.

Our 'jewel in the crown' is the Altar Stone - the "Mensa Tablet" - which we believe dates back to the Saxon period and is still in one complete piece with a cross in each corner and one in the centre which was believed to have been done by a bishop on the day it was consecrated.

Amongst the many other features, there is the distinctive chancel arch which reflects the Norman influence amidst the enormous pillars, and the magnificent tomb of the politician Sir Anthony Irby and his wife Lady Elizabeth Irby, a prominent family who lived in Whaplode.

There is a wealth of history within the walls, and I hope that this book will convey to those of you who read it the same pleasure and sense of affinity with its subject that it continues to afford me, and that you will be able to gain a lively understanding of the colourful history of the noble Church of St Mary's, Whaplode.

Indeed, to add to your further interest and wider appreciation, there will also be available, in due course, its 'sister' book, "Whaplode a journey: Medieval times to the 21st century".

Enjoy.

Contents

Page No.

CONTENTS

CONTENTS

CONTENTS

CONTENTS

CONTENTS

Acknowledgements

To construct a book covering such a wide topic many hours have been spent researching the subject, together with reading how others have viewed the village of Whaplode and its surrounding area, and most particularly, its impressive church - St. Mary's.

Over the years I have gleaned valuable information from the two principal lecturers from Heritage Lincolnshire, namely Tom Lane and Dave Start for their broad knowledge of the subject covering the ancient topography of the Whaplode area in the Lincolnshire Fens, especially the area of Salt manufacturing. I am also grateful for the guidance provided by the now deceased Dorothy M. Owen for her specialist knowledge regarding the religious orders from Medieval times in her book *'Church and Society in Medieval Lincolnshire'* as part of the History of Lincolnshire series.

As regards the history of the Church there have been countless contacts from a wide area of academia, from Cambridge and Oxford, Lincoln, the British Museum, the British Archives, the British Library, and other academic sources, where possible these references have been identified in the bibliography, or within the text. In some instances, individuals have been the source of material, and again where possible these are acknowledged, accordingly. Every effort has been made to ensure the authenticity of information, but there may be areas where information may be regarded as anecdotal and is therefore identified as such.

Much of the material such as the correspondence between the Curator of the Royal Armouries Tower of London, and the Reverend William Henry Gibb (Vicar of St Mary's 1953-1960), was passed to me for safe keeping by the local retired Schoolmaster Ron Clare who was also a past Churchwarden (these documents are now kept in a safe in the Church).

For inspiration in collating, gathering, and researching the subject matter, I would like to acknowledge the part played by Reverend David Carney, which followed a conversation in his study early in my relocation to the area, and my becoming part of the congregation at St Mary's Church, also to John Lord, and a colleague of his, who worked at the Department for Conservation and Preservation at Lincoln University.

In addition, access to the Church's Vestry records held on site, and / or housed at Lincolnshire Archives, would not have been possible without the kind approval of the Parochial Church Council of St. Mary's Church, Whaplode.

ACKNOWLEDGEMENTS

Also, our appreciative thanks to the University of Durham "The Corpus of Anglo-Saxon Stone Sculpture Project" under the guidance of the late Professor Dame Rosemary Cramp and her team(s), and, in particular, Professor David Stoker, and Professor Paul Everson, for their permission to reproduce in full their detailed analyses and conclusions surrounding the examination of the items of 'Saxon' burial stonework found in and around St. Mary's Church.

Furthermore, grateful thanks are due to the Spalding Gentlemen's Society for their co-operation in providing access to one of the few available copies of Revd. John Rhodes public statement issued in October 1900 *"The Tithe Payers of Whaplode versus (The Johnson Foundation) Uppingham School"* and their permission to include extracts therefrom.

All photographs have been taken either by me, Leslie Dingley, or David Brennan, unless otherwise accredited where it has been possible to identify the source. If not known, it is stated as such.

Finally, it would have been an impossible task to have not only gleaned the information but interpreted it into a readable book without the able assistance of my co-author Leslie Dingley, who has broadened the research from my original manuscript of 2016 into areas not previously covered by my original work. Leslie relocated to the village in 2018, and during the time since has collated a great deal of the original research into the history of the church, to such an extent that he had the basis of a book almost complete, whereupon we concluded that, since there was so much more that should be included regarding the history of Whaplode, and St. Mary's Church, with this in mind, a collaboration would provide the most beneficial outcome.

Cyril F. Hearn.
January 2024.

List of illustrations

Cover photograph - St Mary's Church. Aerial view (CH.07.2022)

PART TWO

Introduction

The scope of this book concentrates on both the historical background of the area known today as Whaplode, Whaplode St. Catherine and Saracen's Head, near Spalding, Lincolnshire, belonging to the Elloe Deanery, which helped shape the burgeoning Medieval Town of Whaplode that the area sustained in the early and later Middle Ages, and that of its noble ecclesiastical structure, St Mary's Church ("St. Mary's"), which, prior to the Reformation, was known as The Church of the Blessed Virgin St. Mary, Whaplode.

The name Whaplode is derived from the original spelling of 'Copoloda' which has undergone several variations down the years, from 'Copalade'; 'Coppelade'; 'Capplode'; changing to the usage of 'Quaplod'; 'Quappelad'; 'Qwappelad'; 'Quaphlode'; 'Quappelode'; 'Quappladde'; 'Quapplade' through the 12th - 14th centuries, and also 'Qwaplode' in 1416; and then 'Quaplode'; 'Hoplode'; 'Waplod' and 'Whapload' variously during the Tudor period, finally evolving as 'Whaplode'.

St. Mary's is not only so impressive from the outside, but also on entering it one is overcome by the sheer size and 'Minster' feel to this historic building, which is now nearing 900 years old since its consecration, and over this period there have been numerous enlivened encounters between the clergy of St. Mary's and the Abbots of Crowland under whose 'control' the Church fully existed until 1539, when the Abbey was dissolved. Thereafter, after a short period under the jurisdiction of the Bishop(s) of Lincoln, it was then taken over by the Crown. However, in 1594, the lay responsibility for the Chancel of St. Mary's Church was given to the Archdeacon of Leicester (Robert Johnson), and it was on his death in 1625 that such responsibility passed to the Governors of Uppingham School, under the jurisdiction of Queen Elizabeth I. However, the subsequent 300 years continued to produce controversy, and, latterly, considerable neglect of the Chancel.

Following the ceding of responsibility for the Chancel back to the Crown in 1909, today it resides under the Archdiocese of Lincoln, with the status akin to that attributable to a 'Royal Peculiar' church; such that any stipendiary Vicar of Whaplode requires the Monarch's specific approval, via The Lord Chancellor's patronage, of appointment and subsequent departure.

The architectural history of St. Mary's is of immense importance because of what historians generally now believe to be its earlier Saxon origins, and its subsequent Norman development, and it can rightfully be regarded as a unique 'jewel' in the crown of Lincolnshire's splendid collection of Abbeys and Churches.

There is so much to marvel at within the church, and it has been said there is a 'magical' atmosphere therewithin, and visitors from all over the world continue to enjoy their experience of the St. Mary's 'time machine' through the many centuries of its existence. Without doubt this magnificent church is a 'sleeping giant' in architectural terms, and we sincerely hope that this book will provide an entertaining and interesting read and provide you with an increased appreciation of not only the history of Whaplode, but also that of its distinctive and ancient church of St. Mary's. The book is divided into two sections:

Part One provides the background of the ancient & medieval history of the area surrounding the Parish of Whaplode St. Mary's, embracing the notable moments in the history of the Church, especially its fraught relationship with the Abbey of Crowland, through post Reformation reform, and its subsequent turbulent years of 'fabric' deterioration, until undergoing degrees of restoration in 1909, and beyond, concluding with a selection of more recent events involving the clergy. It also delivers an insight into the history behind all other significant non-architectural features to be found in the Church, including specific works of art, which enhance the fabric of this wonderful Church.

Part Two deals with the important historical documented architectural features and building developments of St. Mary's from its Saxon/Norman origins to date, including commentary on its notable monuments, and other interesting artefacts to be found therein.

Both sections are presented as a compilation from many viewpoints, observations, architecturally, or otherwise; drawn from many sources; Cyril Hearn's own comprehensive research, and many other historians' books, magazines, professional organisations, and periodicals, et al; which provide analyses and/or comments by such historians, building experts, and other contributors. All of which serve to enhance a comprehensive and colourful journey down the years of this wonderful noble church.

Cyril Hearn – Les Dingley.

PART ONE
1.

South Holland and the early Anglo-Saxon
and Roman settlements

An insight into the origins of the early inhabitants of South Holland and surrounding fen areas is provided by H.E. Hallam in *'Occasional Papers No. 6, The New Lands of Elloe'* - Department of English Local History, published by the University College of Leicester in 1954, as follows:

THE ANGLO-SAXON SETTLEMENT OF SOUTH HOLLAND

"Between the first and fourth centuries of our era the Lincolnshire Fenland supported a considerable population of Britons. About a hundred of their hamlets, varying from two or three to a dozen settlement sites, appear on the aerial photographs of South Holland and Kesteven, and their traces still occur in the ploughed fields. No settlement sites appear north of the Hurdletree Bank, in South Holland, and the appearance of Romano-British debris under several feet of estuarine silt in Spalding suggests that the occupation of the Fenland came to a watery end during the fourth and fifth centuries. This probability is important for the study of the settlement of Holland by the Anglo-Saxons, for it means that the earliest invaders would find the mouths of the wash rivers very unsuitable places for settlement. The Anglo-Saxon villages are all on the deposit of mineral alluvium laid down probably in the years after the end of Roman rule in Britain, and we should therefore expect the settlement to be late. Pagan Anglo-Saxon remains occur at Sleaford, Stamford, and Peterborough, which are the first convenient landing places on the Slea, the Welland and the Nene. Nobody has found such remains in Holland, so that the settlers must have been already Christian when they came."

"A few moments' study of the 2½-inch Ordnance Survey map will produce an interesting conjecture on the physical appearance of seventh-century Holland. The traces of ancient sewers and drains form the outlines of a series of spurs or fingers of mineral alluvium, with deep tidal creeks running between them. To these small ridges came the settlers and founded Whaplode, the 'eel-pout stream;' Holbeach, the 'deep-river;' Fleet, the 'tidal stream;' and Gedney, 'Gydda's island.' On the largest spur at the mouth of the Nene-Ouse they settled Lutton, the 'pool town,' with its hamlet Sutton on the south side. The name Holland itself is Anglo-Saxon and seems to mean 'the high land.' The description is apt, for villages of the silt band are several feet higher

1

than the peat fens to the west. The village names support the archaeological evidence by suggesting that the Anglo-Saxons did not settle heavily in Holland until the seventh century. There are three 'ingas' place names, Spalding, Quadring, and perhaps Stenning. The 'Spaldas' appear in the Tribal Hidage of the seventh century. They had six hundred hides of land and were perhaps the people whom later writers styled the 'Men of Holland.' Their name means 'the dwellers by the gulf', which was the area at the tidal mouth of the Welland then much wider than it is now. Spalding is the geographical centre of the county, and its point of focus from very early times."

"Here was Holland's only market in 1086, and Ivo de Taillebois, the Conqueror's Lord of Holland, raised his castle here to guard the lowest crossing of the river. Quadring is the settlement of the 'Haeferingas dwelling in the mud'. This interpretation helps to explain why so few early place names survive, and why two of the three are in Kirton wapentake. The rest of Holland was perhaps still unfit for settlement, but Stenning and Quadring could provide some sort of poor lodgement for a few families, since they were on the raised silt shores of Holland's main estuary, Bicker Haven. Before the twelfth century Bicker Haven seems to have been the outlet of the Slea and the Witham, and its banks were always drier and more prosperous than the rest of the county."

"The late Anglo-Saxon place names, of the seventh century, are well scattered throughout Holland. In Skirbeck wapentake, north of the Witham, there are Butterwick, Frieston, and Leverton. In Kirton wapentake, between the Witham and the Glen, there are Cheal, Doningtom, Dowdyke, Drayton, Frampton, Riskenton, Swineshead and Wyberton."

"In Elloe Wapentake {see below: Elloe Wapentake} *between the Glen and the Nene, there are Gedney, Holbeach, Lutton, Sutton, Weston and Whaplode. These names indicate a heavy Anglo-Saxon settlement in the seventh century, and the one literary source for the pre-Conquest history of the Lincolnshire Fenland is the extraordinary Life of St. Guthlac by the monk Felix."*
[1] (See below-St. Guthlac and the Abbey of Crowland).

With the area having been supplied with so many nutrients accumulated over the centuries from both the debris from the sea-life and the alluvial drain off from the hinterland, much of the soil is of the finest quality, hence the rush to reclaim lands and generate ideal farm land, not just in recent times, but as long ago as during the Roman occupation (evidence of such was found in a field that is now part of Whaplode Drove, where great mounds of Roman pottery shards were discovered during the 19th century).

On seeing the topography of the seabed along the North Sea, between Great
Britain and the near Continent, it is evident that there were raised areas,
presumably where various tribes settled, along with an enormous river delta
that stretched from the west coast of Norway right through the centre of the
forested lands and ending up adjacent to the area we now know as 'The Wash'.
Within the Wash delta, Whaplode can be seen to be present on one of these
land banks surrounded by now extinct water courses (fig.3).

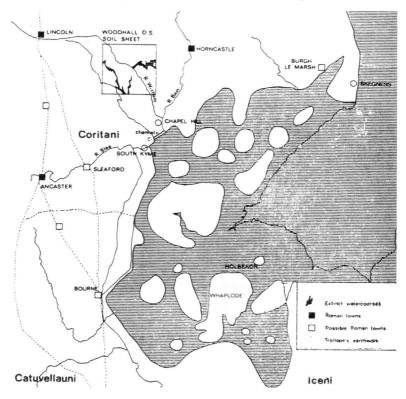

Pre-Roman era map - Lincolnshire Fens (Unknown source) (fig.3)

THE ROMAN INFLUENCE

Under the stewardship of the Romans the Lincolnshire Fens underwent
fundamental change. Having introduced the local inhabitants to square roomed
buildings instead of the traditional round houses (pre-Roman inhabitants built
their dwellings in a circular shape, with a deep trench arcing around from either
side of the main entrance), they also changed the way local people farmed salt
from the nearby sea. Instead of small individual salt-pans, the Romans, quickly
recognising the importance of salt as a bartering commodity, took control and
made it a 'state-controlled' area, including the salt manufacturing. It is said

3

that the huge piles of waste near the saltpans took on the shape and size of irregular hills; thus, giving rise to such village names as Weston Hills, Gedney Hill and other similar places. Salt was such a prized commodity, its true value to the ancient people who inhabited the region was probably the one thing that helped them survive the harsh conditions, especially in winter times when the supply of fresh meat would be so scarce. Salt was not only used to preserve meat and fish stocks, but it was also used for cleansing flesh wounds and a thousand other purposes.

The Romans also introduced vast areas of reclaimed land from near the sea by strengthening and reinforcing the defensive sea banks, perhaps this is reflected today with their association with the more familiar name of the 'Roman Bank' running southwards from Lincoln through many villages and market towns. It is understood that during the Roman occupation the North Sea and Wash penetrated much further inland than they do today, again with suggested being in evidence in the villages of Surfleet-Seas-End, and Moulton-Seas-End, and the following map (fig.4) illustrates the area covered with the dotted lines, which is thought to be the coastline when the Romans occupied the area.

One aspect of the area which has over the years attracted considerable debate is that of the origin of Car(Carr)s Dyke, as to whether it was in existence (certainly parts of it) pre-Roman era (the unearthing of Saxon pottery during excavations along the dyke would appear to support an earlier occupation in particular areas), and/or it was predominantly adapted / constructed by the Romans during the 1st or early 2nd century, and in support of this Stukeley makes the following assessment *"Carsdike must have been projected and done by Agricola* {Roman Governor of Britain 78-93AD} *on his conquest of Scotland."* And when *"the Sixth Legion came to Britain with Hadrian* {Emperor 117-138 AD} *it was concerned with perfecting the Carsdike navigation to Peterborough."*[2]

Importantly, it is one of the greatest works of this county, a considerable canal, or drain, extending some 40-50 miles (albeit, depending on the interpretation of inter-linking extensions, some commentators attribute its length to be close to 85 miles) across the county, from the river Nene, nr. Peterborough, (equally, others attribute the start to be at the river Welland) to the river Witham, near Lincoln.[3] & [4]

Anecdotally, it is also said to be known as the 'Bell-Dyke,' from a tradition that the original 'Great Tom' bell of Lincoln Cathedral was floated on a raft, or boat, on this canal to its destination at the Cathedral, the bell being a gift 'from the Abbot of Peterborough to the Cathedral'.[5]

It is also interesting to see on this map (fig. 4) the Whaplode Fleet or river (as highlighted in yellow). It is believed that during the period following the Roman occupation there were three major trading posts along this area of coastline, these being Kings Lynn in the south, Whaplode in the centre of the coastline and Bicker Haven in the north (Boston as a port was not properly developed until early in the 14th century).

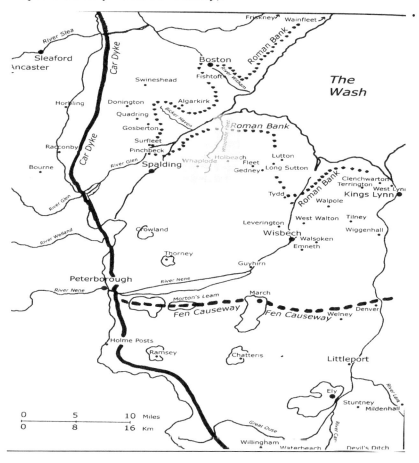

Fenland areas. (John Elms – amateur cartographer) (fig.4).

The Romans were also responsible for creating some of the larger conurbations in this part of the country, a prime example being Lincoln. This was originally a Roman Army Garrison Fort at a place called 'Lindum' which quickly attracted peddlers and traders who sought to earn their livelihoods through selling products to the Roman soldiers. As these settled near the garrison fort, the Roman authorities encouraged them to build permanent homes, such that the area became known as the 'Colony.' It was soon corrupted to a combination of both the Roman name 'Lindum' and 'Colony' - becoming Lincoln. (Notably, the subsequent importance of Lincoln as a local centre is implied by the fact that its early English name *Lindcolun* was derived from its late British name of *Lingolun*). [6]

Although this strengthening, reinforcing and recovery work aided the preservation of reclaimed land from the sea, it did not preclude some of the areas being flooded from the numerous rivers and creeks that naturally converge on the area as they flooded during the spring spate of ice melt. Rather than just accept the inevitable, another series of inland banks were introduced to keep the bog and newly formed fens from flooding the villages and market towns. Part of the evidence for this inland bank can be seen through Jekyll's Bank, Old Fendike Road and Hurdletree Bank; constructed to keep the newly claimed farmland from severe flooding; however, these came after the area was handed back to the local inhabitants, whether they be families derived from the Roman occupation, Scandinavians or travelling tribes.

All this work meant that new and better systems for draining the excess waters away from the threatened villages and towns had to be introduced and, although there is evidence that the Roman occupiers made satisfactory progress with their channels and dykes, the real problems were not solved until the arrival of the expert dyke and dam builders from Holland. Many of the drains and dykes still bear reference to the names of these experts, e.g., Vernatt's Drain.

THE CONCENTRATON OF RELIGIOUS ESTABLISHMENTS WITHIN THE CHANGING COASTLINE

Latterly, when describing the ancient coastlines around Whaplode, unfortunately, it is easy to overlook just how many churches were dotted around the area. In his book *'In Fen Country Heaven'* Edward Storey mentions the Lincolnshire churches that lined the then ancient (Middle Ages) coastline before the major land reclamations, citing Holbeach, Fleet, Gedney and Long Sutton,[7] but as one can see from a map of 1645 (fig.5) there were, in fact, many other churches lining the then coastline, namely, Wycombe Abbey, Weston, Moulton, Whaplode, and Lutton, as well as Sutton St Mary's, which later became Long Sutton.

Extract above showing South Holland coastline - from 'REGIONES
INUNDATAE' (Map of the Fens) by Joan Blaeu, c.1645-1672 (fig.5).

The above map by Joan Blaeu is probably based on a now lost manuscript map
by William Hayward and shows the Fens before they were drained by
Cornelius Vermuyden in the 1650s.[8]

EARLY EVIDENCE OF RELIGIOUS CONVERSION AND TRIBAL
SETTLEMENTS IN THE FENS

In describing the area South Holland, many people make the natural
assumption that having been occupied by so many people from Holland during
the 17th and 18th century, who participated in the many draining projects, the
derivation is attributed to this. However, the real reason is two-fold, firstly, and
primarily, as previously ascribed to by Hallam, that of post seventh century
Anglo-Saxon settlement influences in Holland (the 'High Land'- not needing
drainage, and therefore the area of 'South Highland' was later corrupted into
the district of South Holland), and, secondly, the abundance of religious houses

7

found here prior to and after the Norman invasion in the middle part of the 11th century. It is estimated that with over 140 religious houses and 650+ churches (not including all the outlying chapels associated with the mother churches), there were at one time over 900 places solely devoted to religion in Lincolnshire. It is no wonder that part of it was known as 'Holy land,' from which the corruption Holland lends itself to further interpretation.

From a religious perspective, Lincolnshire also lays claim to be the originator of the only English Religious Order, that of the Gilbertines at Sempringham, established in the latter part of the 12th century, and the only order to embrace both men and women housed together (in separate parts of the same building). Further evidence for the origin of the name not belonging to the settlement of Dutch Engineers in the 17th and 18th centuries comes from the contents of 'The Gough Map' (the earliest road map of Great Britain) with the descriptions for Lincolnshire place names therewithin. The bulk of the content for which is taken from the Bodleian Library's (Oxford) reprint of E.J.S. Parson's *The Map of Great Britain circa AD 1360*', making it one of the oldest formalised maps in existence being over six and a half centuries old.

As highlighted earlier, South Holland consists of almost entirely of alluvial land and is abounded by the river Welland on the west, the coast of the Wash on the north and east, and the South Holland or Shire Drain on the south, which separates it from the Bedford Level.

The central portion, about 5 miles in width, lying on the north and south sides of the main road leading from Spalding to Sutton St. Mary, was enclosed by the banks constructed during the Roman occupation, the northern bank still being known as the *Roman Bank*, as previously mentioned, and the southern bank as the *Ravens Bank.*

On the south of the Ravens bank was a tract of low fen land subject to inundation from any overflowing of the Welland and the Nene, and north of the Roman Bank was the coast of the Wash. The general features and characteristics of the central portions show that it was inhabited in early times, and there are also remains of Roman *Castella (water distribution works)* at Whaplode Drove and Gedney Hill. The villages are all situated in this central portion, and, from the names which they now bear, show that they owe their original settlement to the Saxons, as highlighted by Hallam, in particular, the termination *ton* in Weston, Moulton, Lutton, and Sutton, denoting that they were originally settlements of Saxon Chiefs; the termination *lode* of Whaplode refers to the stream that runs through it; and Gedney is derived from the Saxon Family name of Geden or Gedden. [9]

It does seem, therefore, extremely probable that at Whaplode there existed an early Saxon settlement, not least when one considers the remnants of Saxon Burial stone that have been found in and around St. Mary's, which together with the existence of the church's 'Saxon' Altar stone, gives credence to the view that there did exist a Saxon church (whether wooden/stone), at one time, it being the predecessor to the current 'Norman' Church of St. Mary's, in Whaplode. (See **Part Two**: 1. Early Monastic Estates, and St. Mary's Anglo-Saxon Heritage - Whaplode's Saxon Church).

2.
Whaplode: At the time of the Domesday Book Records

WHAPLODE – ITS EARLY BEGINNINGS

Thomas Allen provides in his book the following description of 'early' Whaplode: *"Whaplode is a village about 2.1 miles west of Holbeach. This town is ancient, and it is distinguished as having been an appendage to the abbey of Crowland, by the names Cappelade, Quappelade, and Quaphlode; the word lade, or its equivalent lode, seems to imply that one of the principal outlets from Crowland waters, was by this cape, or headland, and hence the name of the place, Cappelode."*[10]

A similar description by way of reference to the DB, is provided by WFR in his book, as follows- *"In the Domesday Book this is spelt Quappelode, the village being built on a spit of land elevated above the fens and encircled by drains, or lodes, to keep it free from inundation."*[11]

Allen continues - *"Whaplode, in its original state, was inhabited by a few fishermen, who had erected their huts on this eminence, for the purpose of carrying on their daily employments of fishing and fowling with more convenience than they could otherwise have done by coming from a more distant situation. For this privilege, some acknowledgement was made annually, or perhaps oftener, to the abbot of Crowland for the time being, as lord paramount of these domains; and, as a proof of this statement, we may observe that the principal Manor in this parish still retains the name of Whaplode Abbatis."* {Interestingly, later use of the word (or a derivation of it - Abbatis) as a name, would have indicated a village with a defensive framework surrounding it, partially or fully, arranged on the outside of ditches, consisting of a barrier of felled or live trees with branches sharpened pointing outwards. Such a boundary protection, which would have served to deter intruders to the village, was known as an Abattis, was, latterly, attributed as another method of opposing the enemy's access to a field fortification - *"The First Principles of Field Fortification. Charles Augustus Struensee. London, 1800. Pages, 47, 48"*}.

"As the inhabitants of this cheerless spot were manifestly of the lowest order of mankind, it became necessary, towards their mental improvement, to imbue their minds with the principles of religion and morality; for, in all ages of the world, this has been the most effectual polisher of a barbarous people. To effect so useful and desirable a purpose, one of the early abbots of Crowland erected a small chapel for divine worship, and although we have no

authentic records of the time when it was built or the materials of which it was constructed, yet there is little doubt but that it was originally formed of wood, and covered with thatch, as Spalding and many others in the same jurisdiction are known to have been. When the waters began to retreat, and dry land appeared in this neighbourhood, it became the residence of people of more eminence, such as the Irby and Maynard families, and the wooden chapel was then taken down, and the present stone church erected in its room. King John, when on his march from Lynn to Swineshead a short time previous to his death, established a toll at Holbeach bridge, which is still taken of all persons passing over it (excepting the fishermen of Whaplode and Fleet) during one fortnight before, and one fortnight after Michaelmas, in every year." [12]

This commentary expressed by TA in his book provides an insight into the early life of Whaplode and its inhabitants, albeit little suggestion of the church's Saxon origins.

It is known from the map held at Ayscoughfee Hall that Whaplode was the site of one of three islands within the Great Fen that ran from the west of Pinchbeck, down through southern Lincolnshire and on into parts of Cambridgeshire – the other two islands being located at Thorney and Crowland. However, whilst there are several references to Whaplode in the 'Domesday Survey' (1086) (Refer to pages 886, 902, 906 and 951 therein); these references relate to the ownership of land by Earl Aelfgar (Ælfgar) and Count Alan, and the fact that St. Guthlac of Crowland, and Guy de Craon (Creon) (see below: 3. Influential Landowners in South Holland post the Norman Conquest) also had land in Whaplode, however, there is no mention of the Saxon Church, which is not surprising since the DB was not meant to concentrate on Churches, it was more focused on the ownership of property.

The Abbey of Croyland (Crowland) functioned as the Mother Church for many centuries within the fenland area, its influence having been established in the later part of the eighth century and given the fact that several rivers and streams served the area surrounding Whaplode at the time of the establishment of Crowland Abbey this provided an ideal site for the transportation of goods and cattle from the coastal areas into the hinterland. This proximity of Whaplode 'marshland' to the sea, in early medieval times, was noted in a transfer of land by Lambert D'Oyry, son of Waleran D'Oyry of Whaplode, to Spalding Priory in 1208 (See Appendix II. The Families of De Craon and D'Oyry: II.B. D'Oyry).

Over the centuries, since land had been reclaimed from the sea, it is difficult to plot the precise route of the early medieval Whaplode river. However, given the river 'presence' in the vicinity it can be understood why

Whaplode became an early 'port' for these transportation activities. The mouth of the Whaplode river was to be seen in the area known as 'Saracen's Head', and the river (or 'Whaplode broads' as it became known) meandered, through the village past St. Mary's, inland towards Moulton Chapel, and a dwelling (no longer in situ), situate adjacent to the entrance to St. Mary's churchyard on Church Gate, Whaplode, was hitherto identified, as that of the Harbour Master's accommodation.

Within the last 100 years, as the land has undergone further reclamation, the river has been 'encased' beneath land that has now been built upon, and, where it does surface it flows into the dyke structures.

Extract- Map of Lincolnshire - re Whaplode (Wapland) (fig.6).

Whaplode's medieval position of trading importance is evident from the portrayal on the above map (fig.6): refer 'Wapland'. The sectional extract shown above is taken from a *"Map of Lincolnshire drawn by Humphrey Lhuyd {Lloyd} before his death in 1568 and published in Abraham Ortelius's Atlas in 1573. The map shows the Lincolnshire Wolds for the first time and other areas of local high ground, along with major rivers and key settlements."* https://commons.wikimedia.org/wiki/File:Atlas_Ortelius_KB_PPN36937678 1-010av-010br.jpg

Importantly, given Whaplode's prominence in the early to mid-medieval ages, for such commercial activity, it is quite reasonable to see how the area burgeoned to the point where the population outgrew those of both

Spalding and Holbeach, and lends support to the belief that this was one of the reasons why so many of the aristocracy acquired land in the region, which culminated in their support for St. Mary's, as attested by so many family crests being represented in the church's stained-glass windows, which, sadly, no longer adorn its fabric (see **Part Two** -3. Whaplode's Family Coats of Arms and Stained-Glass Windows).

St Mary's - 1842. Pen & Ink Drawing (fig.7).
Stephen Lewin [TNM, Plate 64]

ST. GUTHLAC AND THE ABBEY OF CROWLAND

The importance of St. Guthlac cannot be underestimated in the development of the Abbey at Crowland, and the subsequent rise of St Mary's as a subordinate 'competitor.'

Guthlac of Crowland (b.Circa.674 - d.11.April.714.CE) was an Anglo-Saxon saint from the Kingdom of Mercia. He is best known for his years spent as a hermit in the Fens region of the East Midlands. Guthlac was born into a noble Mercian family and became a successful soldier and military leader in his teenage years before turning to religious life. He joined the monastic community at Repton in Derbyshire at the age of 24. After two years at Repton, he left to lead the life of a hermit on the island of Crowland. During his years as a hermit, Guthlac became renowned for his holy life and for the miracles he performed. His death is traditionally dated to 11 April 714 CE, which was thereafter celebrated as his feast day. Much of what we know of Guthlac's life comes from the '*Vita Sancti Guthlaci*,' or '*Life of Saint Guthlac*', written by the monk Felix circa 730 CE.

Over the course of the 8th century CE, a monastic community developed at Crowland, following in Guthlac's footsteps. Crowland Abbey was founded in 971 CE, according to the Benedictine Rule, and was dedicated to Saints Mary and Bartholomew, as well as to Guthlac himself. Guthlac was venerated as a prominent local saint ever since, with churches being dedicated to him throughout the area around the Fens in the East Midlands and beyond.[13] The above explains the description of land identified in the Domesday survey of 1086 as belonging to St. Guthlac – a la the Abbots of Crowland Abbey.

Foster provides a translation of the medieval measurement text as regards the Domesday Book, as follows: [14] (See also the formal extracts below of the National Archives original translation). "*Croyland Abbey held manor in Holben (Holbeach) and Copalade (Whaplode). St Guthlac had and has 1 carucate* (an extinct Norman land measurement) *of land rateable to gelt* (the coinage of the day-probably succeeding from the Danegeld - old Norse name for gold payment). *The land is 6 bovates* (the measure of land that could be ploughed by single ox in a year, usually between 10 and 18 acres). *This is now in the demesne* (land attached to a mansion or estate) *1 carucate, and 3 villeins* (tenants/or tenanted land under the feudal system, subject to a lord or tied to a manor, a serf), *having half a carucate and 12 acres of meadow. The annual value in King Edward's time was 20 shillings; it is now the same.*"

In addition, the Domesday Book shows that the Saxon "Earl Ælfgar" (see Appendix I) from whom King William's men had confiscated the lands, had held land up to the time of the Norman Conquest. Foster further translates, as follows: "*Wido de Credun, or Creon,* (otherwise known as Guy de Craon (Creon)) (see below 3. Influential landowners in South Holland post the Norman Conquest), *one of the most fortunate of William's men, had manor in Holbeach and Whaplode. Aleston had 2 carucates and 2 bovates of land rateable to gelt; the land is 12 bovates. Wido has in Whaplode 1 carucate (in demesne) and 4 villeins and 1 bordar with 1 carucate and 10 acres of meadow. The annual value is now £8.0s.0d.*"[15]

It is clear therefore that Whaplode at the time of the Domesday survey held a prominent place in the area under the control of Croyland Abbey, the abbot being the lord of the manor of Whaplode Abbitis (Abattis).

NATIONAL ARCHIVES: THE GREAT DOMESDAY BOOK EXTRACTS
Translations of GREAT DOMESDAY BOOK:

FOLIO 338r

Reference: E 31/2/2/6799

In the same Holbeach and Whaplode, are 5 carucates of land to the geld, which Count Alan held; now they are in the king's hand.

FOLIO 346r

Reference: E 31/2/2/7160 (fig.8)

XI. THE LAND OF ST GUTHLAC OF CROWLAND

In Holbeach and Whaplode, St Guthlac had and has 1 carucate of land to the geld [There is] land for 6 oxen. Now there is 1 plough in demesne: and 3 villans with half a plough, and 12 acres of meadow. TRE worth 20s; now the same.

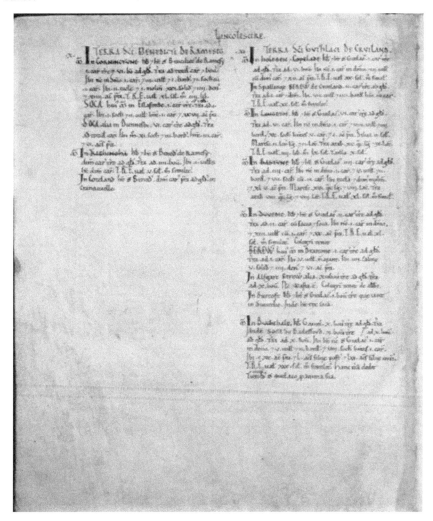

Copy of The National Archives' reference E 31/2/2/7160 (fig.8).

FOLIO 368r

Reference: E 31/2/2/8230

In Holbeach and Whaplode, Alstan had 2 carucates of land 2 bovates to the geld. [There is] land for 12 oxen (pence [sic]. Guy has 1 plough there, and 4 villans and 1 bordar with plough, and 10 acres of meadow. TRE worth 100s; now 8l.

In Spalding, Alstan had 11 bovates of land to the geld. [There is] land [...]. Guy has 1 plough there, and 5 villans and 2 bordars with 1 plough, and a drying-place with salt-pans rendering 4d. TRE, as now, worth 40s.

FOLIO 348v

Reference: E 31/2/2/7256

'ELLOE' WAPPENTAKE (Refer to fig.9)

In Holbeach and Whaplode, Earl AElfgar had 1 carucate of land to the geld. [There is] land for 6 oxen. [it is] a Berewick of Fleet. Count Alan has it, but the king's officers claim it for the use of the king. There are 3 villans with 3 oxen in plough.

In the same places Earl AElfgar had 13 carucates of land 6 bovates to the geld. [There is] land for 9 ploughs and 2 oxen.

WAPPENTAKE (WAPENTAKE)

A 'Wappentake' is ascribed to as being 'assemblies of free men drawn from smaller areas' with the aim of accomplishing the local administration of the shire. The word was Scandinavian, but the institution was not. Most of the 33 wapentakes in the Lincolnshire Domesday have English names (Elloe being one) and the 16 that are Scandinavian in whole, or part, were presumably renamed. The Domesday wapentakes had roots in the distant past, but they were not necessarily the same as they had always been. Some had undergone change, altered by division, combination, or boundary changes over time. They were probably in origin assemblies of the freemen who belonged to the *Lordships*** or royal estates some of which survived as eleventh century *Sokes.***

Several sokes were co-extensive with a wapentake, this may have been because sokes had been enlarged or wapentakes reorganised, and as such, some lordships were originally so large that they comprised several assemblies of freemen. The Scandinavian word *soke* was first used in England in the 10th century, but estates of this kind were much older and had existed in many parts of Britain long before the Scandinavians invaded. Regardless of their origin, with the formation of the Anglo-Saxon kingdoms they were apparently treated as royal, although by the 11th century many were held by laymen or churches.

16

In the 10th century there was a tendency to bring wapentakes, and their equivalents in English England, *the hundreds*, under closer royal control. This led to some renaming, but there is little trace of this in Lincolnshire; only three being named after settlements, all of which were royal estates in 1086 held by the earls before the Conquest. [16]

**Lordships and Sokes.*

In the 11th century a large proportion of the wealth of Lincolnshire gained by the skills and the industry of its people, was paid either as tax to the king or as a tribute to the hierarchy of lords who dominated the economic as well as the social and political life of the region. The lords held estates or manors (the term used in the DB) in which they held land in their own name (demesnes), which was cultivated by tenants, who were obligated to 'work' a set amount of time on the land for the lord. In addition, many manors also had land that was not cultivated by the lord, but owed a 'tribute,' described as a 'soke' (old English *socn,* Latin *soca)*. In the Lincolnshire Domesday, the component parts of many estates are described as *soca.* By a natural extension of the meaning the word came to be used for the whole estate. Many manors had some sokeland, but the description 'soke' is generally reserved for the larger estates that were held under the King by lords who were specially privileged. Sokes were an archaic type of estate, and some of the major sokes of 11th century Lincolnshire can be traced back at least to the 7th century. [17]

ELLOE WAPENTAKE

The tenurial structures of Elloe Wapentake, almost in its entirety, were constituted as a single estate at some period prior to the Conquest. In the map below (fig.9), the shaded 'line' area is the extent of the sea in the 11th century.

During the reign of King Edward the Confessor much of the area was still in the hands of a single lord - Earl AElfgar - who held manors in Tydd, Lutton, and Fleet with various attached Berewick(s) {outlying land belonging to Lords of the Manor for their exclusive use} and sokelands in Gedney and Holbeach and Whaplode which were in the hands of the king in 1086 {refer above Folio 338r}, and the manor of Spalding with appurtenances {rights of way} in Tydd, Pinchbeck, and Holbeach and Moulton which had passed to Ivo Taillebois by the time of the Domesday inquest {see National Archives reference Folio 351v}. The two remaining interests in the wapentake interlock with this extended group and were clearly derived from it. The Abbey of Crowland held a manor in Holbeach and Whaplode, with a berewick in Spalding, and probably sokeland in Pinchbeck, which was similarly granted by Earl AElfgar {refer above Folio 346v}.[18]

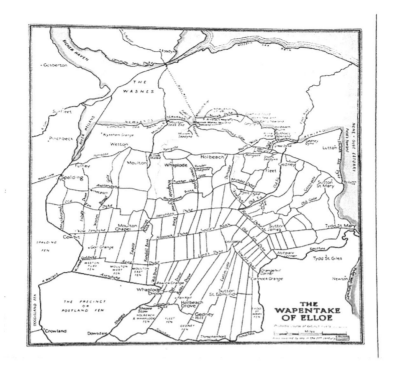

Middle English ELLOE WAPENTAKE Map (undated) (fig.9).
(Source Unknown) (H.E. Hallam – The New Lands of
Elloe: 1954).

View of St. Mary's from SSW (fig.10).

Equally, Æthelstan {Alstsan} held manors in Holbeach, Whaplode and Spalding, with appurtenances in Tydd, Weston/Moulton, and Pinchbeck in an extended estate that was evidently created in much the same way (refer above Folio 368r).

Interestingly, the land held by the Saxon Earl Aelfgar in Elloe Wapentake, as highlighted under the above reference *FOLIO 348v,* which had been confiscated, was passed to Count Alan, who had married a daughter of King William.

In the twelfth century 'The Men of Holland' also claimed the fen to the west as common to the wapentake. On the death of King Henry II in 1189 they invaded Great Postland Fen, which the Abbey of Crowland claimed as part of its patrimony and began to divide it up between them. The long and inconclusive dispute that followed shows that their case was perhaps dubious *['English Justice between the Norman Conquest and the Great Charter 1066-1215.' By Doris M. Stenton. (1964). Pages 154-211.],* but by the same token it stands to demonstrate that South Holland Fen was the undisputed right of the Elloe communities. The point is an important one. At first sight Crowland Abbey's liberties and pretensions within a common community might seem to have prompted the dispute. However, in reality, it was not a simple squabble between neighbours. It was more a clash of communities.[19]

Arguably, such underlying tensions merely served to exacerbate the subsequent discordant relations between the Abbots of Crowland (Croyland) and the clergy at Whaplode, which were to become a running sore in the development of St. Mary's over the next four centuries.

3.

Influential landowners in South Holland post
the Norman Conquest

PRINCIPAL LANDOWNERS AND TENANTS-IN-CHIEF

Such was the 'benevolence' of King William following the Conquest, with the affirmation of Landholdings amongst the erstwhile Barons, and other landowners, that the DB in 1086 reveals the landed wealth of such Tenants-in-Chief (in receipt of land gifted directly by the Crown) was heavily concentrated.

In 1086, the Royal demesne was worth £17,800, about 23% of the total, and there were 15 'class A' landholders {£750+ per year} who between them held 26% of the total; this means that just 16 individuals controlled almost half of the kingdom's landed wealth. Classes B and C {£200-£750 per year}, comprising 59 Tenants-in-Chief account for the next quarter or so of the kingdom's wealth; 132 Tenants-in-Chief in classes D and E {£40-£200 per year} accounted for most of the rest; with the remaining 5% held by more minor landholders. In other words, King William assigned 90% of the landed wealth of England to about 150 people (including himself). [20]

Whilst the available data on post-Conquest Norman land ownership is subject to debate and interpretation (and a margin for error) it is estimated that the Church, already a major landowner at the conquest, together with the monasteries, held possibly a *quarter* of all useable areas. William preferred land to be in the hands of the bishops rather than the abbots because the former had to pay feudal duties to him whereas the monasteries did not. Their dues went to the Pope.[21]

The ownership of a great swath of post Conquest land holdings, and their subsequent movement and expansion thereof, was later confirmed in the *Testa de Neville "The Book of Fees" Vols 1-3: 1198-1293* - the record of which was published in 1921/23. In Vol I the following statement is made: *"In 1242, as in 1212, the returns from Lincolnshire were singularly elaborate, giving a great deal of information that had not been demanded by the king's writs. It would even seem that the persons responsible for them had access to historical notes of some sort, presumably supplied by the sheriff or the Exchequer."* [22]

As regards the 1242 inquisition held in Elloe Wapentake, there also appears the following narrative under the heading of 'HOYLAUND-WAPINTACIUM DE ELHOU.'

*"Inquisico facta in wapentantacio de Elhou per sacramentum horum
subscritorum, scilicet Lambert de Quappelage, Roberti de Ory, Algeri de
Hulmo, Johannis de Fulne, Willelmi filii Hugonis de Spalding,' Prioris Cluny,
Ranulph de BlakeweU, Alcxandri Clerici de Quappelad,' Galfridi filii Eduse,
Willelmi le Clerk' et Willelmi filii Galfridi de Sutton'..."*[23]

The above is broadly translated as follows - in 'Elloe Wapentake
within the region of Holland' – 'An inquisition made in the arms of Elloe by
the sacrament of these underwriters, viz, Lambert de Quappelage {Whaplode},
Robert de Ory, Alger de Hulmo, John de Fulne, William, son of Hugh of
Spalding, Prior of Cluny, Ranulph of Blakewell, Alexander the Cleric of
Quappelad {Whaplode}, Galfrid the son of Edus, William the Clerk, and
William the son of Gaurid of Sutton........'

Notably, amongst the above names, are three in particular: Alexander,
the Cleric of Whaplode (Vicar of Whaplode 1242); Lambert de Whaplode – A
landowner in Whaplode (not to be confused with Lambert D'Oyry, who had
died in 1230); and Robert D'Oyry (D'Ory) another member of the influential
D'Oyry family in Whaplode and Gedney. (See Appendix II.B.).

WIDO (GUY) de CRAON (CREON/CREDON/CRODON, or CROUN) [Circa 1050-1121]

Guy de Craon, as a Tenant-in-Chief, was one of those fortunate few to whom
King William distributed / re-affirmed land ownership. In his 'Itinerary' Dr
Stukeley indicated that *"the family of Craon, Credon, Crodon, or Croun, was
one of the most illustrious in France, and the barony of Croun the first in
Anjou."* He gives a pedigree of the family which commences in the year 940
with Andrew de Croun, Lord of Croun, and Guy or Wydo (Wido) was,
according to this pedigree, in the fifth descent from Andrew. [24]

The father of Wido (Guy) was likely Renaud de Nevers (Craon), son
of Robert "le Bourguignon" (the Burgundian) de Nevers. Renaud had married
Enoguen (Domita) de Craon, the heiress and daughter of Robert de Vitre and
his 1st wife the 'Heiress de Craon' - daughter of Guerin de Craon – and Renaud
de Nevers subsequently assumed the role of "Seigneur de Craon". Although
Wido's parentage remains uncertain, most genealogical sources would appear
to agree that it is chronologically consistent if Wido is 'another' son of Renaud,
not least because of the references to his grandson Maurice suggest a
relationship with "Seigneurs de Craon."

Notwithstanding, Wido de Craon accompanied William the Conqueror
to England, and for his services to him in the Conquest he was rewarded with
upwards of fifty parishes in Lincolnshire and several in Leicestershire, in all

totalling sixty-four townships. Amongst the parishes awarded to him in Lincolnshire within Elloe Wappentake were those of Moulton, Pinchbeck, Weston, Holbeach, Tydd (St. Mary), Spalding and Whaplode, and, out with Elloe, notably land around Boston, and at Burton (Penwardine), Butterwick, and the sizeable lands at Frieston, where he established his principal barony. All these holdings and the remainder were either held in his capacity as Tenant-in-Chief, or as the immediate Lord over the people living on the land who paid taxes to the Tenant-in-Chief.[25]

The nature of Wido's subsequent land distribution from his extensive holdings, and those of his descendants, together with the gifting of land to church institutions, had a lasting impact on the development of Whaplode and the region of South Holland for several centuries, such holdings forming the basis for the numerous disputes as to land supremacy between the various factions in Lincolnshire.

Crest of Wido de Craon (fig.11).
Geni.com/people/Guy-de-Craon (2022-Henn Sarv)

See Appendix II.A. for further information with regard to the principal de Craon family members descended from Wido de Craon, and his 'attributed' father, Renaud de Nevers - Seigneur de Craon, who were all benefactors in the region.

FULK III d'OYRY/ORY/OYRi or OYRii, [Circa 1160/5 - 1231]
This family is not to be confused with the D'Oyly family – also with descendants from the Norman Conquest, but whose lands were principally in and around Berkshire and Oxfordshire.

The origins of the D'Oyry family are not known, although it is a possibility that the surname is derived from Oiry in Champagne, France. Notwithstanding, historians depict the family splitting into French and English establishments with landholdings in Aumale, in Normandy, France, together with land in Gedney and Whaplode in Lincolnshire, England.

The father of Fulk III d'Oyry remains unconfirmed, although, it is suggested by some that it was a Simon Fitz ('son of') Baldwin d'Oyry of Gedney, However, notably, Baldwin was Rector of Gedney, and died in 1189, and there appears to be no confirmed evidence that he had a 'legitimate' son, (see Appendix II.B). It is more likely that Fulk III's father was Fulk II d'Oyry, who had died by 1189, and was the son of Geoffrey d'Oyry, (see Appendix II.B). This would appear to be supported by the following observations:

a)   It was Geoffrey's widow, Emecina, who gave the churches of Gedney and Whaplode to Crowland Abbey, a gift that was confirmed by her son and grandson, both named Fulk.[26]

b)   A later confirmatory acta of Bishop Hugh of Avalon implies that there was indeed a Fulk, son of Fulk, d'Oyry, involved in a dispute over land in Whaplode in 1230. (See below- 4. Claimants to the ownership of the Parish Church of St. Mary's - The Consecration and Confirmatory Acta).

Fulk III d'Oyry became an important landowner in Gedney who gained early additions to his lands from the Countess of Albemarle (the English derivative of Aumale** in Normandy), as subsequently confirmed by King John in 1202, and later by the grant of further land rights in 1227 from King Henry III. Fulk III subsequently married Matilda le Strange, who shared with her sister (Emma) in the inheritance from her father, Ralph le Strange, of lands in Norfolk. [**During his lifetime Fulk III was steward to the counts and countess of Aumale, in Normandy, who also held lands in Holderness in England]. [See Barbara English (BE) – *The Lords of Holderness 1086-1260 – A Study in Feudal Society' - 1979*].

In the South Aisle within St. Mary Magdelene Church, Gedney, there is a damaged 13th century effigy of a cross-legged knight, which it is suggested, represents Fulk III d'Oyry.

In 1189 Fulk III was one of the "Twelve Men of Holland" who mounted an invasion of the precinct of 'common marshland' in Crowland to assert land ownership rights. Fulk III, together with Gerard de Camville, Thomas Moulton, Conan fitz Ellis (see **Part Two**: 3. Whaplode's Family Coats of Arms and Stained-Glass Windows), and others, began one of the greatest medieval lawsuits, against the Abbey of Crowland and showed the Fenlanders in their fiercest and most independent mood.[27] Two other notable members of the 'Twelve' were Alexander de Whapplelode (Vicar of Whaplode) and Richard de Fleet.

Thereafter, there followed numerous depositions to King Richard I by the Abbot(s) of Crowland to assert their rights given by Henry II, all of which were rebuffed by challenges made by the Abbot of Spalding, and it was not until 1 April 1202 that final confirmation was attained of the charter of Henry II setting forth the bounds of Crowland. [28]

Fulk III was the father of one son, Geoffrey, who died a single person after 1236, and three daughters all of whom shared in the inheritance as 'Ladies of Gedney'; Ela, who married Robert de Constable, of Burton-Constable, Yorkshire; Emecina, who married Ralph de Gousel, of Flintham, Nottinghamshire; Alice, who married William de Beaumont of Groton, Suffolk.

The Seal of Fulk d'Oyry (fig.12).
The above as redrawn from a damaged original in the Brymor
Jones Library, University of Hull. (BE. Page. 148, plate 13).

WALERAN d'OYRY [b. circa 1120 -d. post 1165]
THE WHAPLODE CONNECTION
Waleran was the second or third son of Emecina (wife of Geoffrey d'Oyry) and was in possession of sizeable lands in Whaplode given to him by either his mother, or his brother Fulk II. Waleran's wife is named as Margaret, and, although not stated, she is likely to have been the daughter of Alexander of Ingoldsby, with property in North Stoke, since in 1212 Waleran's son and heir, Lambert, held a knight's fee there in concert with Osbern of Ingoldsby. In addition to his heir, Lambert, Waleran had four sons: Fulk and Geoffrey, who were, at one point, the joint incumbent parsons at St. Mary's Church, Whaplode; and Thomas and William. The date of his death is not known, but the Nave of St. Mary's was built within his lifetime <u>and</u> that of his brother Baldwin who was rector there prior to his death in 1189/90.[29] See Appendix II.B. for further information on other principal members of the D'Oyry family.

4.

Claimants to the ownership of the Parish Church of St. Mary's

Parish Churches were being founded in increasing numbers, especially from the first half of the eleventh century, usually by one or more landowners who paid for the erection of the building and endowed it with land (glebe) and a house site (toft) for the priest, and who, thereafter, 'owned' the profits of the church, that is the profits of the obligatory tithes and offerings. The contribution of a tenth, or tithe, of all the produce to the support of the church had also been introduced into the Anglo-Saxon church, and by the tenth century was already incorporated in the legal codes. From the very beginning of most of the parish churches it provided the major proportion of funds which supported their priests, and the customary offerings, important though they were, can never have yielded so much except in city parishes. (See below - 5. The evolvement of Church Income and Clergy Stipends).

Even when the under-tenants dwelling in the parish contributed to the endowment of the church, and this seems to have happened quite often, the advowson *[the process for appointing a parish priest in England]* and the profits remained with the principal owner. The proprietary and territorial way of regarding the parish churches continued extraordinarily strong throughout the twelfth century. The same 'territorial' attitude allowed landowners to endow monasteries with churches and with lands, including even those lands which had been given to the churches by their men.[30]

St Mary's North side towards North Transept (fig.13).

THE CONSECRATION AND CONFIRMATORY ACTA

The official consecration of the Norman church of "The Blessed Virgin St. Mary, Whaplode" is generally accepted as having been in 1125. Other suggested dates of 1130 & 1140 do not align with the architectural evidence of the early Norman Chancel Arch and the four Norman bays in the east end. From its consecration, the ownership of the church at Whaplode, and control over the surrounding land, was contested by the monks at Croyland (Crowland) Abbey over many years, and this was only resolved when the monks established their rights by law, finally, before the Bishop of Lincoln, in 1447.

These disputes had continued to rage long after the DB in 1086 had delivered apparent determination of land holdings, and there were numerous subsequent decrees by Bishops that were made in succeeding years to affirm such land ownership, and entitlement to tithes and offerings, as demonstrated by the following:

EXTRACTS FROM ENGLISH EPISCOPAL CONFIRMATORY ACTA

i)   1067-1185 Vol. I. Lincoln.

Acta of Bishop Robert Chesney. No. 102

'*Confirmation for the monastery of St. Guthlac, Crowland, of the churches of Gedney, and Whaplode given by Emecina wife of the late Walter de Cantelu, saving the agreements between the monastery and Baldwin d'Oyry during the latter's lifetime. (19 December 1148 x18 April 1161).*' [31]

Acta of Bishop Walter Countances. No. 302. Castle Acre - Crowland

'*Notification of a settlement made in the bishop's presence about a parish boundary agreement between the churches of St. Mary, Whaplode, and All Saints, Holbeach, said to have been made in the time of bishop Alexander, which has been the subject of dispute between Baldwin d'Orly (rector of Whaplode) and G.(rector) of Holbeach. The boundary is to be 'Chotwere' and 'Scaldcryk.' Those persons living between this line and Whaplode church are to pay tithes and offerings to Whaplode and be buried there. An exception is made in the case of tithes of the salt-pans of 'Houtbrokene' and tithes of the lands of four named parishioners living between the boundary line and Holbeach church, all of which are to be paid to Whaplode church. 1184.*' [32]

ii)   1186 – 1206 Vol. IV. Lincoln.

Acta of Hugh of Avalon No. 44. Crowland Abbey

'*Grant to the abbot and monks of St. Guthlac, Crowland, permitting them to convert the church of Whaplode in usuos suos, after the deaths of Geoffrey,*

Fulk and Hugh, {D'Oyry family members} *who now possess the church,
paying to the monks one hundred shillings a year. The monks shall present a
perpetual vicar to the bishop. The vicar shall receive all the offerings of the
church, except sheaves. He shall pay the monks two and half marks a year and
shall be responsible for all episcopal duties.'* {There follows the attached
footnote, which provides more expansive information surrounding the
involvement of the d'Oyry family}. *['The church of Whaplode was given to
Crowlands long with Gedney church, by Emecina successively the wife of
Geoffrey d'Oyry and Walter de Cantelu (cartulary fos. 76r. 106r, pd by K.
Major. The D'Oyrys of South Lincolnshire, Norfolk, and Holderness (1130-
1275 (priv.pd. Lincoln 1984) app.i no.14 and was confirmed by various
members of the d'Oyry family (ibid.nos.3,6,7). The churches were confirmed
by bp Robert Chesney (EEA I no. 102) and by archbps Theobald and Richard
of Canterbury (K. Major op. cit. nos. 5, 8, 9; EEA ii nos. 118-19 and by popes
Lucius III and Urban III (PUE iti nos. 364,386. Hugh the chaplain and Fulk
and Geoffrey had been admitted to the church by Robert de Hardres, canon of
Lincoln and vice-archdn (cartulary fos. 76v-78r, no. ix-no 77 in foliation
sequence) and a second charter of vice-archdn Robert (fo, 78r, no.x) institutes
Geoffrey and Fulk (described as brothers, the sons of Waleran d'Oyry) to the
perpetual vicarage of the church. Robert was vice-archdn from 1183 until he
became archdn of Huntingdon (by 1192 at the latest) and these charters may
have been issued sede vacante after Walter of Countances's translation from
Lincoln to Rouen (for vice-arcdn Robert see Reg. Ant. Vii 206 & n.).'
'Alternatively, the second of Robert's charters could indicate that Hugh the
chaplain had died or resigned (since he is not mentioned) and that it was issued
at a later date (before 4 April 1192). If this is the case, then bp Hugh's charter
must date before 1192 since it mentions the three incumbents. This actum was
possibly the charter of bp Hugh exhibited in the case between Fulk son of Fulk
d'Oryr and abbot Henry of Crowland over Whaplode church in the king's
court in Trinity term 1230 (CRR xiv no. 169).The grant was apparently not
effective, and the church was again appropriated to Crowland by bp Richard
Gravesend on 11 December 1266 (cartulary fo. 8or, no. xxii); the abbey was
indicted into corporal possession of the church following a mandate of the bp's
vicegerent dated 1 July 1267(Iibid. Fo. 80v, no. xxv). A vicarage was ordained
by bp Gravesend in January 1269 (Iibid. fos. 80v – 81v, no. xxvi: Rot. Grav.
33-4). For the whole question and disputes between Crowland and the d'Oryr
family.(See K. Major, op. cit. 9-15 and app.i, nos. 2-15)].'* [33]

PARISH BOUNDARIES

The proper name of the complete parish is '*Whaplode St. Mary, Whaplode St. Catherine, and Saracens Head.*' The latter part of the name-Saracens Head-raises questions as to why this parish should be so different from other nearby parishes, which all have hamlets named after saints.

In medieval times 'Saracen's Head' was known as Saltney, which means "Island of Salt." This name was derived from the mound which stands up to 15 feet high in a meadow covering several acres on the sea side of the 'Roman Bank' and is a relic of the salt making days of the region. The nearby road leading into the village of Whaplode is known as "Saltney Gate." [34]

SALTNEY (SARACEN'S HEAD) – A LINK WITH THE CRUSADES

DMO makes reference to *"the 'hospital' of St. John Baptist in Fleet, which was to become the manorial chapel of St. John Hospitallers' estate at Winstow."*[35] {Winslow-part of the Hospitallers' Commandery (a district under the command of an order of Knights) of Skirbeck, which was handed over to the Hospitallers, circa 1230, by Thomas Moulton}.[36]

DMO continues *"It is possible that there was also a hospital of St. John the Baptist at Salteneia; the single reference to it, in the Crowland cartulary, suggests that it lay to the north-east of Saltney Gate which links Holbeach to Whaplode."* [37]

These references provide the implied direct link with the 'Crusades', via those deigned 'Knights Hospitallers' who were the protectors of the Order of the Hospital of St. John of Jerusalem, which was formed in England in the early 12th century. Other suggestions proffered as to the origin of the name 'Saracen's Head' are; that the name was derived from that of an ancient drovers' inn within the hamlet which was so named because it was the ambition of anyone returning from the Crusades to bring home the head of an 'infidel' or Saracen [not being a Christian]; a claim that examination of a mid 19th century map of the village reveals that the boundaries of the village form 'literally the shape of a Saracen's head.' Notwithstanding, as mentioned earlier, indirect links do arise via the families of de Craon and D'Oyry, who were not only benefactors of the church within the region, but had members of their families serving in the Crusades. (See Appendices II.A. and II.B.).

WHAPLODE'S ROYAL CHARTERS

St. Mary's, along with many other churches that experienced the medieval times post the Norman Conquest, have records of being granted various Royal Charters. This custom appears to have developed sometime during the Anglo-

Saxon period, evidence of which is recorded in the dealings with Medeshamstede Abbey – the original name of Peterborough Abbey. Essentially it was a simply a method underpinning the allocation of much needed wealth for the establishment of the clergy throughout the country. It appears to have been common practice for the Norman Barons, together with the various Kings from William through to Stephen, to establish their own clergy within the hierarchy of the religious establishments throughout the country; the inclusion of the various charters granting markets and fairs therefore meant that the order for procuring much needed finances for the clergy was secure.

In 1255 King Henry III granted the Abbot of Croyland (Ralph Mershe) a weekly market on a Saturday for Whaplode, as well as a fair on the vigil and feast day of the Assumption of the Blessed Virgin (August 15th- a date which is still regarded as the ceremonial birthday of St. Mary's) and for 6 days afterwards. Further Royal Charters were granted in the following years, under the reign of Edward, 1300; 1303; 1307. The last of the Charters in 1307 coincided with the death of Edward I, and it was, simply, a re-iteration of the first Charter granted by his father King Henry III in 1255. Since these fayres (fairs) were held on the feast days of the saint to whom they were dedicated, it can be assumed that the church of St. Mary, at Whaplode, was already known as St. Mary's, Whaplode, even as early as the 13th century.

Whaplode's Royal Charters are listed, as follows, in the *"The Gazeteer for Markets and Fairs in England and Wales -1516."* [38]

WHAPLODE 5324 3240. J 334 Subsidy £480.

Market *- (Charter) Sat; gr 10 Jun 1255, by King Hen III to Abbot and Convent of Croyland [Crowland]. To be held at the manor (CChR, 1226-57, p. 448). In 1281, the Abbot of Croylaunde was holding the market (QW, p. 402).*

Fair *- (Charter) vf+6, Assumption of Mary (15 Aug); gr 10 Jun 1255, by King Hen III to Abbot and Convent of Croyland [Crowland]. To be held at the manor. The feast is stated to be the Assumption (CChR, 1226-57, p. 448). In 1281, the Abbot of Croylaunde was holding the fair, the feast of which was given as the Assumption of Mary (QW, p.402).*

The following citation from the National Records Office provides greater clarity around the 'Market' charter listings:

"The Abbot of Croyland, by a grant, 39 Henry III (in the year 1255), obtained a weekly market on Saturday for Whaplode, and a fair on the vigil and day of the Assumption of the Blessed Virgin (August 15) and six days afterwards."

WHAPLODE'S OUTLYING CHAPELS

Owen refers to the early settlements of outlying Chapels in the vicinity of St. Mary's, at Whaplode St. Catherine (Fenhall), Aswick Grange (which is still recorded on present day maps at the junction of Hagbeach Drove and Eaugate Road, northwest of Whaplode Drove) and a parochial chapel at Whaplode Drove for the easement of those who guard the banks of the rivers and ring bells as warnings against floods from the Fens. [39]

Two further chapels are also highlighted; a chantry chapel of St. John (referred to above – that of St. John Hospitallers), and the manorial house (chapel) endowed as being the only rural friary in Lincolnshire dedicated to the 'Friars of the Holy Cross'- otherwise known as the "Crutched friars" at Whaplode. [40] However, this Holy Order, which was one of the earliest houses of the order in England, founded by the patron, Robert d'Oyry (D'Ory)(see Appendix II. B) as the convent of St. Mary *de Novo Loco*, and confirmed by Pope Innocent IV in a 'Papal Bull' issued April 1st 1247, only lasted a few years since such foreign 'splinter' orders not only attracted little interest from the local people, but also hostility from bishops, in particular, Bishop Grosseteste of Lincoln, and as a consequence it folded in 1260, with the property being given back to the heirs of Robert d'Oyry, his daughter Elizabeth and her husband Adam of Hagbeach who subsequently, but prior to 1269, granted the property to the Priory of Spalding in return for 20 marks of silver. [41] & [42]

It was recently discovered that there was a Chapel serviced by the monks of St. Mary's Church at the junction of Wallis Gate, Bush Meadow Lane and Stockwell Gate, the site of the 'Ellis Cross'. (The connection to the family of Conan fitz Elias/ Ellis, who had land in Whaplode in the 12th century, is covered within Appendix VIII and **Part Two**: 3. Whaplode's Family Coats of Arms and Stained Glass Windows).

At this site, during some amateur archealogical work carried out in 1989 by Ken Lowe, a Lincolnshire metal detectorist, several religious items were recovered including a Papal Bulla (a Papal ring, which is now on display in the Peterborough Museum along with other artefacts relating to the finds at Ellis Cross). Examples of the finds (below) were recorded in *the Collector's Magazine "The Searcher" August 1989,* and relate to Pope Honorius IV (c.1210 to 3rd Apr 1287), born Giacomo Savelli, who was Pope for two years from 1285 to 1287. During his unremarkable pontificate he largely continued to pursue the pro-French policy of his predecessor, Pope Martin IV (1281-85). Notably, he was the last Pope to be married before he took Holy Orders, however, he was widowed before his Pontificate.

| Pope Honorius (fig.14). | Papal Bulla - Obverse (fig.15). | Papal Bulla - Head (fig.16). |

A further two chapels, which were directly serviced by St. Mary's, have also been identified. Holy Trinity chapel, however, its location is not known, and one at the property of Sir Robert d'Oyry (de Ory), for which a charter was given by Bishop Grosseteste at Nettleham (Netelham) in January 1238 - principal extract herewith: *"Omnibus, etc. Noverit universitas vestra, nos, dilectorum in Christo filiorum, Abbatis et conventus Croylandie, patronorum ecclesie de Quappelad et domini Willelmi de Bagleye, ejusdem ecclesie rectoris, interveniente consensu, concessisse, et hac presenti carta mea [sic] confirmasse, dilecto filio Roberto de Ory, militi, et heredibus suis, ut in perpetuum habeant capellam in curia sua versus mariscum de Quappelad, sine fontibus et campana, et cantariam per proprium capellanum in eadem, sumptibus propriis et oneribus, et quod panem benedictum et aquam benedictam ibidem percipere valeant sibi et hospitibus suis, et domestice familie....."* [43]

Foster provides a translation of the above, as follows: *"......... given by consent of the abbot and convent of Croyland, patrons of the church of Quappelad (Whaplode) and Doms William de Ragleye, Rector,* {William Ragleye (not Bagleye) is identified as the Rector of Whaplode in 1238} *whereby the Bishop granted and confirmed to Robert de Ory,* {D'Oyry} *Knight* {However, Foster inadvertently transcribes 'Ory' as 'Cry'}, *and his heirs, license to have a chapel in his court towards the marsh of Quappelad, and to receive Holy Bread and Water for himself, his guests and servants."* [44] (See Appendix II.B).

In all there were known to be eight such Chapels belonging to St. Mary's, and many of these were established before the end of the twelfth century. Further evidence for some of these Chantry Chapels was discovered during the excavations for the construction of the Heraldic Suite between 2004 and 2006. (See **Part Two: 6.** The 'lost' chapels of St. Mary's).

There are lots of inconsistencies regarding the ownership of the St. Mary's Chancel in the early years, although allegedly it was suggested that a researcher at De Montfort University in Leicester came across evidence that the monks working on the reconstruction of Croyland Abbey in the late 12th century were, in fact, from Peterborough Abbey, and that it was these monks who worked on the construction of St. Mary's, albeit they were resident at Croyland at the time. Although it would seem that Croyland Abbey had control of the manor and church at Copoloda (Whaplode) during the construction of St. Mary's it was not long before the ownership was being disputed, as substantiated by the number of references in the history of Croyland Abbey involving disputes taken to law.

In the circumstances, such disputes as to ownership and the ensuing prolonged conflict between the Abbey and Convent of Croyland and some of the wealthy Barons who resided in the area, who no doubt provided much needed funds to maintain, or continue with the development of the church of St. Mary's, would have impeded progess, accordingly.

Much of this period coincides with the rule of King John (r.1189-1216) who, due to his poor handling of armies (his lack of leadership credentials had been evident since his youth) and the fact that he lost much of the French possessions gained through William the Conqueror's lineage, (hence the 'nickname' John Lacklands) forced him to raise taxes,. However, the barons rebelled and forced upon him the 'Magna Carta' in 1215 – in essence a 'peace treaty' designed to establish land ownership as agreed between the King and the rebel barons, and when Henry III (r. 1216-1272) succeeded John, the barons retained much of their powers making constant challenges to the Bishops and Abbots throughout the land.

As highlighted earlier, with Fulk III d'Oyry's involvement therein, it was in 1189 that the Abbot of Croyland (Robert de Redinges) found himself embroiled in a dispute over the rightful ownership of the church, which was being contested by the Prior of Spalding supported by the "Twelve Men of Holland". Ultimately, Hugh de Puiset, Bishop of Durham, settled the dispute making each of the Holland men plead their piece and pay a fine.

A record from the Abbot of Croyland (Ralph Mershe - 1253-1281) refers to great expense and long suits at law, to gain the manor of Gedney and the church of Whaplode. As the church had for years previously belonged to the Abbey, (Emecina d'Oyry having given both churches, at Gedney and Whaplode, to the Abbey in the middle to latter part of the 12th century - see also reference to an earlier advowson from Alan de Craon – as mentioned by Revd. Geo. Oliver - Appendix V), no doubt the local barons who held sway during King John's reign, and the early years of King Henry III, had somehow appropriated the rights.

In 1268, according to an extract from an order written by the Bishop of Lincoln (Richard de Gravesend:1258-1279 - see Appendix III) it was decreed that the church at Quaplode (Whaplode) be protected under the Abbey and Convent of Croyland's care in perpetuity, saving that the Abbot would undertake to maintain the chancel of the church, and that they take care of and repair, and find books, vestments, and other necessary ecclesiastical ornaments after the cessation, or decease, of the incumbent Vicar Simon.[45]

Despite the appropriation of the church of Whaplode in 1268, Richard of Crowland - the Abbot of Crowland (1280-1303) - was called upon to defend the rights of Crowland to the advowson of Whaplode, and he gave 40 marks to Robert de Hakebeth for his *quitclaim* (a formal renunciation of a legal claim for a right to land).

In 1321, yet another twist to the rightful ownership occurred, when William Calthorpe, a sizeable landowner, remitted all his rights to the manor and advowson of Gedney, Whaplode, and Holbeach to Croyland, which, might appear odd, at first sight, since these had previously been established in law in favour of the Abbey and Convent of Croyland (Crowland) in both 1245 and 1268, a point that Foster makes in his book, and he comments, accordingly: "*It is most improbable that Croyland ever willingly parted with the patronages of the churches, and one is at a loss to ascertain how William Calthorpe became possessed of any rights in them.*"[46]

However, it transpires that in 1927, Colonel C.W. Carr-Calthrop, in his comprehensive book on the genealogy of the families of Calthorpe & Calthrop, cited the most probable answer to the apparent 'ownership' dispute, that being a link by marriage of an ancestor to a descendant of Sir Fulk III d'Oyry, Lord of Gedney, whose father was most likely the son of Geoffrey D'Oyry who had married Emecina, from whom the gift of Gedney and Whaplode churches to the Abbot of Croyland had originally emanated.[47]

CROWLAND'S ROYAL CHARTERS

Crowland was the site of a monastic house founded in the early 8th century by Æthelbald, King of Mercia (Charter:S.82.AD 716), and dedicated to St Bartholomew from its foundation,which was destroyed in the late ninth century, but re-founded in the late tenth century. This was the only monastic house in Lincolnshire at the time of the Norman Conquest, and Crowlands Royal Charters are contained within the listings of the *"The Gazeteer for Markets and Fairs in England and Wales -1516",* [48] as follows:

CROWLAND 5241 3103 1334 Subsidy £50

Market - *(Charter) Wed; granted 24 Oct 1257, by King Henry III to A and C of Crowland (CChR, 1226-57, p. 476). In 1281, the Abbot of Crylaund [Crowland] was holding the market (QW, p.396).*

Fair - *(Prescriptive) f, Bartholomew (24 Aug); recorded 1136 & 1154, when King Stephen granted the Manor of Croiland [Croyland] a fair (feria) of six days, namely three days before the feast of Bartholomew and three days after (Regesta, iii, no. 252). This grant does not include St Bartholomew's day itself, presumably because a prescriptive fair was already held on that day. Fair recorded in 1227 (CChR,1226-57, p.17). In 1281 the Abbot of Croylaund* [Croyland] *was holding a fair beginning eight days before the feast of St. Bartholomew and lasting for eight days after the feast, which he claimed ab antique (QW, p402).*

As a consequence, one can see why successive Abbots at Croyland Abbey and Convent were keen to take issues of controversy to the 'Courts', since it was in the interests of some of the elders and noblemen of the time, in order to keep the Abbots on their toes, that they should challenge rightful ownership especially if they had manor houses in the area.

From all of the above evidence, given that there were many contentious issues regarding the proper ownership of the church of St. Mary's, not least when one considers the fact that there was not just one Abbey interested in holding sway with the inhabitants from as far back as the ninth century, then it is reasonable to presume that hostilities would continue to prevail in that area. Subsequently only to be aggravated further as Croyland sought to expand their ownership of lands in the area during the eleventh and twelfth centuries. Evidence of this is seen by the number of challenges they put before the Bishops of Lincoln and Durham, usually claiming lands that were defined by bordering dykes or river, a practice that was to reverberate when Spalding Monastery, backed by the powerful Baron Ivo Tail-Bois (Taillebois) a relative of William the Conqueror, reneged on their loyalty to Croyland after the defeat of Hereward the Wake.

The following extract from 'Papal Letters 1138-1304' does serve to confirm that it was not only St. Mary's that encountered aggression from the Abbots of Croyland when it came to disputes concerning the ownership of land connected with the parish churches under their 'control'.

1240. R15 GREGORY IX 14 Kal. May Lateran (f.68d.)

"Mandate to the bishop of Coventry and Lichfield, and the treasurer and precentor of Lichfield to warn and induce the abbot and convent of Croyland to restore to the church of Castre, (as referred in DB – this is now known as Caistor, in West Lindsey), *of which R. cardinal of St. Eustace's is rector, a portion of the marsh belonging in common to the abbey and the said church, which they detain."* [49]

Notwithstanding, another extract does demonstrate a degree of Papal compassion towards penitents visiting St. Mary's on festival days, in common with other churches, as extracted from 'Papal Letters 1362-1404', as follows:

1363. I. URBAN V 6.Id. Sept. Avignon (t.144)

"Relaxatio, during ten years, of a year and forty days of enjoined penance to penitents who on the principal feasts of the year visit the church of St. Mary's Cuappelade, in the diocese of Lincoln." [50]

St. Mary's - The South Side and South Porch door (fig.17).

5.

The evolvement of Church Income and Clergy Stipends

INCOME

By the 12th century, the maintenance of churches was paid for, predominantly, by income from a three-fold source:

a)   An endowment, of land or rent charges on land (the glebe), had been made by the founders and tenants at the time of a church's consecration, and this was sometimes increased by later gifts.

b)   Tithes (tenth parts, payable annually), of corn, hay, and wood (the greater tithes), of other crops and young animals, and of the profits of trade, milling, fisheries, salt-making, and other personal activities (the lesser tithes), were becoming customary during the twelfth century.

c)   Customary offerings made by parishioners to the church or the priest, which, though they differed widely from parish to parish, everywhere formed a substantial portion of the priest's endowments.

Many 14th and 15th century boundary definitions were concerned with the tithe of land recently brought into cultivation, where no exact line had ever been known. Holbeach and Whaplode were among those parishes which had troubles of this sort, with the result that the bishops, acting as arbitrators, were called upon to make the final decision. Equally, the definition of the parochial area was important to secure that part of the church's income which derived from the offerings of its parishioners. In particular, the Abbey of Crowland, concerned to establish the boundaries of their tithe areas, succeeded in 1370 with the definition of the boundary between Holbeach and Whaplode.[51]

In 1288 it was recorded that the three wealthiest churches, whether or not the vicarages were taken into account, in the Holland Deanery were Long Sutton, Holbeach and Whaplode.[52]   Clearly, the level of income receivable by a church was a determinant as to the number of clergy a church could support, and in this respect Owen refers to comparative findings from the Foster Library PROE179/7/35 indicating that in 1376 St Mary's Whaplode had 10 Priests, 1 Deacon and 2 sub-Deacons, actually living on the premises in a room attached to the north side of the Bell-tower. Comparatively, in 1526, the number of clergy was only 5. *(H. Salter's edition, A subsidy collected in the Diocese of Lincoln in 1526, Oxford 1909, pp. 62-8).*[53]

These living quarters were necessary for the Clergy to service the eight outlying Chapels, together with the four Altars (one of which was the main High Altar being regarded as separate to the Chantry Chapels) which were part

36

of the main Church buildings. Access to these 'rooms' was gained via the *Monks' steps* (a turret staircase), which, in accordance with tradition at that time, were situate behind the stone 'Rood Screen' (See **Part Two**: 2. The Architectural Structure and Principal Fabric Heritage of St. Mary's – The Stone Rood Screen).

We can only speculate when the 'Rood Screen' was destroyed, however, the turret steps, which date from the late 13th early 14th century, remained in situ and provided the access to the 'Singing Loft' (formerly the 'Rood Loft') used by the Church Band. These *Monks' steps* (as they are often called) are still in place today. (See below – The Church Band).

The Bell Tower – West Face (fig.18).

ENDOWMENTS AND WILLS

Endowments and Wills often provided a regular donation of income to a church on set dates, and Allen highlights that in 1821 the status of the parish and two notable endowments, was as follows:[54]

"This parish, in 1821, contained 341 houses and 1744 inhabitants." [By comparison, more recently, in 2021 the population of Whaplode was recorded as 3515].

Allen continues:

i) *"It was recorded that the benefice is a vicarage, valued in the King's books at £16.14s.9d. It is in the patronage of the crown."* (See below - 7. The prelude to the final handover of responsibilities in 1594, and the turmoil beyond -The Lord Chancellor's Patronage of St. Mary's).

ii) *"That in 1708 Elizabeth Wilson left a small estate, which now let for £12. a year, to the schoolmaster for the time being, to teach as many of the poorer sort of children to read, as the salary amounts at twopence per week. The Schoolroom adjoins the church."* (See below- 9. Specific artistic and commemorative contributions to the fabric of St. Mary's - The Charity Boards- and **Part Two:** 6. The 'lost' chapels of St. Mary's - The North Transept (Lady Chapel)).

iii) *"An ancestor of Lord Boston built six alms houses, for six poor widows, with an allowance of ten-pence a week to two of them; and from the same source, thirteen two-penny loaves are given to as many poor persons, who attend divine service in the church, every Sunday from the beginning of November to the end of April. This donation only occurs once in two years."* (See below- 9. Specific artistic and commemorative contributions to the fabric of St. Mary's – The Charity Boards).

Indeed, Foster draws our attention to a very early will recorded in Gray's (Bishop of Lincoln 1431-1435) Register, as follows: *'Thomas Alderman of Quaplode, chaplain. Feast of St. Benedict Abbot, 1442 (fo.113]. To be buried in Quaplod church yard. To every altar** in the church, iiijd'(*3d).'[55] {** this refers to the number of chantry chapels within the church, where wealthy landowners made an endowment to the priest for the individual (sometimes family) celebration of mass for their souls}. It is thought that there were, perhaps, as many as five separate chantry chapels, however, Foster acknowledged the existence of three. (See **Part Two:** 6. The 'lost' chapels of St. Mary's).

Today, the church remains reliant on such benefactors (more recent or otherwise) together with public donations and gift aid payments, or subscriptions (the taxpayer receives relief thereon and the Church receives the amount of the tax benefit), supported by grants and applications made to various funding sources in support of specific heritage projects.

TITHE RETURNS

Originally, the collection of the 'Tithe' represented a diversion to religious uses of around one tenth of England's agricultural wealth, this 'tax' was intended to sustain parish priests, maintain church buildings, and provide alms for the poor, but religious corporations could appropriate parish tithes to their own purposes, and could even 'sell' the tithes before collection. By way of comparison the Tithe Return of St. Mary's in 1431 was recorded as £7.0s.0d, and some 50 years later in 1481, the return showed a record of £7.6s.8d.

In 1594 Robert Johnson, Archdeacon of Leicester and founder of Oakham and Uppingham Schools in Rutland, was granted the parish tithes collected on behalf of St Mary's by Queen Elizabeth I. However, on his death in 1625, the ownership of the tithes was passed to the Governors of Uppingham School, who proceeded with the same neglectful attitude towards the 'maintenance' of the chancel and the clergy, as the previous tithe collectors, and ultimately, the Governors were to hand back their 'Chancel' responsibilities back to the Crown in the early 20th century. (See below: 7. The prelude to the final handover of responsibilities in 1594, and the turmoil beyond - Robert Johnson & St. Mary's - Uppingham School).

Foster refers to Maurice Johnson Esq.,[56] writing about the Whaplode Vicarage in 1749, wherein Johnson commented that the church records of 1676 indicated that all the tithes had to be paid at Easter as well as tithes on all animals, crops etc., and a tithe for which all persons over 14 years of age had to pay the Vicar 2d a year, also took place on Easter Day.

Other particular tithes are referred to by Johnson therein: The cost of having a 'Churching' {the blessing of the Church to the mother} after the birth of a child was $7^{1}/_{2}$d., 4d for a registering a baptism and a 1/- to register a wedding, however, for the marriage in the Parish a couple should pay to the vicar's discretion not exceeding 5/- to register their marriage, but if you lived outside the parish you had to pay 13/4d. For burials, if the burial took place in the church the cost was 6/8d, whereas burials in the chancel cost 10/-, but if you came from another parish the cost was 13/4d in the church, and £1 in the chancel. [57]

Notably, in 1676, a lengthy tithe dispute arose when the Revd. John Thomas, Vicar of Whaplode (1662-1688), filed a bill in the Court of the Exchequer against John Fowler and others, for the vicarial tithe. In this claim he referred to the instruments given by the Bishop of Lincoln in 1268 and admits the Rectory to have been of 'Old impropriate by Virtue' of it, or some other instruments, whereby the Vicarage was endowed, and that his predecessors, the Vicars thereof, had or ought to have had, the tithes, and he demanded the tithes mentioned. Among the numerous things chargeable were 'herrings taken in the parish or by parishioners abroad the sea, title in kind to the said vicars.' [58]

THE COMMUTATION OF THE TITHES

The system of church tithes ended with the Tithe Commutation Act 1836, when tithes were replaced with a commutation payment, and in St. Mary's case its tithes were commuted to £1,600 (at 2022 relative prices this would be worth approximately £180,000), to which reference was made in 1858 within the *'Topographical Dictionary of England' by Samuel Lewis, 7th edition,* wherein the parish of Whaplode St Mary is described as follows: "*The living (vicarage) is valued in the king's books at £16.14s. 9½d, and in the patronage reference to which of the Crown, impropriators* [assigned to a lay proprietor] *the trustees of Uppingham School. The great tithes have been commuted for £1,600, and the small for £553: the vicar has a glebe of 5 acres.*"

Unfortunately, latterly, in 1900, such was the parlous state of the fabric of St. Mary's arising from absence of necessary spending, Revd. John Rhodes, who was appointed Vicar of St Mary's (1898-1909), badgered the governors of Uppingham School so much that they subsequently gave up their 'ownership', and responsibility for the chancel, and thereby any claims on the parish tithes, in favour of the diocese of Lincoln, and the Crown. (See below: 7. The prelude to the final handover of responsibilities in 1594, and the turmoil beyond - Robert Johnson & St. Mary's - Uppingham School).

CLERGY STIPENDS

The payment of the tithes to the church by lay people, together with offerings, endowments, and other avenues of income to the church (e.g., collections), provided the underlying support, whether monetarily, or in goods and produce, to enable the church to provide a degree of regular income to its clergy, in the performance of their pastoral duties. This 'income' support to the clergy became known more formally as a 'stipend'- a fixed amount of money intended to provide financial support to a person, particularly to help cover living expenses.

Owen comments that *"in 1526 the average gross stipend of a rector was £12.13s. 8½d., which after various charges were met was on average net £9 9s.6¾d. Similarly, a vicar had an average gross payment of £9.9s 1⅓d. and net £6.13s.1½d. The vicar's portion was sometimes a flat payment, but more often a share of the tithe and offerings, and this might vary very considerably with economic conditions and the state of the population. The vicarage of Whaplode, which was appropriated to Crowland, was estimated in the late fifteenth century to be worth £28.18s 8d., which was partly made up of 67s. 8d for Cokwax {candles provided by householders who had hearths in use} and Romepenny {Peter's pence - an annual tribute of a penny paid by each householder in England to the papal see} from eleven score and twelve {232}, omitting forty-nine widows' houses, oblations of twenty-four score and four {484} persons, eight score {160} new communicants at easter, and offerings in the chapels of Holy Trinity, St. Katherine, and St. John Baptist. Out of it he found two parish chaplains at £6 each and their keep and chambers, maintained a house, and paid the holy-water carriers during the three days of principal offerings. By comparison, in 1526 Whaplode's value was estimated at £16.6.8d. gross, which included finding a chaplain at £5.6s.8d."*[59] (The comparative purchasing power of £17 in 1526, given the relative movement of RPI over time, translates into £15,400 at 2022 prices).

It is not known from these figures who was in direct charge of the clergy, as there were a few deviations from the usual terminology to describe some of the incumbents. It is without doubt that some of the clergy would have been supported by income raised from the private devotions said within the various Chantry Chapels, together with their added responsibilities for maintaining the various Chapels in both the Marshes and Fens.

Interestingly, the priests that served these institutions across England at the time of the dissolution appear to have been a group of rather elderly men, and according to information gathered in chantry surveys which had been carried out across six english shires (Essex; Kent;Linc;Warwicks;Wilts;Yorks) in 1548, it was established that the average age of chantry priests ranged from 47 to 55 years with nearly 8% being over the age of 70, which, when compared to their respective dates of institution, seemed to give credence to the hypothesis that many such priests may have regarded their posts as equivalent to retirement pensions - i.e. holding 'office' in perpetuity, until death, so to speak. [60]

There follows two examples of Papal letters issued in connection with St. Mary's about the deliverance of specific benefices arising from incumbency.

Firstly, one issued in 1290 releasing the Abbey & convent of Croyland to pay a pension to an Italian canon, hitherto *charged* to the Parish church of Whaplode.

1290 3 NICHOLAS IV Kal. July. Orvieto. (f.43.)

"R. papal chaplain, abbot, and the Benedictine convent of Croyland, are freed from the payment of a pension of 80 marks sterling, charged on the parish church of Quappelade, in the diocese of Lincoln, granted to their uses, hitherto

held by Francis de Foliano, canon of Reggio (in Emilia), between whom a question had arisen, the said canon having died at Rome, so that the church may be held entirely to their uses." [61]

Secondly, issued in 1502, providing the Vicar of Vaplod (Whaplode) with certain benefices for life (dependent upon his incumbency) - as follows:

25 June 1502 ALEXANDER VI 731 Reg. Lat 1103. fos 235v – 236v

"To Thomas Everard, BDec. perpetual vicar of the parish church of Vaplod, d. Lincoln. Dispensation - at his supplication - to receive and retain for life, together with the perpetual vicarage of the above church, one, and without it, any two other benefices, etc. [as summarised in CPL, XVI at no. 583]." [62]

However, unfortunately, the Reverend's receipt of such benefices was somewhat short-lived since Magister Thomas Everard resigned his post as Vicar in 1505.

As an example of the nature of 'stipends' provided, herewith, a list of those registered as Curates of the Parish of Whaplode, for which stipends were recorded within the *'Clergy of the Church of England Database, [CCEd] 1503-1803'*:

- 1769 - John Northon - £40.
- 1771 - William Betham - £40.
- 1776 - Robert Benson - £40.
- 1784 - Thomas L Howell - £30 plus surplus fees + use of a house.
- 1792 - James Gifford - £50.
- 1798 - John Grundy Thompson - £40 plus surplus fees + use of a house.
- 1803 - Samuel Oliver - £70 plus use of a house.

Clearly, historically, individual parishes both raised and spent the vast majority of the church's funding, meaning that clergy pay depended on the wealth of the parish, however, since the mid-19th century, all Clergy stipends (salaries) have been governed centrally by the Church of England and are paid out under the authority of the area Dioceses.

In 1948 the Church Commissioners ("CC") were established as a merger of the Queen Anne's Bounty, and the Ecclesiastical Commissioners, following the passing of the Church Commissioners Measure 1947 by the National Assembly of the Church of England. As a body corporate the CC administers the property assets & funds of the Church of England, and in so doing, manages central diocesan expenditure such as the running of diocesan offices, and also funds clergy pay and housing expenses (in 2022, an amount of circa £260 million per annum across all dioceses), meaning that clergy living conditions no longer depend on parish-specific fundraising.

THE PARISH QUOTA

Most parishes, however, give a portion of their money to the diocese as a "quota" or "parish share". While this is not a compulsory payment, dioceses strongly encourage and rely on it being paid; it is usually only withheld by parishes either if they are unable to find the funds or as a specific act of protest.

Over the years the level of this quota has risen, understandably, as can be seen by comparing the Lincoln Diocesan Trust and Board of Finance 'Tribute' Letter of February 1958, as sent to St. Mary's Churchwardens (Appendix XIX) wherein the amount requested of St. Mary's was £97. 15s. 0d, with the extract from the St. Mary's Income & Expenditure Account for the Year ended 31st December 1991 (Appendix XX. A.), which shows that it was levied at a rate of £12,932. To put that 1991 contribution into perspective the 'quota' for the year ended 2022 was £15,000.

6.

Further disputes between the Abbots of Crowland and the Vicars of St. Mary's.

Doubtless, as other sources of income diminished, the churches became increasingly important, and this may explain Crowland's acrimonious disputes in the late fifteenth century with the vicar of Whaplode concerning long running disagreements surrounding the maintenance of the surrounding embankments, the provision of desks and stalls for the chancel, and the ownership of the churchyard trees[63] as follows:

THE MAINTENANCE OF THE EMBANKMENTS AND THE WHAPLODE FLOOD. 1439

The maintenance of causeways, bridges and dykes in the marshes had long been a source of strife for over 100 years, not least because landowners (principally the monasteries) were seen to be responsible for their prolonged neglect of sustained maintenance of embankments, etc, and there had been much friction between successive Abbots and the surrounding townspeople of Crowland, Moulton and Whaplode.

In 1433 there was achieved a settlement whereby the Abbot of Crowland should rebuild the embankment between Brotherhouse and Whaplodes-dike, and keep it in repair for forty years, but, if the rainfall was very excessive, he was not to be held responsible for any overflow.

However, in 1439 there were heavy storms, and the water overflowed the embankment on the south side of the precinct, which happened to be out of repair, and inundated the common lands of Whaplode. Accordingly, the Abbot was presented for default before the commissioners of sewers, who pronounced that he was bound to repair the embankments. With great efforts the Abbot succeeded in getting the judgement reversed. At an inquisition held at Bolingbroke, before the sheriff of Lincoln, the jurors swore that the Abbots of Crowland their men and tenants, had never repaired the embankments, *'either for the safety of the lands adjoining, or for the purpose of keeping out the water running between the embankment or for the easement of the people . . . or any one of them, nor ought of right to repair the same . . . but only for their own easement, advantage, and profit, at their own will and pleasure'.* [64]

THE MAINTENANCE OF STALLS AND DESKS. 1446/7

In 1446 a dispute arose between the incumbent Vicar of St Mary's and the Abbot of Croyland regarding the rightful maintenance of the church's stalls and desks in the chancel. The Vicar (John Pynder: 1433-1466) cited the declaration of the Bishop of Lincoln in 1268 (Richard de Gravesend – see Appendix III) to the effect that Croyland had the responsibility for their repair and replacement. The Abbot (John Litlyngton), who undertook several disputes with local clergy and Churches, took the Vicar to court. The case was heard at St Mary Arches, in London, where the court ruled in favour of the Abbot, leaving the Vicar to pay the Abbot's costs *(5 marks)* as well as making good the various items requiring repair. [65]

In 1447 the same abbot had a dispute with Thomas d'Acre, in another costly litigation, however, this time the Lord Bishop of Lincoln (William of Alnick) decreed that the Abbot of Croyland (John Litlyngton) had the right of manor and lordship of Whaplode, *except for the tenants of Thomas d'Acre (Lord of Holbeach) who resided in the Whaplode area.* This decree distinguished the areas governed by the Abbot to being, the church and manor of Whaplode, the authority of his church leet, the fair and market, and that he and his predecessors had franchise, and liberties, pertaining to the view of 'francopledge' {pledge of peace} from the time of Henry III (1216).[66]

THE HARVESTING OF TREES – THE WHAPLODE RIOT. 1481

February 1481 saw the beginnings of the Whaplode riot when a dispute arose around the harvesting of the trees in the churchyard. The Abbot's bailiff Alan Dawson reported to the Abbey at Croyland on February 13th, informing the Abbot that the townspeople intended to cut the trees down. The Abbot charged his bailiff to inform the clerics and the townspeople that the trees belonged to Croyland Abbey, and that they were forbidden to harvest them. The townspeople responded by sending a deputation of three men (Richard Keele [Vicar of Whaplode 1479-1501], William Haltoft and Robert Andrewe) on the Thursday prior to Ash Wednesday. The Abbot was unmoved but would send his steward (Lambert Fossdyke) to deal with the matter. When Fossdyke arrived with two others (John Okeley and Simon Herris) the people were already cutting down the trees, Fossdyke declared to the crowd the Abbot's rights to the churchyard trees and told them they were forbidden to proceed any further.

The crowd's response was one of belligerence, declaring that even if the Lord Abbot appeared himself, they would not only continue cutting down the trees, but they would also cut off the Abbot's head. Some of the woodcutters began to approach Fossdyke in a menacing manner, and he fled for his own and his men's safety and was rescued by the clergy on taking him into the vestry for sanctuary. The Vicar, Richard Keele, locked

45

them up inside the church for their own protection, however, he handed the key to William Haltoft on the understanding that the men were to remain there until an agreed letter had been written for delivery to the Abbot, not only demanding the right to continue to cut down the trees, but to include a claim for exculpation of the people for their conduct.

The letter also asked that the Abbot hand his sealed response to Alan Dawson, who was ordered by the people to have their response back in Whaplode by 6.00pm that evening. If he failed to complete his task due to any delay by the Abbot, then he was to remind the Abbot that the townspeople would require two sacks, in which they would return the head and body of his steward. The Abbot conceded under such duress for the sake of Fossdyke and his colleagues, following which William Haltoft received the response at 7.00pm, and he released Fossdyke and the other men, all of whom returned safely to the Abbey.

To punish the rioters, the justices were asked to meet and form a jury, chosen by the bailiff of Elloe Wapentake. The assembled jury not only acquitted the people of Whaplode, but also found the Abbot and his men guilty of affray; proceeding to indict them for it. The Justices did not accept the verdict and hastily appointed another meeting in Spalding, where two of the men, namely William Lambe and Thomas Echard, were found guilty of the affray, whereupon the Abbot appealed to the Bishop of Lincoln (John Russell) to ex-communicate several of the Whaplode people.

As a result, in 1482 there were four men (Thomas Milner, William Haltoft, Thomas Echard and William Joiner) who were sentenced to go in procession at Whaplode on Palm Sunday in their shirts and barefoot, holding wax candles, before the Vicar to receive three strokes of the rod; Haltoft, Milner and Joiner were also required to process at Croyland Abbey on Easter Day carrying a deed they had received from the Abbot. They were to dress only in their shirts (no girdles to be worn), and barefoot carrying wax candles to the high altar. They knelt on their knees confessing their crimes to the Abbot, who commanded them to lay the deed on the High Altar, from there they processed to offer their candles to St Guthlac. On receiving their confessions, the Abbot ordered the men never to lay violent hands on any clergy, during the remainder of their lives, they were then absolved of their sins. [67]

The Whaplode Riot of 1481: Scene outside the Church Tower
of St. Mary's – the clergy rescue the Abbot's steward,
Lambert Fossdyke. Drawing by Anthony Barton (fig.19).

A more comprehensive account of this dispute is included as an appendix
within Foster's book.[68]

7.

The prelude to the final handover of responsibilities in 1594, and the turmoil beyond

OWNERSHIP OF AND RESPONSIBILITY FOR ST. MARY'S CHANCEL
When one considers all the attendant issues, together with the fractious nature of the relationship between the townspeople of Whaplode and the Abbots of Croyland, it is understandable that Croyland would seek to remove itself from the duties and burdens of dealing with such a restless constituency.

Following the legislative dissolution of the monasteries introduced under Henry VIII, which was completed by 1540, the Benedictine church of St. Mary's Whaplode underwent significant changes in the manner of its operation. As a result of the changes brought about by the Reformation, together with the emergence of Protestantism as the religious order to be followed throughout the Kingdom, albeit there was a brief period, between 1553-1558, when Queen Mary claimed the throne; much of the lifestyle within the towns and villages also changed. No longer were people subject to the laws imposed by the Abbot and his agents, instead much of the influence of daily life was now being directed through wealthy aristocrats and landowners, and since Whaplode had attracted many such families during its 'boom town' years, there were plenty of people available to support the church.

In 1544 the incumbent of St. Mary's, Mgr. Robert Baynthorpe resigned, whether this was in response to the 'Dissolution of the Monasteries' is not known, but from the time of Henry's marriage to Anne Boleyn there was the beginnings of a schism within the religious orders and the monarchy. By 1561 the term 'Vicar' was being used to describe the incumbent, following the death of the previous incumbent Dom. Robert Browne, by grant of the late Abbot of Croyland.

In 1594, St. Mary's, which had hitherto been under the 'control' of the various Abbots of Croyland until the Abbey was dissolved in 1539, and thereafter under Diocesan Bishops on behalf of the Monarch (a short period aligned with Queen Mary), was placed into the ownership of the Archdeacon of Leicester - Robert Johnson, as an impropriator (assigned thereto as a lay proprietor of the 'Chancel'), by Her Majesty Queen Elizabeth I, and upon his death the responsibility for the 'Chancel' was to pass to his successors, the Governors of Uppingham School, again on behalf of the Monarch.

ROBERT JOHNSON: ST. MARY'S & UPPINGHAM SCHOOL

Robert Johnson (1540-1625) founded two 'free' Schools - Oakham in 1574, and Uppingham in 1584. Johnson was Rector of North Luffenham, during that time, and later became Archdeacon of Leicester (1591-1625). The schools were both unique in their pursuance of a free education, especially for the poor families of the districts. However, since one of the stipulations for continued attendance was a constant attendance record, such a situation at once deprived the least well-off families of a much-needed income. It was customary practice at that time for children to be employed, usually in the more menial tasks which could not easily be performed by adults.

In addition to his remuneration as Archdeacon, and Rector of North Luffenham, Johnson also received additional income from four other Churches (which included the tithes received from St Mary's Church, Whaplode). He also founded the Hospitals of Christ in Oakham & Uppingham and was one of the eight founding members of Jesus College at Oxford University. In recognition of his foundation, a statue of Johnson can be found on the Victoria Tower at Uppingham School.

By way of interest, whilst genealogical records are not conclusive as to his earlier ancestors, it is known that Robert Johnson was one of seven children of his father, Maurice Johnson - MP for Stamford (b. circa 1480 - d.1551), who married Jane Lacy. Examination of such records suggest that a Francis Johnson (d. before 18.05.1616) was one of Robert's brothers - if this is correct – it would imply that Francis, who married Elizabeth Thorogood, was the great, great, great Grandfather of Maurice Johnson, Esq., F.A.A. Barrister-at-Law, who was the founder of the Spalding Gentlemen's Society.[69]

Queen Elizabeth I bestowed a Royal Charter on both schools in 1587 as a direct consequence of the generous funding Robert Johnson had been providing to the schools and the hospitals, and elsewhere. Johnson was also a close friend of William Cecil - 1st Baron Burghley, who was responsible for the building of Burghley House near Stamford and was also a confidant of the Queen.

It is understood that the Royal Coat of Arms of George III, which hangs over the Chancel Arch in St. Mary's, is directly connected with the association that St. Mary's had with the Royal School at Uppingham. (See below: 9. Specific artistic and commemorative contributions to the fabric of St. Mary's - The Royal Coat of Arms of George III - 1773).

POST 1625 - THE GOVERNORS OF UPPINGHAM SCHOOL

The events that led to the responsibility for the Chancel of St. Mary's being removed from/given up by the Governors of the Estates of the Foundation of Robert Johnson, Archdeacon of Leicester (vis. Uppingham School) are quite extraordinary.

The Governors of Uppingham School took over the lay responsibility for the 'Chancel' of St. Mary's (as assigned to them as impropriators) on behalf of Queen Elizabeth I on the death of Robert Johnson in 1625. Whereupon they continued to wantonly take the 'appointed' tithes down the centuries, for any use other than the maintenance of the fabric of St. Mary's, and over many years successive Vicars repeatedly pleaded with them to expend money thereon, to no avail. However, such was the Governors' antipathy to such requests, that after years of neglect only £400 (approximately a quarter of the annual tithes that were being received) was spent on rebuilding the Chancel in 1818, with the result that a great deal of 'heritage' was destroyed leaving a nondescript 'modern' chancel bereft of any architectural significance. In this context, St Mary's tithes were commuted in 1836 to an annual value of the order of £1,600, which, at 2022 comparative prices, would translate into approximately £180,000.

REVD. JOHN RHODES v THE JOHNSON FOUNDATION

OCTOBER 1900: THE PUBLIC CAMPAIGN BY REVD. RHODES

In October 1900, Revd. John Rhodes, Vicar of St. Mary's (1898-1909) undertook a very public campaign to harangue the Governors and highlight their appalling neglect and dismissal of any need to maintain the fabric of the chancel of St. Mary's Church. In so doing he produced a public booklet – frontispiece as below (fig.20) (courtesy of the Spalding Gentlemen's Society).

Therein, over fifteen pages, he delivers a strongly worded indictment of their prior failure over 300 years in receipt of said tithes (an average of £1,600 pa) and specifically the previous 50 years, to spend the necessary money in fulfilment of their obligations. In so doing, on page 5, he refers to the damning remarks made by Sir George Gilbert Scott in his report on St. Mary's, as follows: *"I am persuaded that you are all quite unaware of the condition of that portion of the fabric for which you are responsible. The late Sir George Gilbert Scott, 42 years ago, in his report of the church, spoke of the extraordinary beauty and magnificence of the nave, and added that the Chancel is reduced to the lowest possible architectural character and a perfect blot on the beauty of the Church. Some of the details he described as beneath criticism. The ancient beauty and extent of the Chancel has been frightfully mutilated, for two aisles have been wholly destroyed and the roof lowered……"*

His strength of feelings around this subject is clearly demonstrated in extracts from pages 10, 11 & 13, as reproduced hereunder [his *'bold'* highlights] : *"……I submit the Rectors* [Governors of Uppingham School] *ought to reckon **the spiritual and material needs of the Parish have first claim on the Tithe,** but instead of this the narrowest possible interpretation has been put upon even their legal responsibilities. That this is so, I have only to remind the reader of the description given above of the state of the chancel in 1898. It has since been roughly colour-washed (and a useable stove provided by the Rectors in place of the broken one), and a carpet laid in the Sanctuary, and a few ornaments added by parishioner and friends.*

***The Rectors have failed to fulfil their legal obligations.** But I have, some will think, a yet more forcible argument to bring against the Rectors, because this argument is based on their own contention. They say they do not dispute their legal responsibilities. Now, the law requires that the Rector shall **"preserve and repair" the Chancel,** and the Deed granting the tithe of Whaplode to the Governors of Oakham and Uppingham Schools, says: "and we will acquit and hold indemnified the said Governors to us and our heir…….except as regards the agreements and burdens which any farmer or farmers of the premises by reason of these indentures and demises are held to discharge or pay therein…………"*

Rhodes continues *"……...The Agreement referred to is a Grant, 26th Elizabeth* [26th year of Elizabeth I reign]*, to Katherine, Thomas and Robert Pulvertoft, to "farm" the tithe of Whaplode, in which it is specified they "shall at their own proper costs and charges well and sufficiently repair, support, sustain, scour, purge, and maintain the Chancel of the parish Church of Whaplode aforesaid and all houses and buildings, and likewise all hedges……..and all necessary repairs to the premises, in and by all things, from time to time whensoever it shall be necessary and fitting. In the eighteenth century, they have so far failed to observe this requirement that they allowed the Chancel and its aisle or aisles to fall into a ruinous condition, and then an attempt was made by them or on their behalf to induce the Parishioners to re-build the fabric. **This attempt to escape even this fragment of service for their £1,600 of annual tithe was frustrated by the then Curate-in-charge, the Rev. Samuel Oliver.** The Rectors then saddled the parish with this hideous parody of the splendid fabric with which they were entrusted. **£400!!** being the entire cost of the new Chancel - thus sum having been much more than saved by the*

51

annual reduction of maintenance and repairs on the smaller building. A large group of buildings which formerly stood to the West of the Church have been entirely erased from the face of the earth , presumably because of the neglect of the Rectors to fulfil their covenanted duty………………"

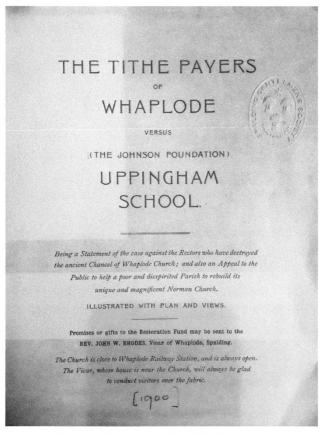

Frontispiece of Revd. John Rhodes' public Statement on the state of the fabric of the Chancel of St. Mary's Church. - October 1900 (fig.20).

In a response to an earlier request by him to the Governors for £100 per annum to be set aside for twenty years to accumulate at compound interest for re-building the Chancel, he further states, as follows:

"They unanimously declined to make even this tiny effort to help the parish they injure" and he includes a copy of their letter in reply, in which the following is stated: '*The Governors are unable to see their way, insomuch as the Chancel is not in any state of dilapidation, to expending any larger sums of money than are necessary for the maintenance of the Chancel in good repair, having consideration to the educational and charitable*

*demands to which they are liable under the trust. Believe me, Yours truly,
H.R. Finch.'*

Whereupon he concludes: *"This answer is evidently given under the
complete misconception of the whole question, and I do not doubt that when
the Rectors have had time to assimilate the other side of the case and
recovered from their first annoyance at this extremely painful publicity –
painful alike for me as for them – they will make strenuous efforts to make
amends to the Church and parishioners."* [70]

MAY 1901: THE AFTERMATH – A PUBLIC PETITION IN SUPPORT OF REVD. RHODES

His forthright conclusion in his Statement of October 1900 had been that the
sum of £3,000 would not only be necessary, but also that he expected that the
Governors **would** pay it, to rectify matters, and in May 1901 a public petition
was raised in Whaplode in furtherance of the Vicar's aims and submitted to
Edward King, Bishop of Lincoln, to gain his backing.

Sadly, the Vicar's plea was to no avail since no support was
forthcoming from the Bishop. Worse still, the aftermath of the Vicar's public
'denunciation' of the Governors led to the errant action of the Governors by
taking the Vicar to the County Court to recover from him 'Tithe' monies not
paid over (albeit this itself was 'illegal' since he could not be held responsible
for such), but the Vicar failed to challenge the claim, and his property was
seized for public auction in restitution thereof.

APRIL 1907: REVD. RHODES' CONTINUING CONFRONTATION

Undeterred, in April 1907, the Revd. John Rhodes continued to regale the
Governors in his sermons for their irresponsible actions, and this publicity
added to the interest being shown by various organisations who, since prior to
the turn of the century, had also been pressing for work to be carried out to
rectify the deplorable state of the fabric of St. Mary's. (See Appendix XII).

JUNE 1909: THE GOVERNORS CEDE THEIR RESPONSIBILITIES FOR THE CHANCEL BACK TO THE CROWN.

The outcome of this confrontation was that ultimately the Governors ceded
their responsibilities, as impropriators, for St. Mary's Chancel back to the
Crown, and in 1909 the Crown Lands and Estates, acknowledging such land
ownership, following a request from the new Vicar, obtained Treasury sanction
for a contribution of £35 (at 2022 comparative prices – circa £4,000) towards
the costs of repairing the fabric of St. Mary's Church, as detailed in the
National Archives Record: T1/11035/11956. (See Appendix XIII – Crown

Lands and Estates documentation June 1909: Contribution towards costs of repairing the fabric of St. Mary's Church, Whaplode).

Fortuitously, a year earlier, the new Vicar - Revd. Ed. W. Brereton M.A., who took over from Revd. John Rhodes and had taken up the cause, also pursued The Society for The Protection of Ancient Buildings for action, given their interest in the state of St. Mary's since being approached by Revd. John Rhodes in 1904, and as a result, in 1910, the Society contributed £10 towards the cost of the works (see Appendix XII).

THE LORD CHANCELLOR'S PATRONAGE OF ST. MARY'S

St Mary's Church (along with many other churches) has a particular standing within the hierarchy of Church governance, in so far as it is aligned with those churches that are classified as being of a 'Royal Peculiar' status, whereby any change in a stipendiary appointment is required to be sanctioned by the Monarch of the day. [71]

Whilst St. Mary's is not a 'Royal Peculiar' church *per se*, examination of the Church & Parochial Church Council ("PCC") records highlights that due authority for any appointment or vacation of the post of a *'permanent'* Vicar has been sought from the Lord Chancellor, who, it would appear, has been the patron of St. Mary's Whaplode since medieval times.

Historically, this unique situation arises from the 14th and 16th centuries whereby the Ecclesiastical patronage of the Lord Chancellor was part of the patronage of the Crown. The exercise of the Crown's parochial patronage being divided between the Monarch and the Lord Chancellor. In the 14th century the poorest livings (Church benefices), those less than 20 marks, were passed to the Lord Chancellor, and in the 1530's it was those less than £20, and the Crown retained those livings that were worth more than these amounts. Therefore, this basis of assessment was in place when the monasteries were dissolved under King Henry VIII, and the Crown was the major recipient of their parochial patronage, and currently, if the value of the benefice is more than £20, the appointment is made by the Monarch acting on the advice of the Prime Minister, whereas if the value is under £20, the Lord Chancellor makes the representation in the Monarch's name.

Consequently, the value of a benefice in the 16th century is the determinant as to whether the Monarch or the Lord Chancellor makes the appointment in the 21st century, and since 1964 the patronage rights of both the Lord Chancellor and Her/His Majesty have been dealt with through officials based in Number 10 Downing Street. Comparatively, the Lord Chancellor either exercises patronage solely or shares patronage for approximately 442 parish livings and 12 cathedral canonries in England, and such benefices where the Lord Chancellor appoints only makes up 5.5% of English livings.[72]

To put the above into context, in 1526 St. Mary's Church was still under the control of the Abbot of Crowland, with a value of estimated at £16.6.8d (DMO, Pages 135-136). However, the Abbey of Crowland was dissolved in 1539, and thereafter, as evidenced by the Clergy of the Church of England database (CCEd) *(1540-1835:Lincoln Diocese, ID:8606 - Whaplode Parish)* for a short period of time, St. Mary's fell under the jurisdiction of successive Bishops of Lincoln, until March 1554 when John Blades was formally appointed Vicar by the new Patron, Queen Mary (r.1553-1558). By way of comparison, our sister church, All Saints' Church, Moulton, received their first patronage appointment – that of Richard Russell, Clerk - by The Lord Chancellor in 1540.

Therefore, in 1594, whilst Queen Elizabeth I had appointed Robert Johnson, as lay proprietor, who would be responsible for the fabric of St. Mary's 'Chancel', as Monarch she continued to retain the direct responsibility for the nomination and appointment of the St. Mary's Clergy. and her ecclesiastical representative would have been 'The Lord Chancellor' – given that St. Mary's had a *'living'* less than £20.

The earliest record within the Parish Records of the subsequent involvement by the Monarch in the appointment of a *'permanent'* [formally termed as *'perpetual'* in CCEd] Vicar, can be seen in an entry dated 15th November 1613, wherein it is recorded that *"William Holden, clerk, M.A.* [Vicar of St. Mary's 1613-1650] *was presented by the King* [Elizabeth I had died in 1603 and was succeeded by King James I] …… *with the Mandate for induction from the Archbishop of Canterbury, the See of Lincoln being vacant."*

Centuries later, in February 1883, the following is recorded *" The Lord Chancellor has bestowed the vacant living of Whaplode, Lincolnshire, on the Rev. John Collin, Great Ayrton Vicarage, Northallerton, Yorkshire. The living is worth £700 per annum and a house and garden."*

A copy of a letter dated 10th February 1927 sent to the Churchwardens by William Swayne, Bishop of Lincoln (1920- 1932) (fig. 21) together with an extract from the minutes of a PCC meeting held 16th May 1977 (fig.22), confirm the continuing practice.

Today, the ecclesiastical administrative duties of the Lord Chancellor, fall under the Patronage (Benefices) Measure 1986 which sets out the formal procedures that are followed, and the Church Appointments Team in the

Cabinet Office in Downing Street continues to play a substantive role in the determination of the selection of candidates for office, however, ultimately, representatives of the relevant parochial church council must approve any candidate.[73]

10. 2. 27.

My dear Churchwardens.

        I am grateful to you for your letter of Feb. 4th. I am forwarding it by this post to the Eccl. Secretary of the Lord Chancellor. The Lord Chancellor is the patron of Whaplode. I can of course make no promises, as the Lord Chancellor may have already offered the benefice to some one, but I will do my best to secrue that your suggestion will be favourably considered.

I think your suggestion is thoroughly sound and I personally will be very glad if we could secure the Rev. H. C. Holland as Vicar of Whaplode.

    I am

        Very sincerely yours

          S. V. Lincoln:

Copy of Letter from Bishop of Lincoln to St. Mary's Churchwardens. 10th February 1927 (fig.21).

A Meeting of the Parochial Church Council of St. Marys Whaplode was held in the Village School on Monday 16th May 1977 at 8. 0p.m. with Canon Colin Evans in the Chair.

28 Parishioners and P.C.C. Members were present.

Received from Dr. Deverell, and Mr. David Green.

The Minutes of the Meeting held on the 29th June 1976 were read confirmed and signed. There were no matters arising.

Canon Evans announced that the Lord Chancellors Office had approved the appointment of the Rev. Ogdens successor, namely the Rev. Lancelot Carter. It is understood that the Rev.Carter hopes to move in to the vicarage this summer.

Extract from minutes of PCC meeting 16th May 1977 (fig.22).

8.

A chronology of pastoral / other events occurring, together with non-architectural fabric features introduced

VILLAGE DANCERS & SECULAR ACTIVITIES

In the early 16th century, invariably, the larger villages had their own companies of players who performed plays, or ceremonies, e.g., the Assumption of the Blessed Virgin, whose costumes were provided by the parish, and who took their play, whatever it was, round the neighbouring parishes, and collections would be taken up by respective parishes to pay for the performers.

Whaplode's tradition of customary dancing was extended through much of the century. By way of example, in 1514 on Plough Monday a man bequeathed 12d to the dancers' light in the parish church, and the parish also received 12d from the 'lumini de le dauncers'. In 1524, Whaplode players performed at Sutterton, and in 1562-3 the Morris dancers of Whaplode were paid for their appearance at Long Sutton.[74]

In Holbeach, the 'Holbeach bells' were used to call the scattered parishioners to a secular meeting, and the bells must often have been used to give warnings of disasters, especially where floods were likely. The use of the 'lantern lights' at Moulton and Whaplode churches, for which bequests were made in 1514 and 1526, were undoubtedly used for the same practical purpose. [75]

THE EARTHQUAKE

On 25th May 1671, Whaplode St. Mary's Church suffered the consequences of an earthquake. The evidence of this traumatic event can be seen from viewing both aisle walls (especially the south aisle wall – it should be noted that these aisles were widened between 1380 and 1460). Further evidence can be viewed from the steps of the Chancel, when looking towards the west window, one can see that the first of the Transitional Period arches on the right leans slightly to the north. (See **Part Two:** 2. The Architectural Structure and Principal Fabric Heritage of St. Mary's: Late Norman-Early English: Transitional Period (1130-1190)). In all other aspects these sturdy Norman bays have never varied more than + or - 5mm, as recorded in regular surveys conducted in the church every 10 years. The last one was completed in 2010.

THE CHURCH CLOCK

The Church clock stands on an elevated platform within the clock room, at the second-storey level of the Bell Tower. Access to the clock room is gained via the narrow spiral staircase situate at the south west corner of the Bell Tower, in which there are 41 +2 stone steps to the clock room, and a further 12 narrow wooden steps on a ladder, with one hand rail, leading up to the wooden encased 300-year-old clock mechanism.

Close-up of the Clock face. (fig.23)

The original mechanism of the clock required it to be manually re-wound every 46 hours. However, during the 1960's the clock stopped working, and in 1970 it was dismantled, with the mechanism rebuilt by a local engineering firm (D.A. Green & Sons Ltd), and subsequently elements were also replaced in 1977, but the clock mechanism continued to suffer its 'age'.

The wooden encased Clock mechanism (fig.24).

Latterly, in 2008, after close inspection from three expert clock repairers, the PCC, in consultation with John Ablott, the Lincoln Diocesan Advisory Committee clock expert, concluded that the time and stroke mechanisms should be completely overhauled, repaired, and the manual re-wind replaced with an automated electronic re-wind and strike.

View of pre-electric
'going train' (fig.25).

View of electronic
'going train' (fig.26).

A funding appeal was launched in November 2008, which raised more than £10,000, and, following the receipt of the Lincoln Diocesan Advisory Committee certificate of authorisation in 2009, the work was commissioned and subsequently concluded in 2012, and it was during this period of work that the date of the manufacture of the clock was determined as having been circa 1718-1720.

In 1976 there had been raised a suggestion that the diagonal (diamond) framework markings on the East face of the Tower above the dial were associated with an even earlier dial (figs.105-106 provide a view of these markings). However, following consultation with Clockmakers - 'Smith of Derby' - this was discounted, given that "*such a dial would have been quite enormous, perhaps 9 or 10 feet in diameter, to be enclosed in such a framework. The marks, being incised, suggest that some kind of 'roof' may have been there, but even that seems a little unlikely as it would have been too close to the arcade decoration.*"

More recently, a lithograph of the Church dated circa 1810-1830 (see fig.181) has been found, which would suggest that there was simply a more pronounced diamond style stone framework in position at one point, which has been worn down by weather, within which was housed the 'circular' clock face and its mechanism.

A detailed synopsis of the workings of the original 'going train' and 'striking train' of the clock, together with photographs of the pre-electronic 'original' mechanisms can be seen on the St. Mary's Church, Whaplode website, https://whaplodechurch.co.uk wherein it is indicated that the likely cost of the clock would have been between £12 - £25 circa 1720. £20 in 1720 is comparable to more than £5,000 at 2023 prices.

THE CHURCH BELLS

It has been suggested that the first introduction of bells in Churches was through the Venerable Bede. Allegedly, he was responsible for the ringing of a bell to indicate certain times of devotion during his time at Jarrow in the 8th century, and the inclusion of church bells was to become commonplace in Western Europe by the 9th century.

Five of the present six bells in situ at St Mary's were made by Henry Penn, a Bell founder of Peterborough, who was responsible for hanging bells in twenty-six Lincolnshire churches over the period 1708 until 1729 when he supplied a whole 'ring' of bells (the name given by bell ringers to a set of bells hung for English full circle ringing) to the church of St. Peter and St. Paul, in Bourne, Lincolnshire. The original five bells of St. Mary's, having been hung by Penn in 1718, have undergone minor alterations throughout their life, with the fourth bell being recast in 1933. The bells were initially rehung in the autumn of 1888, when extensive repairs were made to the belfry at a total cost of £138 (repairs (£128) and re-hanging).

The Bell frame is officially listed as being of historical importance with Historic England under a Church Heritage Record reference: CHR 30152, and the six bells are recorded under CHR reference 30150.

To reach the Bell room, using the spiral staircase, a further 26 +2 steps beyond the clock room are required to be negotiated. Once inside the Bell room, a glance upwards at the roof will reveal two large timber beams, each supporting a king-post, and each with two braces, across which is a cylindrical timber complete with through mortice holes in relevant places, which it is believed is the remaining evidence of a capstan winch used by Penn to lift the St. Mary's bells into place (the mortice holes being for the wooden levers).

It is rare to find such substantial remains of old lifting equipment, and therefore, it possible that the present roof was at one time much higher, not least because there is insufficient space under the current roof to allow enough space for the levers to clear, or for any operatives to stand. Indeed, examination of the brickwork of the Tower battlements would appear to point to an earlier roofline of two feet (or thereabouts) higher than the current one.

View of the rear two bells' wheels framework (fig.27).

However, there are no records to suggest that either a pyramid or spire were part of the topmost area of the Tower at an earlier stage. (See **Part Two:** 2. The Architectural Structure and Principal Fabric Heritage of St. Mary's. Late Norman-Early English: Transitional Period (1130-1190) - The Bell Tower).

View of front four bells' wheel framework (fig.28).

Inscriptions were various and common on most church bells when made by the respected founders from around Britain. Those appearing on the five original Whaplode Bells are identical to those appearing on five of the six bells (Vicars'& Churchwardens' names aside) that were hung by Penn in 1729 at Bourne, Lincolnshire.[76]

Whilst Foster provides a correction as to the inscription on the third bell being 'IT' not 'ET,' the notice below (fig.29) can be seen in the church, and records how each of the six bells at St. Mary's are inscribed, together with details of their hanging and casting. The Latin inscriptions to be found on the five respective bells, as shown on the notice, can be translated, broadly, as follows: [77]

Second:	"I praise the true God. 1718 Henry Penn, Founder"
Third:	"It shouted to the heavens. 1718"
Fourth:	"As the world, now we have joy and grief. 1718"
Fifth:	"James Bolton & William Owen, Churchwardens. I call the people to gather the clergy. 1718"
Tenor:	"John Rustat, Vicar. I warn the living to mourn the dead. 1718"

St. MARY's CHURCH, WHAPLODE: RING OF SIX BELLS.

	DIAMETER	NOTE	WEIGHT Cwt. Qtr. Lb.			INSCRIPTION
Treble	2'-5"	D#	5	1	19	EVA WRIGHT 1932 19(founders mark)33
Second	2'-7½"	C#	6	1	2	LAVDO DEVM VERVM 1718 HENRICVS PENN FVSOR
Third	2'-9⅝"	B	6	1	25	ET CLAMOR AD CÆLOS 1718
Fourth	2'-10⅜"	A#	7	3	17	VT MVNDVS SIC NOS NVNC LAETITIAM NVNC DOLOREM 1718 RECAST 1933
Fifth	3'-2¼"	G#	9	0	10	IAO DOLTON OVLS ONE CWS. PLEBEM VOCO CONGREGO CLERVM 1718
Tenor	3'-6¼"	F#	12	0	14	IOH RVSTAT VICAR DEFVNCTOS PLANGO VIVOS MONEO 1718

The Bells were also completely re-hung in 1933.

Bell inscriptions - Notice in Church (fig.29).

An earlier re-hanging of the original five bells occurred in November 1888 at a cost of £128. 7s, and the subsequent service of re-dedication of the bells, conducted by the Vicar, Revd. John Collin, took place at evensong on 19th November 1888. There was a very large congregation in attendance including eight local clergymen, together with the Bishop of Lincoln, and his chaplain, and the singing was much enlivened by a cornet, and it was reported in the local papers, as follows:

"Dr Edward King (Bishop of Lincoln; 1885-1910) undertook the formal ceremony of re-consecration of the bells, after which, he gave a practical discourse on the use of bells, from the text Exodus xxviii., 33, "Bells of gold."

The 2nd Bell inscribed with 'Henry Penn' –
Bell Founder (fig.30).

"Dr King reminded those present of the use of bells and the lessons they should teach at all times, more especially on New Year's Eve and Easter day. Dwelling at length on the use to which they were put at weddings, his Lordship remarked that many marriages were contracted out of sheer necessity occasioned too often by the misconduct of the contracting parties. The state of matrimony, he said, was too mysterious and too holy a thing to be ridiculed or entered into with thoughtlessness, and marriages of necessity were not occasions for rejoicing, and at such times let the bells keep silence. The vast audience were moved with the Bishop's words."

Coinciding with the subsequent recasting of the fourth bell and re-hanging of the other four, in 1933, there was a sixth bell (the Treble) installed, made by John Taylor, a well-known Bell Founder of Loughborough, and inscribed 'Eva Wright 1932'. The dedication is associated with Eva Wright (died 25th June 1932) who was the wife of George Nutt Wright, a local farmer, whose residence was at the old manor house of the Irby family in Whaplode.

The Bell framework was later to be repaired and renovated, also by John Taylor, at an overall cost of approximately £813 in 1984, with 50% of the cost being borne by The Mary Bass Trust Fund.

Arrival of Church Bells at St Mary's 22nd May 1933 (fig.31).

Also, to be found on the wall within the Ringing Chamber are the records of three Peals.

First record: *Dated 27 February 1775*
A ring of 10,080 changes or 84 Peals was completed by - William Jackson; Richard Harwood; William Money; Stephen Davis and Richard Pottenger, who raised and settled the Bells in 7 hours and 25 minutes.

Second record: *Dated 31 October 1953*
*A visit by the Lincoln Diocese Guild of Bellringers on Saturday 31st October 1953 with a Peal of 5,040 Plain Bob minor in seven different extents. The ringers being - *Pte. P. G. Butler (treble); †Mrs G. R. G. Butler (2); *John Graham (3); *Harold Oliver (4); G. R. G. Butler (5); George Coleman (Tenor - 12cwt conducted by G. R. G. Butler. *First Peal, †First Peal inside in the method.*

Third record: *Dated 31 October 2023*
A Peal of 5040 Plain Bob Minor in 2h. 54 mins, in celebration of the 70th Anniversary by the Butler family and friends, a Peal of 5040 Plain Bob Minor on 31st October 1953, with 3 first peal ringers and 1 first peal inside.

The Treble Bell- inscribed 'Eva Wright-1932' (fig. 32).

View from inside the 'Ringing Chamber' (ground floor
of the Bell Tower) (fig.33).

THE CHURCH (VILLAGE) BAND

In the 18th century church services were also enlivened by music and singing
in many places. Allen makes the statement that *"In 1748 a gallery* (the 'singing
loft') *was built at the east end of Whaplode church to accommodate*

parishioners who were 'skilled and experienced in Psalmody.'[78] (Psalmody-the act of singing psalms and hymns). However, this assertion has subsequently been proven to be not entirely correct - the gallery was simply a re-configuration of the original 'Rood Loft,' elements of the structural fabric of the loft having survived the Reformation - sadly, even this 'constructed' gallery was eventually removed in 1844, but the turret stairway (the *Monks' steps*), which led to it, is still in situ. (See **Part Two** - 2. The Architectural Structure and Principal Fabric Heritage of St. Mary's – The 'Rood Loft').

View of the Monks' Steps entrance, leading to the dormitory,
and the 'Rood Loft' (latterly - 'Singing Gallery') (fig.34).

The Monks' Steps entrance - as now closed off (fig.35).

View from the top of the Monks' Steps, looking down Nave
towards the West End of the Church (fig.36).

THE DOUBLE REED BASSOON

By way of example of the popularity of some of these village bands, as many
as 30 people, accompanied by musical instruments, sang the psalms in Bourne
parish church in 1791, and Bassoons were the most frequently mentioned
instruments in churchwardens' accounts.[79] Indeed, the only remaining
evidence of Whaplode St. Mary's Church (Village) Band is the large Double
Reed Bassoon, which used to hang in the South Aisle for many, many, years
(as noted by Arthur Mee [AM] on page 414 in his book) but is now stored
safely within the Vestry at the East End of the Church. However, its structural
beauty is captured by a framed picture of a replica of this '6-keyed instrument'
which can be seen in the West End of the Church and is shown below (fig. 37).

The bassoon is believed to be from around 1790-1810, as
manufactured by William Mullhouse of 337 Oxford Street London (taken from
an article in *'The Double Reed' – Vol.24. No.3. 2002*), and in 2006, in a letter
to the Churchwardens of St. Mary's, Dr. H. La Rue, Lecturer/Curator of the

Bate Collection, and of the Musical Collections in the Pitt Rivers Museum, and also a Fellow of St. Cross College, Oxford, confirmed that such bassoons were commonly in use in such bands at the end of the eighteenth century.

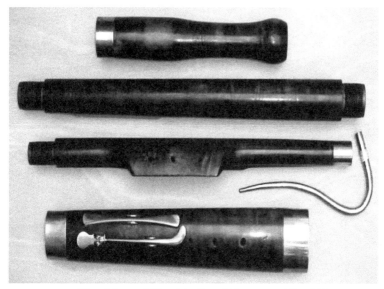

The 6-keyed Double Reed Bassoon (fig. 37)

THE CHURCH ORGAN

The original Church organ was installed at some point between the years 1854-1864. Built by Mark Noble of Norwich it was repaired in 1882 and placed on a platform and positioned in the entrance to the South transept leading to the Bell Tower. It is described in the National Pipe Organ Register ("NPOR") as having had a '*Front of 5c-9-5c dull grey pipes*'. [Ref: N14428]. At a later stage it had been moved to be situated alongside the entrance to the North Transept (see Schematic plan of the Church - 1909 (fig.68), however, it would have been moved back to its current position on the opposite (south) side of the church, adjacent to the turret staircase leading to the 'Singing Gallery' (formerly the 'Rood Loft'), when the renovation of the North Transept window and roof took place in 1909/10.

The 'Noble' organ was subsequently replaced in 1949 by the current 'Compton' organ - a Miniatura Model No.3; rank extension organ: Diapason, Flute, Gemshorn, built in 1948 by John Compton Ltd. (NPOR front description – '*Plain case encloses organ; gold display pipes at front in shallow towers either side and two flats between*'. [Ref: K01296]).

The detailed specifications of both organs can be found on the NPOR web-site:
The National Pipe Organ Register - NPOR

The 'Compton' Organ in situ: Adjacent to the 'Rood' turret staircase
(fig.38).

The 'Compton' organ was given to the church by the widow of William Kilham Wright, and his two sons, as a token of their affection and remembrance of him.

Dedication plaque to W.K. Wright adjacent to the
'Compton' Organ (fig.39).

A particular favourite of the congregation in the 20th century was the organist, Mr Thomas William Walker, who began playing the organ at the Church in 1923. He was to become an ever-present organist and received a cheque from the PCC in 1973 on completing 50 years in the post, and he continued to play for the services at the Church until the mid-1990's when he found it difficult to play, as he was having problems with his hearing.

However, although Thomas ceased to play for the services, he would play 'freely' afterwards, and people would remain simply to listen to him. He continued to play whenever possible, until his death on 12th March 2006, a few days after his 100th birthday.

THE BRASS EAGLE ECCLESIASTICAL LECTERN

In 1874 a wooden Lectern was purchased for the expense of seven pounds. However, in 1918 the gift of a beautiful brass eagle ecclesiastical lectern was bestowed on the church by Isabellina Wright, in memory of her husband Carden Wright, and his years of service as a churchwarden of St. Mary's.

The Brass Eagle Ecclesiastical Lectern (fig.40).

The dedication inscription to Carden Wright on the base (fig.41).

PRIVATE BAPTISMS

The rite for private baptism, which provided for cases where there was 'great cause and necessity' was used in ways that suited the personal circumstances of parents, although, generally, the clergy were thought to be bound privately to baptise a child, whether well, or ill, when required to do so. However, in scattered fenland communities it was less easy to arrange prompt public baptisms as laid down in the prayer book.

At Whaplode, infants were said in 1845 to be brought to the clergyman's house 'generally on or about the third day'. Here he was to some extent in control of a situation in which he acquiesced, since in a parish where 'a vast number of infants die' private baptisms were an attempt to ensure them the burial service that the Prayer Book denied the unbaptised.[80]

WORKHOUSES AND 'FREE' PEWS

During the latter part of the 18th and the early 19th centuries Whaplode supported the inhabitants of a local workhouse (poorhouse) for the poor families and focused on the importance of religious instruction and cleanliness.

In 1816 there being no regular attendance upon the religious duties by the people in the workhouse, it is recorded that the Revd. Oliver, who had for many years been endeavouring to bring about such regulations, and the Master of the Workhouse that year being *Tonsor* General [*latin:* Barber General: "Tonsure" – the practice of cutting or shaving some or all of the hair on the scalp as a sign of religious devotion or humility], proposed the following order:- "*By order of the Vestry No shaving to be done for hire after 9.30am on a Sunday Morning and every inmate is hereby ordered to attend Divine Service, with the Master and Mistress, twice every Sunday and sit in the* {free}

71

places appointed for them in the parish church. Under pain of being taken before a Magistrate and to be dealt with accordingly to the law. Signed by Revd. Oliver, Churchwarden, the overseer of the poor and five other people."

In the furtherance of this, the poor people were allowed into the church to be part of the services, and on a floor-plan dated 1849-1854, as found in the Church records, there appear as many as 20 pews marked as 'free', being reserved for people from the workhouse, albeit, the occupants of these pews, whilst they could hear the service, they could not necessarily see the service being performed by the priest because of where the pews were positioned. There remain today a few rows of such *Free pews* so marked to be seen in the North Aisle. Given that parishioners were 'expected' to contribute for their seating at services, the cost of providing such 'open' seats at Whaplode Church in 1850 was met by voluntary contributions. [81]

On 8th June 1866 at a meeting of owners of property and ratepayers of the Parish of Whaplode, a resolution was passed to the effect that "*consent was given to the Guardians of the poor of the Holbeach Union* {Poor law unions were set up in geographical areas embracing a number of parishes who were jointly responsible for the administration of poor relief in their areas and each governed by a board of guardians - the Holbeach Union covered the parts of Holland} *selling by private contract to the Revd. J.F. Francklin* {Vicar of Whaplode, 1859-1883} *for the sum of nine pounds the following premises that is to say a small plot of land whereon the lock-up formerly stood, under the provisions of an Act of Parliament* {Poor Law Amendment Act 1834} *to facilitate the conveyance of Workhouses and other property of Parishes and of Incorporations or Unions of Parishes*".

The subsequent Local Government Act of 1929 abolished Poor Law Unions and the responsibility for public administration and assistance of poor relief was transferred to county and county borough councils.

GENERAL IN-HOUSE MAINTENANCE

The church underwent several changes during the early to middle part of the 19th century, including the cleaning of the West End to remove ochre, lamp-black (soot) and whitewash, with the remainder of the Church being cleaned in 1846.

During the 18th and 19th centuries the church was heated by a series of pot-bellied stoves. These were at one time used to reduce the number of bats, and one occasion three large stoves were used to burn sulphur to eradicate them, which resulted in the demise of over 500 bats, however, the bat population thrives (a protected species since 1981) to this day.

North Aisle stove chimney 'hole'   Lady Chapel stove chimney 'hole'
(fig.42).   (fig.43).

The only evidence we have today of this heating system is a circular hole for a stove's chimney in the panelling of the North Aisle roof near to the present-day heating system, together with one in the Lady Chapel – these to funnel the fumes out of the church (see above figs.42 and 43).

View of Pot-Bellied Stove - undated, but before 1973 (fig.44).

The above photograph (fig.44) appears in the Church records and can also be seen in the book *'South of the Wash, Tydd St. Mary to Spalding', 1995, by J. Latham and others. [JL.II, page 86].* However, whilst the date of the photograph does not appear in either the Church records, or in the book, the date is certainly *before* 1973 since the Mary Curtois painting can be seen hanging above the Chancel Arch and it was taken down in 1973, being replaced with the Royal Coat of Arms of George III. (See below: 9. Specific artistic and commemorative contributions to the fabric of St. Mary's – 'Christ in Glory'- Oil Painting on Canvas and Zinc Plate - 1907).

Whilst the Victorians craved cleanliness through everywhere being scrubbed clean, it was not until the early part of the twentieth century that the use of candles for the purpose of lighting the inside of the church was discontinued. This was due to the introduction of electric lights, but the method of heating introduced by the Victorians with three or four pot-bellied stoves continued well into the 1950's, by which time they were converted to burning coke, instead of wood. There was also a change to the way the church was heated through the introduction of piping throughout the pews, which carried heated water from the stoves.

Unfortunately, the inclusion of another pot-bellied stove to warm the south side of the church necessitated removal of part of the original timbers to incorporate another chimney, the gap for which remains to be seen in the rafters. Church records show that a request was made in 1974 to remove the stoves, however, it was not until 26th April 1976 that the stoves were finally removed from the church.

A SELECTION OF PASTORAL EVENTS IMPACTING THE CLERGY

EXTRACTS FROM ST. MARY'S VESTRY MINUTES/ WHAPLODE PARISH REGISTERS:
1771 – Churchwardens' Accounts declare a deficit
An early Income and expenditure statement highlighting monies owed to the officers, in the sum of £12. 3s. 8¾p to be recovered from parishioners, is shown within Appendix XX. B. The relative value of such at 2022 prices would be circa £1,900.

1801- an unusual request, that lit up the streets
John Hinning – an Attorney from Holbeach – died, and he expressed the desire to be interred at Whaplode at Midnight by torchlight, requiring men to be stationed between Holbeach and Whaplode churchyard with lighted torches.

1802 – Memorandum of Revd. Samuel Oliver

When the Revd. Samuel Oliver first came to Whaplode as Curate he found the Vicarage premises in a deplorable condition. The House, and its Appurtenances, Gardens, Grounds, and the Churchyard had been let together for £10 per annum. There had not been a cartload of manure worked into the garden or the grounds for ten years, and the greatest part of the resulting hay sold. The garden was a complete bed of rubbish, the grounds without fences and the churchyard fence was not able to be seen. All the land was considered as common pastures and stocked as such by everyone who chose, and the pigs belonging to the neighbouring houses were always in the garden.

He had come to the parish on Lady Day 1802, only to find that the premises all but the house were let by a tenant until the following Michaelmas, and, in the winter, little could be done. No sooner were the grounds (all three and a half acres) fenced, he got the whole garden in good condition and raised and planted about three hundred gooseberry and currant trees, as many raspberries, about two hundred willows: six elm, ten walnut, ten apple, seven filbert, three pear, three cherry, twelve plum, a Siberian crab, and some shrubs. In addition to all this he expended twenty pounds in repairing and improving the buildings!

1804 to 1811 – Revd. Samuel Oliver - Collections

The collections in the church between 1804 and 1811 were a cause for concern. The lowest for a year was recorded in 1804 as £1.8s, and the highest reached in 1811 being £2.11s.9d. Because Revd. Samuel Oliver was having trouble with the parishioners' collection being taken at the Holy Communion, a service which followed Matins when most of the people were leaving, he started having the collection taken at the service of Matins. After being a Curate for nine years in the parish of Whaplode, on 23rd March 1811 it was recorded that it was the first day he was able to get possession of the Registers of the parish, despite asking several times, from the Vicar the Revd. Dr Fisher of Charter House, and by Robert Collins the Parish Clerk. Subsequently, the Revd. Samuel Oliver found in the Registers, errors, false entries, and corrections in many places, and arising from this he recorded his displeasure with Robert Collins in the Parish books.

1820 - Upon the accession of King George IV to the throne

The Vicar, the Revd. Samuel Oliver planted one American and four English Walnut trees, all from seed-nut 12 years ago, and he declared that henceforth they would be called 'Royal Nut trees.'

1821 – Extract from Revd. Samuel Oliver's Annual Report

"On 28th May, & three subsequent days the population of the Parish was taken (by Act of Parliament) by Mr Longstaff, the Overseer of the Poor, taking Mr Roberts, the Vestry Clerk, to assist him. I also went round the Parish, in my ecclesiastical capacity, & found 152 Persons in the minority; & eight couples who notoriously cohabit, as man and wife, together! Four of these couples call themselves Methodists, & regularly attend the Meeting Houses! One couple held a Meeting in their own House! Two couples are within the degrees of Affinity! And five couples have had children born!! I likewise found another couple who will not acknowledge that they sleep together; tho' they both sleep in one room!!!" [Exclamation marks – as expressed by the Revd. Oliver].

1885 - Almshouses

It is hoped the parishioners are coming round to the Vicar's suggestion to levy a voluntary rate of one penny in the pound for re-building the six Almshouses, which had been built by an ancestor of the Lord Boston. Latterly, these were demolished in the 20th Century.

1896 – The case of the 'Muffled Peel'

In 1896 a lady named Harriett Dawber died. She had attended every Service at Saint Mary's Church Whaplode over a number of years; her husband was the owner of the Bell and Bowl Public House at Whaplode. When the lady died on the evening of the funeral the bell ringers thought it would be nice to ring a 'muffled peel.'[82] One of the bell ringers went to ask the vicar, but the vicar was out, and as a muffled had to be rung on the day of the funeral and before 9pm they started to ring. The Vicar heard the bells ringing and went to stop them, on entering the tower he grabbed the rope from one of the bell ringers then let go of the rope, the rope went up then came down round the bell ringers neck, two of the other ringers stopped their bells one grabbed the rope from around the bell ringer's neck, the other bell ringer pushed the vicar out of the tower and locked the door. The Vicar then went to see the policeman to complain and have a court case made against the bell ringers for locking him out of his church. The bell ringers heard about this, so they went to the policemen to have a court case made against the vicar for nearly hanging a bell ringer. Both cases were arranged for the same day at Spalding, when both parties arrived at the Court House in Spalding, they agreed to call both cases off. The reason the vicar did not want the bell ringers to ring a muffled peel was because Harriett Dawber's husband was a publican. The Vicar at the time would be the Revd. J. Collin and four of the bell ringers were Herbert and Joe Lawson and Frank and Fredrick Barker the fifth ringer is not known.

1908-10 /1911/12 – Churchwardens' Accounts et al

Appendices XVII and XVIII provide an insight into typical income and expenditure within the parish in the early 20th Century with copies of Churchwardens' Accounts for 1908-09: 1909-10 and 1911-12, together with the Accounts of the Vicar's Fund for 1911-12.

1933 - Vicar found £1,000

In January 1933, the Vicar of Whaplode the Revd. H C Holland (Vicar 1929 – 1944) had a pleasant surprise when he opened a registered envelope to find ten £100 notes. On a plain sheet of paper was written "*I enclose £1000, the interest on this to be used towards church expenses in the name of the vicar and churchwardens".* The note was not signed and there was no indication to show who the generous donor was. The letter was posted in Yorkshire (£1,000 in 1936 would be comparable to that of £80,000 in 2022).

1969 – Enlarged Parish responsibilities

In 1969 with the re-organisation of the Parishes associated with Holbeach, St. John's Holbeach Fen having been a distinct Parish since the 1880's was included in the responsibilities of the vicar of St Mary's Whaplode. This was in complete contrast to an earlier request in 1959 for Saracen's Head to be separated from Whaplode PCC, which was met with strong objections and, ultimately, was not pursued.

1979/1983 -Extracts from Revd. Lancelot Carter's Annual Reports

The Revd. Lancelot Carter served as Vicar at St. Mary's for a period of eight years 1977-1985.

1979

"*There is saying among the more cynically minded of my fellow Clergy that during the first year of a new Vicar in his Parish he can do no wrong, during the second year he can do no right and by the third year nobody cares what he does. That puts me half way through the doing no right period, If that is so, you must be more charitable than most parishes, or I am more deaf than most clergy. The only complaint that I've heard recently, and that in a very roundabout way, is that you can't always hear what I am saying at the back of the church. There are two possible cures for this, and I suggest we try them both. I will try to speak more clearly, and those of you who can't hear me might try sitting nearer the front; there are, alas, plenty of spare seats."*

1983

"I think the thing that concerns me most about the life of our church at the moment is summed up in that rather ugly word 'outreach'. The church does not exist primarily as a sort of holy club for the benefit of its existing members, but to bring the Gospel of Christ to those who do not yet know Him, or who have turned their backs on Him. I am very conscious of the fact that for every one person in the church on a Sunday morning, there are fifty people in the parish who are not there. What are we doing, what can we do about this? What can we do to attract more children and young people. A large proportion of our congregation are no longer in the prime of youth."

EXTRACTS FROM INDEPENDENT PUBLICATIONS

1876 - The Vicar of Whaplode and Pope Joan

On 19th September 1876, The Lincolnshire Free Press, Boston and Spalding, South Holland, and Eastern Counties Advertiser ('LFPBS') was requested to publish an exchange of letters between the Revd. John Fairfax Francklin, MA, Vicar of Whaplode (1859-1883), and Mr William Clement, the village schoolmaster.

The content of three letters between 9th and 12th September under the heading of - The Vicar of Whaplode and Pope Joan - centred on a rancorous discussion surrounding Mr Clement's recent conversion to Catholicism, in which Mr Clements states that *"....you have written me an angry letter and call me a pervert for having submitted to the Holy Catholic Church, in which, at my baptism, I professed my belief".*

Unrepentant, the Revd. Francklin, having challenged Mr Clements that his reliance on certain authorities was in error, wrote that he would await his further research but *" ...you are a very slippery individual, and as hard to be caught and held as an eel."* The correspondence continued and resurrected an argument pursued some 300 years earlier (1560) between John Jewel (Bishop of Salisbury) and Thomas Harding (Roman Catholic Priest & Controversialist: b.1516-d.1572) over the existence of a 'Female Pope'. This exchange of views attracted so much media attention that a pamphlet was printed under the same title. [Reference: *"British Newspaper Archive: LFPBS - 19th September 1876."* Also see '*The Female Pope: The Mystery of Pope Joan' – 1988,* Rosemary & Darrell Pardoe].

1891 - Charges against the Vicar of Whaplode (Bishop Tayler's Primary Visitation, 1552)

At a meeting of the Society of Antiquaries of London held Thursday March 19, 1891, W. E. Foster, Esq, F.S.A. delivered a 'curious' account of a presentment (a formal charging document) raised in 1552, which listed 12 specific charges made against Dom. Robert Browne, Vicar of Whaplode, who had been installed as Vicar in 1546.

In his presentation Foster recounts *"In the first visitation of the Bishop of Lincoln held at Donnington 26th September 1552, presented by Thoms flete, George littilbury, John bandre, Thoms Idon, Alya dawson, Richard Williamson, John Martyn, and John Chapman, the elder".*

Foster then proceeds to list all the charges levelled against Robert Browne, amongst which are the two principal charges, which centred on his co-habitation with a woman of 20 years of age, or thereabouts, who was not his wife – as follows:

i)   *"Ffirst the yycar hathe kept a woman of th'age of xx yeres or theiraboute by the space of thre yeres till the ixth day of June last past, vnder the colr of his wyff, but nit maryed, to the evyll example of other."*

ii)   *"Itm where the constables with other of the peryshe went about with a pryvye watche, and heryng that said vicar had straungers lodged with hym in his house, came amongst other their pgresse thither the vicar being founde suspycyously (that is to say) the wenshses clothes on hys bedde and she in her smocke, w'out other clothes was in the same wherein was but one bedde for theym both, the vicar saynge to her Avaunt hoore I had rather haue spent alone and when they laid it to his charge he said yf any woman were in with me what then she is my lawfull wyffe yit they were neither maryed nor axed in churche, but nowe they be axed & bene this monthe, but not yet maryed."*

It does appear that all the other charges levelled against Dom. Robert Browne were a collection of complaints of the nature; that he had sowed discontent; that his sermons were inaudible; that he was not conducting appropriate teachings of children; and that he had obtained his 'benefice' unlawfully. In summation, a litany of transgressions seemingly to attempt to remove him from office.

However, he continued as Vicar for some years, until his death in 1561. [Reference: *"Proceedings by the Society of Antiquaries of London. Nov 28, 1889 - Jun 18, 1891: 2nd Series: VOL XIII."* Pages 268-270. Digitised by University of Toronto. Int. Archive].

1904 - Vicar of Whaplode complains about inappropriate grave adornments
In the June 4, 1904, edition of 'The Garden' there was the following entry:
*"Floral emblems in churchyards – We cut the following from the Daily Mail
of 23rd ult* {May}:

> *The Vicar of Whaplode* {at the time the Vicar was Revd. John Rhodes}
> *in his parish magazine, asks residents to note that he cannot approve of jam
> pots being used to decorate graves. Even earthenware wreaths in glass cases
> are not approved of, and these, when broken, will be removed. Flowers are
> preferred, or for permanent memorials may be made with the vicar for simple,
> inexpensive, wooden crosses. Those who use real flowers he hopes will remove
> them from the graves when faded."*

The editor of the publication comments therein that whilst he was
sympathetic to the personal wishes of those wishing to display such as a token
of remembrance and affection, nevertheless, "…..*while they are satisfying
their own kindly impulses, they are destroying the beauty of the churchyard,
and bringing into it an element of vulgar tawdriness that is wholly in
opposition to what should prevail in the consecrated space of ground where
we lay our well-loved dead to rest*."

[Reference: '*The Garden, an illustrated weekly journal of gardening
in all its branches. 1871-V65-1904.'* University of Massachusetts Collection.
Digitised by Amherst Libraries. Int. Archive].

9.

Specific artistic and commemorative contributions to the fabric of St. Mary's

THE CHARITY BOARDS

It was from the early to mid-17th century that some of the charitable bequests associated with the church were organised. There are now only three of the 'Charity Boards' remaining that had been created and which hung over the North Porch for many centuries. In 2005/06, the Boards, which were in a serious state of disrepair, and barely legible, were taken down, treated, conserved, and restored by a group of students at Lincoln University Department of Conservation and Restoration, as part of their final year project – a co-operation between St. Mary's and the University. The work took the best part of a full year to complete, and the Boards are now fully legible, protected from the bats, and sit within illuminated glass frames. These tablets are now a worthy testament to the memory of benefactors to the parish of Whaplode, and embrace dates from the 17th to the 19th centuries, as follows:

Board 1

1st - *24 strike of beans payable every year out of the Impropriation of Whaplode and to be distributed amongst the poor of this Parish during ye season of Lent.*

2nd - *A dole of forty shillings pr. an. (per annum) and given in the last Will and Testament of the Lady Horden and John Walpool Esqr (Esquire) to the poor of Whaplode forever and payable forever and payable out of certain lands called Haltoft now belonging to ye Right Honourable the Earl of Stamford.*

3rd - *The aforesaid Lady Horden and her son John Walpool Esqr (Esquire) given also by the last Will and Testament ye sum of Five Pounds pr an (per annum) forever to ye Minister of Whaplode for ye time being payable out of ye lands above mentioned.*

4th -*There is an Almshouse founded by ye family of ye Irbys in this Parish of Whaplode to lodge six poor widows which Almshouse is to be kept in good repair and two of the six widows in it are to receive two penceper week each forever out of the estate belonging to ye successors of that family.*

Board 2

5th - *Erasmus Avery of Moulton Gent (Gentleman) in his last Will bearing the date February 18th 1653 gave unto the poor of Moulton and Whaplode Fifty-Two shillings pr. an. (per annum) to be distributed in Wheaten Bread to each Town successively Two shillings every Sunday beginning the first Sunday in November and ending the first Sunday in May.*

6th - *Elisha Wilson buried November 3rd 1704, and Frances his wife gave to the Schoolmaster of Whaplode for the time being two cottages and two acres of freehold land for ever now rented at Five Pounds Ten shillings pr. An. (per annum) to the intent he should teach so many of the poor inhabitants' children at two pence per week each as the annual rent of the estate above mentioned shall amount to.*

Board 3

Jacob Davey of Holbeach Gent (Gentleman) who died February 2nd 1833 by his last Will dated January 26th 1833 did leave to the Churchwardens and overseers of the Parish of Whaplode in the County of Lincoln and their successors in office forever a rent charge of Five Pounds per year payable out of the house and lands in the possession of Mr Ashley Palmer to be by them on the Feast of St Thomas yearly distributed amongst ten of the poorest widows residing in and belonging to the said Parish of Whaplode.

The Three Charity Boards (fig.45).

THE ROYAL COAT OF ARMS OF GEORGE III - 1773

The Royal Coat of Arms of King George III (fig.46).

The painting is described in the book "*Royal Arms in Lincolnshire Churches*" *by Jennifer S. Alexander and Geoffrey F. Bryant – 1990.* Published by Workers Educational Association, Barton Humber. Pages 32 and 53 - reference 109, as follows:

"*Above the Chancel Arch. Painted on canvas c.3' by c 4'. Arms of 1714-1801 in good condition. 'G R III 1773' above Arms. R. Weston (?) R. Pearse (?) Church wardens. BULLARD Painter' on the lower edge. Mantling ermine and or.*"

A closer view of the painting determines that Messrs '*R. Weston* and *R Pearse*' are, in fact, J (John) Moslin and T (Thomas) Pears, both of whom were the Churchwardens in 1773, and interestingly, in 1742/3 there was a local man named Valentine Bullard who was also a churchwarden. This may provide a 'Bullard' family connection, but it remains a matter of conjecture.

The painting would have been commissioned in 1773 (George III had ascended to the throne in 1760) quite likely by the Governors of Uppingham School, who, upon the death of the prior benefice, Robert Johnson - Archdeacon of Leicester, in 1625, had gained the rights of the Chancel. The Governors had gained a Royal Charter from Queen Elizabeth I in 1594, and following the death of the Archdeacon, 'ownership' of the St. Mary's Chancel formally passed to them. As mentioned earlier, their 'ownership' was ultimately ceded back to the Crown, circa 1909.

Sadly, following the installation of the Mary Henrietta Dering Curtois painting above the Chancel Arch in 1907, the Royal Coat of Arms was placed on the wall at the back of the Church for many years in the area now occupied by the Heraldic Suite, and it was only in March 1968 at a meeting of the Whaplode PCC that the wife of the Reverend Ogden (Vicar 1960-1977) commented on the need for its restoration. Subsequently, on 10 September 1971, the PCC agreed that the painting should be restored, a quote for restoration of £35 having been received by the Vicar from the Studio of Ecclesiastical & Commercial Art at Newark-on-Trent.

Finally, following its restoration, at a meeting of the PCC on 16 October 1972, it was decided that in view of its value it should be exchanged with the existing painting above the Chancel Arch - that being the Mary Curtois painting (see below: 'Christ in Glory' - Oil painting on Canvas and Zinc plate 1907), and in February 1973 the Royal Coat of Arms of George III painting was placed on the wall above the Chancel Arch, where it remains to this day.

'CHRIST IN GLORY' - OIL PAINTING ON CANVAS AND ZINC PLATE - 1907

This unique painting by Miss Mary Henrietta Dering Curtois (1854-1928) has, latterly, hitherto hung on the west wall in the north transept of the church, until very recently, when it was taken down and placed within the Chancel, resting against the South wall, pending examination by Lincoln University Conservation Department. It is unusual in two aspects, one of which is that it is an early form of a montage, that being a pictorial combination of sheet metal and canvas. The second is that it depicts members of the community of Whaplode at the time of the painting - providing a historic local portrait.

Mary Henrietta Dering Curtois was the eldest daughter of the Revd. Atwill Curtois, of Longhills, Branston. Lincolnshire, and as an active member of the Forum Club London she gained considerable reputation as a speaker and lecturer but was principally known for her work as an artist. One of her most notable works - that of the painting of a ward in Lincoln County Hospital (exhibited 1882 in the Royal Academy and Paris Salon) - was given to the Usher Gallery, Lincoln, and she also gave other pictures to Crowland Abbey and Long Sutton Church.

This remarkable painting, commissioned in 1907 and presented to St. Mary's, was painted in the Pre-Raphaelite style, with 'children of Whaplode' forming the supporting figures surrounding the figure of Christ (fig.47).

"Christ in Glory" - Oil painting on canvas and zinc plate (fig.47).

It is described as '*a wonderfully bold and original treatment of the subject "Christ in Glory" – Especial interest centres on the fact that one of the angel's faces is modelled upon an early picture of the artist's mother. {Central angel with distinct black hair in the foreground represents an early portrait of her mother}. The figure of Christ is several feet high and whole picture is on a colossal scale which serves to accentuate rather than mitigate the beaty of the treatment.* '[83]

As highlighted above, in 1972/3 the wife of Revd. Cyril Newton Ogden (Vicar:1960-1977) was instrumental in the replacement of Miss Curtois' painting of 'Christ in Glory', which, since its commission had hung on the wall above the Chancel Arch, with the newly restored painting of The Royal Coat of Arms of King George III.

View of Miss Curtois' painting above Chancel Arch:
circa 1949 [AM] (fig.48).

Thereafter, the 'Christ in Glory' painting sat on the wall at the west end of the church (in the place previously occupied by the Royal Coat of Arms), until the construction of the Heraldic Suite in 2006, whereupon, having been taken down for a period of time, the Curtois painting was left facing the wall in the North Transept with a hessian overlay placed over the front of the picture. As a consequence, the rear attracted usage as a 'pin-cushion' for a myriad of items thereon. The resulting damage left the picture in a distressed state, and independent estimates in 2014 for its repair and renovation exceeded £10,000.

West End of Church - Pre 2006: View of Mary Curtois'
Painting in the former place of the Coat of Arms.
(1973-2006)(fig.49).

Unfortunately, over the succeeding years, little has been achieved in raising the money to attend to any repairs, and the painting, having deteriorated more, currently sits against the south wall of the Chancel, having been taken down from its most recent position in the Lady Chapel, whilst it awaits a conservation survey. It is estimated that the resultant work for it to be restored to its former glory would likely cost in excess of £25,000, at 2023 prices. A funding project to undertake this task is currently under consideration by the PCC, in consultation with Lincoln University Conservation Department, which, if successful, will see the painting re-hung in a more protected space on the South wall in the Chancel.

THE MADONNA & CHILD (WOODEN SCULPTURE)

On the east side of the main window in the North Transept is the figure of a Madonna and child carved from a solid piece of African mahogany. This modern carving was commissioned from the Guild of Lincolnshire Artists and Sculptors by the wife of William K. Wright and donated to St Mary's in 1967.

It is the work of a local man, John Grimble, who taught Art at Boston Grammar School. He was Chairman of the Lincolnshire Artist's Association for 1962/63. Beneath the scuplure there also sits the dedication plaque to Emily Wright.

Dedication plaque to Emily Wright.
(1855-1965) (fig.51).

A letter dated August 1979 is reproduced below from John Grimble following a request from the Vicar, Revd. Lancelot Carter, for some restorative cleaning of the sculpture.

Madonna and Child (wooden sculpture)
(fig.50).

JOHN GRIMBLE

Address removed

Boston, Lincolnshire

11 August 1979.

Dear Mr Carter,

Re: Mother & child Figure - African mahog: Whaplode Parish Church.

You spoke to me about cleaning this carving a month or so ago, and I replied " contact me at the beginning of September"

I now find that I shall be at home and could make a start straight away, if you will give instructions to have the figure taken down, and for me to be informed - I will collect.

All this relies upon your willingness to permit me to exhibit this work at the Autumn Exhibition of the Lincolnshire Artists' held in the Usher Gallery Lincoln Oct 13 to Nov 11 '79.

I'm sure the son of the Engineering Firm close by the Church would arrange to have the figure taken down - it is supported by a bolt in the wall - just like lifting it off a hook.

Yours sincerely
John Grimble

Letter from John Grimble - re: restorative cleaning (fig. 52).

THE TEN FOOT LONG 'DAN HAGEN' OAK 'COMMUNION' TABLE

There is a fine ten-foot-long oak table situate in the North Transept, which has been used on occasions for Holy Communion. The table was made by Dan Hagen of Ingham, Norfolk, in 1972. Employing a pre-1700's early English construction technique of using pegs and wedges, the craftsman has made a table worthy of the church.

The ten-foot-long Dan Hagen Oak table (fig.53).

COMMEMORATIVE PLAQUES

THE WRIGHT FAMILY

In addition to the dedication of the 'Treble Bell', the Organ, the Brass Eagle Ecclesiastical Lectern, and the Madonna and Child Sculpture, as mentioned earlier, there are two other family memorial plaques to be found in the church, representative of a family which continues to support the Church to this day, as follows:

i)   On the wall of the South aisle, adjacent to the South door, in the memory of Isabellina Wright, the widow of Carden Wright (d.1910), who was the brother of Richard Wright, the father of George Nutt Wright.

Dedication plaque – Isabellina Wright (fig.54).

ii)   Also, on the wall of the South aisle, between the two stained-glass windows, in memory of Henry Carden Wright, whose bequest enabled the bells to be rehung in 1933. Henry was the second son of William Kilham Wright, who was a brother of George Nutt Wright.

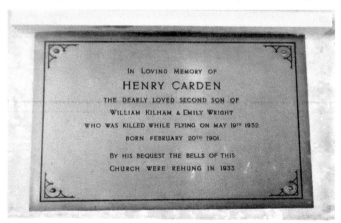

Dedication plaque – Henry Carden (fig.55).

HENRY CHURCHILL McNEIL-SMITH

On the wall in the North Aisle is a dual plaque commemorating:-

a)   Henry Churchill McNeil-Smith, who died whilst on active duty – April
     27, 1916. on his Majesty's ship Russell – was the son of Revd. H.B.
     McNeil-Smith. *[Vicar of St. Mary's in 1913]*

b)   Mary St. Barbe, who was the wife of Revd. H.B. McNeil-Smith, and
     mother of Henry, died at Whaplode Vicarage on November 19, 1916.

Dual Memorial Plaque : McNeil-Smith Family (fig.56).

BENJAMIN GRANT & FAMILY

Two Memorial Plaques – Benjamin Grant & Family (fig.57).

On the south aisle wall, adjacent to the First World War Memorial Stained-Glass window, is a *'marble scrolled plaque and a gilt monument with cherubs, palms, skulls & festoons'* with regard to Benjamin Grant (d. 24.02.1716 - Age.52) and his family, depicting commemorations to his wife Ann (d. 06.04.1734 - Age 62), and his five children who all died in infancy (fig.57).

FRANK DRING

Adjacent to the Chancel Arch, alongside the remnant of the Stone Rood Screen, is a memorial plaque to Frank Dring and his wife, Ethel Jane. A benefactor to the Church, Frank held the position of Churchwarden at St. Mary's for a remarkable 53 years (fig.58).

Dual Memorial Plaque : Frank & Ethel Jane Dring (fig.58).

OTHER MEMORIAL INSCRIPTIONS, MONUMENTS AND SLABS TO BE FOUND IN THE CHURCH: PRE-RESTORATION

In 1888, William Foster recorded in his book a list of inscriptions, monuments and slabs that he viewed as being within the church prior to its restoration, together with highlighting a similar record by *"Mr Morton, of Boston in 1843 in his book – "An Account of the Churches of the Division of Holland, in the County of Lincoln."*

The list, extracted from pages 48-50 of W.E. Foster's book, is reproduced in Appendix XIV, however, it should be noted that a number of the slabs and their respective inscriptions, as referred therein, are, sadly, no longer identifiable, and/or visible.

10.

21st century improvements to facilities

NEW HEATING SYSTEM - 2002

The residue of the former 'Pot-Bellied' Stoves Heating system was itself replaced with under seat electric heaters, but proving to be unsafe, they, in turn, were replaced with overhead infra-red heaters. Finally, in 2002, these were superseded by a much debated, and at times, controversial, system of gas heated warm air. The location for which proved to be the most controversial, since siting such large equipment into a 12th century building generated an unusual amount of interest and delay, inevitably perhaps, from countless people and organisations who were concerned as to the impact on the fabric of the building and surrounding grounds.

Eventually, after a good deal of wrangling and arbitration, between interested groups, the PCC agreed that the available space provided by the unused North Porch would be a suitable location and ensure easier access for all the required services of gas and electricity, disturbing only a fraction of the consecrated graveyard. This location was also served by the water and drainage system for the church, which would prove to be most useful when another project was planned four years later. (See below: New Room Facilities-The Heraldic Suite – 2006).

Ventilation system for the warm-air heater (fig.59).

IMPROVED LIGHTING - 2002

During the regular inspection of the church lighting and electrical supply system it was found that much of the wiring, etc., would require replacement, as it could pose safety concerns, which meant that the church had to be quickly adapted for the use of temporary lighting, or else face closure during hours of poor light.

Ironically, the unfortunate absence of stained-glass windows in the residual state of the church, (extremely sad from the historic perspective of the Church) (see **Part Two:** 3. Whaplode's Family Coats of Arms & Stained-Glass Windows), proved to be a blessing in disguise when these projects were underway, for a major contributory factor to the decay of the wiring and lighting systems was the constant threat of salts being drawn to the surface of the interior walls through the ever changing temperature of the building, which was exacerbated by the inadequate ventilation caused by the absence of windows that can be opened at all levels of the church (presently, the only windows that can be opened are those situated in the both the north and south clerestory, which have to be managed by extensive ropes, and, therefore, are not altogether easily maneuverable).

With hindsight, and on reflection, the position of the North Porch heating system as now situate directly opposite the main entrance to the church through the South Porch is, arguably, not best placed given the potential for an immediate escape of warm air directly across, and out of the church, upon the opening of the main doors.

NEW ROOM FACILITIES - THE HERALDIC SUITE - 2006

It had been also proposed around 2001/2 that consideration should be given to the construction of a toilet, and work area to provide teas and sandwiches, for both the congregation and visitors (other churches in the vicinity had started to have these facilities installed), however, funding sources appeared limited, and resistance was met to the degree of work required.

The project was resurrected again in 2003, and the new Committee reviewed various innovative ideas for funding. At a cost of nearly £150,000, it was decided that rather than seek a narrow 'church' funding option, the resource should be sought from numerous providers, such as

    i). Local Authority

    ii). European Community Grants

    iii). Local Church Charities

    iv). Area Tourism funding

to ensure that it did not impact on other local provisions, not least the requirements for both the Village Hall and the nearby Methodist Church Hall.

Completion of the Suite was achieved in 2006, and hailed as a tremendous success it has provided community benefit not only by reason of its presence in the Church, but also from the sharing of the project management experience gained by the Churchwardens of the day – Messrs. Cyril Hearn & Roy Willingham – with many other organisers of local and county wide projects, including similar improvement changes (toilets & office space) made to St. Botolph's ('The Stump') at Boston.

      The story setting out the requirement, the planning, and the eventual construction of the Heraldic Suite is contained within two portfolio folders, available for public inspection, to be seen in the West End of the Church providing invaluable guidance on issues raised in its construction.

The North-West corner - prior to the construction of the Heraldic Suite (fig.60).

The North-West corner – following the construction of the Heraldic Suite (fig.61).

Entrance to the new 'Heraldic Suite' (fig.62).

The name given to the rooms - "THE HERALDIC SUITE" - was in recognition of the many wealthy families that have supported the church over the centuries. (See **Part Two**: 3. Whaplode's Family Coats of Arms & Stained-Glass Windows – Colonel Gervase Holles' Report). Their various Coats of Arms are to be seen within the new Suite displayed on the wooden framework partition separating the Meeting room and kitchen facilities from the other parts of the structure.

The Heraldic Suite – Coats of Arms I (fig.63).

The Heraldic Suite – Coats of Arms II (fig.64).

11.

Layout plans of St. Mary's Church

There follows a series of plans that show how the outline & interior layout of St. Mary's Church has changed since 1800.

i) **Undated - but likely to have been post 1800 but before 1818**

This undated plan (See below fig.65) is held within the church records and is likely to have been early 19th century, because it precedes the rebuild of the Chancel circa 1819/20 and displays the position of the school room, which was situate 'outside' the North-East 'transept' for many years prior to 1829, but also shows the following:

a)   Two aisle seats along the North wall for the Choir. These were removed arguably when the overall seating was changed upon the rebuild of the North Transept.

b)   The position of the 'twin' pews in the North & South Aisles are centred on the Norman pillars. Once the North transept was rebuilt the pews were reconfigured to sit against the walls in both aisles, and in single rows aligned with the pillars (See 1846 plan below).

c)   The Pulpit occupying a position in front of the 2nd column in the North Aisle of the Nave leading from the Chancel. It now sits in front of the 1st column.

d)   The position of only three rows of *Free pews* on the South Aisle wall. These would be increased to around twenty - circa 1849-1854 - sited not only in the North and South Aisles, but also in the North Transept.

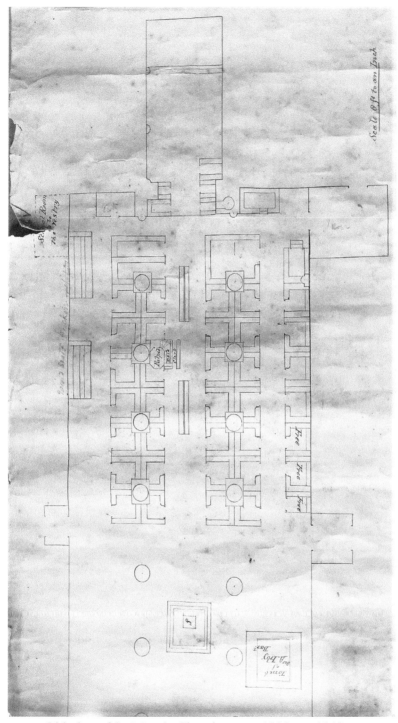

Old plan of St. Mary's Church – post 1800 pre.1818
(fig.65).

ii) **1846**

This architect's plan (fig.66), albeit primarily configured for the purpose of identifying the plumbing system within the church, serves to confirm the re-positioning of the benches /pews.

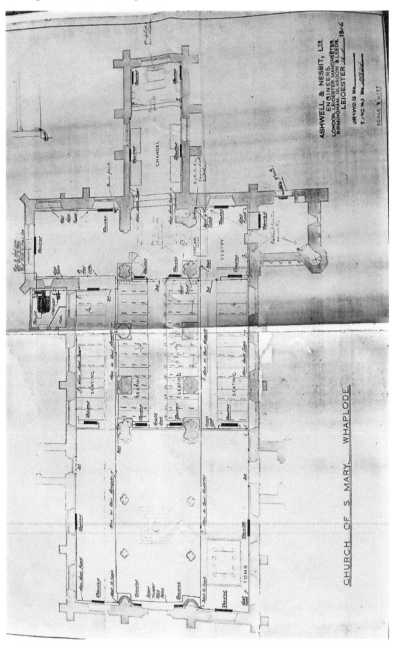

Architect's plan of 'plumbing' within St. Marys' - 1846 (fig.66).

iii)   ***Circa 1870***

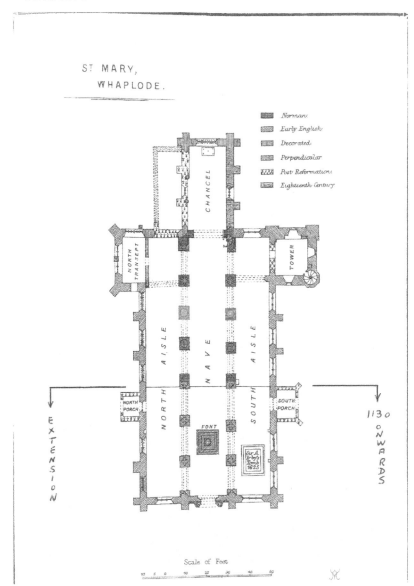

Architectural Timeline layout plan of St. Mary's Whaplode – circa 1870,
with West End extension dateline highlighted thereon (fig.67).

The above outline plan is taken from WEF, p24, and it also appears in MJE,
p.245. The earlier original Chancel chapel outline (north aisle top left – now
demolished) is portrayed alongside the 1818 re-configured Chancel.

iv)   ***Circa 1900, and presented in 1909 (The outline of the building reflects the 1870 Plan)***

This plan of St. Mary's Church below (fig.68) was presented at the Royal Architectural Institute in March 1909 [84] for the purpose of their discussion on the reparations required. Like the plan drawn up by William Weir, Architect, it is essentially the same outline as that of the 1870 plan as displayed above in (fig 67).

However, thereon we have overlaid where the new Heraldic Suite is now situated – Area enclosed **A, B, C, D** - and it also highlights other aspects of the interior of the Church that have subsequently undergone movement or removal, as follows:

    i)   Two of the 'Pot Bellied' stoves

    ii)   The Church organ is shown outside the North Transept, it was later to be moved to the South side.

    iii)   The former resting place of the ancient Altar Stone was alongside the excavated stone coffins- within the area now known as the 'Heraldic Suite.'

    iii)   The indication of the existence of the original panels of a Jacobean pulpit in use as screen/cupboard in the 'old' Vestry adjacent to the North Transept – prior to the reclamation and restoration of the Pulpit

In addition, there was a further re-arrangement of some of the pews/benches following the 1909/10 refurbishment.

The original plan also figured in Revd. John Rhodes publication in 1900 wherein he set out his complaints against the Governors of Uppingham School (See above : *October 1900 – The Public Campaign by Revd. Rhodes)*.

Re 1900/1909

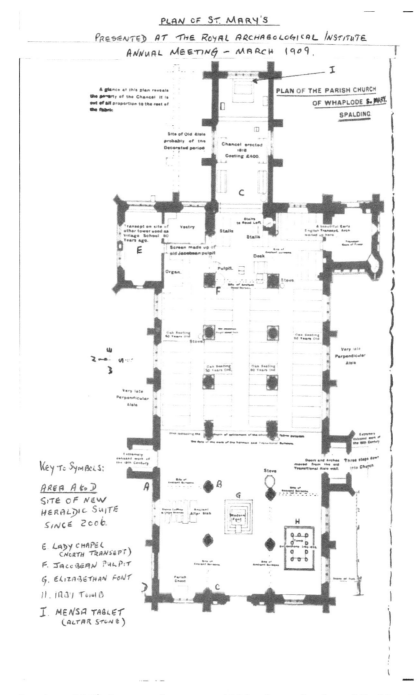

Overlay of 20th Century changes on 1909 schematic plan of St. Mary's (fig.68).

PART TWO
1.
Early Monastic Estates and St. Mary's Anglo-Saxon Heritage

St. Mary's Church (in one form or another) having survived for over nine hundred years at the time of writing has undoubtedly undergone considerable changes from its early beginnings in 'Saxon Britain,' but most notable, as recorded, those of its 'Norman' heritage from the early 12th century.

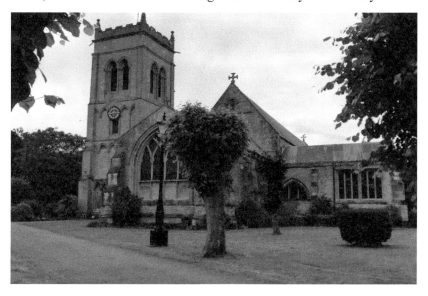

View from ENE inside main gate (fig.69).

IMPACT OF VIKING RAIDS AND THE CONQUEST OF LINCOLNSHIRE
The Viking raids and conquest (793-1050) caused immense changes in the institutions and organisation of the church in Lincolnshire. None of the abbeys and nunneries founded in the early ninth century survived the desecration onslaught, however, the continued existence of markets at some of their former sites, long after the disappearance of these monasteries, where people gathered from time to time to buy and sell, an activity that had been closely linked to the festivals celebrated in those religious communities, implies that the sites retained their local importance.[85]

MONASTIC ESTATES: PRE-NORMAN CONQUEST
Prior to the Norman Conquest the largest monastic estate was at Peterborough (Medeshamstede), and there is no reason to believe that any monastery had

acquired much land north of the Welland in the 100 years before 1066. The only monastery in Lincolnshire on the eve of the Conquest, Crowland, was the northernmost of a group of Fenland houses that were revived or re-founded in the reign of King Edgar.[86]

Crowland's revival is dated at between 971 and 984, and it underwent a chequered existence over the next hundred years suffering from several fires, and finally, following yet another fire in 1091 the monastery was destroyed. Such was its self-proclaimed importance, at least 15 charters were forged after that disaster to provide documentary evidence for its privileges and possessions. Many of these were later included in a fantastic history of the abbey attributed to Ingulf, the abbot at the time of the fire in 1091, and their inclusion has therefore cast doubt on some of Ingulf's historical commentaries. The church subsequently underwent re-building, and it was finally consecrated in 1114.[87]

In 1050 almost all of Lincolnshire churches were still timber buildings, but in the following decades there was a dramatic change as dozens of them were re-built in stone.[88] However, whilst most surviving Lincolnshire churches were not built-in stone until after the Conquest there is good evidence that many of them stand in pre-Conquest churchyards, implying the existence of an earlier church. Many more early churches can be identified by means of Anglo-Saxon stone sculpture in the form of architectural details, or grave monuments, whole or broken. Much of this sculpture is embedded in the later fabric of churches, but some pieces are free standing in churches or churchyards.[89]

However, while most of the fragments of sculpture found come from free standing monuments and therefore cannot prove the existence of stone churches *per se*, they do provide good evidence for the existence of churchyards, and, as many of them can be dated, if only within broad limits, they not only supplement the evidence of the DB, but also show that some of the churches already existed a century or more before the compilation of the DB.[90]

WHAPLODE'S SAXON CHURCH

There was likely a pre-Conquest church of some sort in Whaplode, which was the pre-cursor to the building of the grand Norman one that dominates the skyline of Whaplode of today. (See **Part One:** 1. Whaplode: South Holland and the early Anglo-Saxon and Roman Settlements).

Indeed, Foster commented in his book "*there is little doubt there was a Saxon church at the time of the Domesday survey*" in 1086, [91] a belief supported by the earlier commentary by T.N. Morton in 1843 as to the church being '*rebuilt soon after the conquest*',[92] and with the subsequent discovery of burial stonework in and around St. Mary's Church being dated as early to middle 11th century, all of which would seem to support this historical position.

Confirmation of the dateline of this burial stonework arose from the extensive analytical work of the Corpus of Anglo-Saxon Stone Sculpture Project conducted by Durham University, which began in 1977, and which has since documented the earliest Christian field monuments from free-standing carved crosses and innovative decorative elements, to grave markers, across all counties in England. Its comprehensive findings for Lincolnshire, published in 1999, provide a fascinating insight into early Anglo-Saxon burial sites across the County, and therewithin are their results of the examination of the three pieces of 'burial stonework' found at St. Mary's Whaplode. (See Appendix IV - "The Corpus of Anglo-Saxon Stone Sculpture – Whaplode Stonework 1999" in which their findings are reproduced in full).

St. Mary's Saxon Burial Stonework on display - exhibit 02-386
Re: The Corpus of Anglo-Saxon Stone Sculpture (fig.70).

The principal piece of the Saxon stonework, as examined by the University of Durham, is housed within a glass cabinet which can be seen outside the Heraldic Suite in the West End of the Church (fig.70). The three fragments of Saxon stonework are recorded under Lincolnshire Heritage HER reference MLI22198. Heritage Gateway - Results

THE CROWN JEWEL OF ST. MARY'S CHURCH

There is without doubt one feature that excels all other of this magnificent church, the consecrated Altar stone table *('Mensa Tablet')*. The *Mensa Tablet* is inscribed with five consecration crosses, one at the centre and one at each corner. When the altar was consecrated these five crosses (symbolising the five wounds of Christ) would have been anointed with holy oil, however, it is not known when the crosses (maybe four initially, followed by the central 'fifth' later –this is pure speculation) were made in the stone. Some historians make the point that this 'custom' was practised in some places as early as the 6th and 7th centuries,[93] and others refer to such customs (of four or five crosses) beginning much later, not least highlighting the formal canonical decree which enforced the practice of five crosses in 1536.[94] & [95]

It is thought that the limestone *Mensa Tablet* could have been sourced from the now extinct quarrying site of Barnack, near Peterborough, at which there was some evidence found that the Romans were the first to quarry. Whilst more than one kind of stone was quarried, Barnack stone – *"Oolitic Lincolnshire Limestone"* - provided a great deal of the stonework for Crowland Abbey, and the Cathedrals of Ely and Peterborough. However, it is more likely that the source was from another extinct quarry at Alwalton, near Peterborough. *'Middle Jurassic Fossiliferous Limestone,'* known as 'Alwalton Marble' is a brownish-grey stone, and was also used in the Cathedrals of Lincoln, Peterborough, and Ely, and in many parish churches from the late 11th century.

At the time of the initial construction of St. Mary's, the Abbey at Croyland was served directly by monks from Peterborough Abbey (This was previously known by its Anglo-Saxon name 'Medeshamstede' which was changed to Peterborough during its restoration by King Edgar and the Bishop of Winchester in the 10th century – following its earlier destruction at the hands of the Vikings in 864) as Croyland had been sacked by the invading Danes. It remains pure speculation that St. Mary's Altar stone was brought to the original church by the settling monks from Peterborough Abbey, as they sought to convert the heathen people to the Christian way of life, not least because the Altar stone is of a different limestone composition to that of the 'Barnack' stone, which is to be found in the rest of the building. In the circumstances, it is believed that the *Mensa Tablet* predates any of the St Mary's original Norman buildings, which serves to add more credence to the existence of an earlier Saxon church being here in Whaplode.

The *Mensa Tablet* [Dimensions: Length- **7 feet 2 inches**: Width- **2 feet 10
inches**: Depth- **6 inches**] sits on a substantial oak altar framework encased by
a separate oaken cover frame with a glass 'window' inset therein to allow
viewing of the tablet. The cover frame together with the smaller glass
'window' (dimensions: length 7 feet 4 inches: width 2 feet 2 inches) afford
protection to the *Mensa Tablet* from light and damage, and the height of the
Altar framework from top to bottom is 3 feet 4½ inches.

In the circumstances, a photograph of the full *Mensa Tablet* is not
practical, and therefore only an artist's impression of the top surface thereof is
shown below (not to scale) (fig.71).

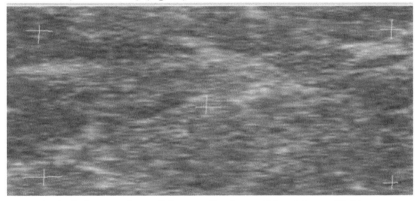

Artist's impression of the top Surface of the *Mensa Tablet*
(Altar Stone) (fig.71).

During the Reformation commenced by Henry VIII, and extending
into the Puritan era, there was a zealous movement generated by the *reformers*
to rid the churches, as well as the Abbeys, and Monasteries, of anything
remotely identifying the buildings with Roman Catholicism, to the point where
great works of art, and/or artefacts and were destroyed, or sold off to the local
inhabitants, or whomsoever proffered money. In no part of England was the
ugly business of gathering the spoils pushed on with greater vigour than in
Lincolnshire, where there was encountered open revolt and defiance, and no
less than 37 religious houses were passed into the king's possession. [96]

Such was the vast array of Altars, chancery screens, tombs,
gravestones, paintings, pews, choir stalls, bells, etc, etc., and even entire
buildings with effects, that were placed 'under the hammer' at public auctions,
some churches, or in several instances portions of buildings, were only saved
by the prompt action of people who, by an offer of ready money, redeemed
them from destruction. Thus, the parishioners of Crowland paid £26 for the
north aisle of their church, and £30 for two of the old Abbey bells.[97] {The

relative purchasing power of £56 in 1536 at today's prices would be in the region of £38,000}.

With the threat of destruction, it was customary practise for churches to remove their Altar stones, burying them, or breaking them into small pieces and, on occasion, placing them in the pavement of the church, especially near a doorway, in order that they might be most readily and effectually desecrated and worn, and on occasions the upper surface would be turned downwards to prevent further destruction or desecration.[98]

Alternatively, such consecrated slabs would be put to base uses; as identified in statements recorded by King Edward VI Commissioners; *thus, in Lincolnshire alone, one became a sink for a kitchen, another a fire-back, a cistern-bottom, a hearthstone, a stile in a churchyard, a pair of stairs (this by the parson) and a bridge*.[99]

Whilst there were those churches that managed to escape the full wrath of the early reformation onslaught, the re-erection of some stone altars during the reign of Queen Mary angered the Puritans so much that, ultimately, they passed a Parliamentary Ordinance in 1643 directing that all altars and tables of stone be utterly taken away and demolished, together with the removal of all manner of other religious artefacts.[100] The result was that very few survived this further onslaught of such residual wanton destruction. Albeit they can be found dotted across the country, by way of example, St Michael, Brimpsfield, in Gloucestershire (in use as a stile until 1937- rededicated in 1971); St Martin, South Raynham, East Anglia (was a step into the chancel - rededicated in 1980s); Holy Trinity, Stratford upon Avon, Warwickshire (discovered in Victoria's era under the floor of the Becket Chapel, and rededicated).

Fortunately, for St Mary's, this particular Altar stone was removed to a place of safety and remained hidden from sight for over two hundred years, only coming to light when the incumbent Vicar, Thomas Bateman (who was a non-resident vicar at the time, circa 1780, usually leaving the day to day running of the church to a curate or curates) happened to see what appeared, at first sight, to be large slab of limestone rock protruding from the base of a dyke, within a quarter of a mile of the church. Upon investigation he discovered the identifying consecration marks, as described above, which encouraged him to have it returned to St. Mary's. Thereafter, because the *Mensa Tablet* had been taken away, upon its re-installation the Altar and/or the Church would have been consecrated anew, in accordance with the Ecclesiastical canons.[101]

It is not known precisely when the Vicar/townspeople of Whaplode decided to remove the complete *Mensa Tablet*, but it is likely to have been in the middle to late 16th century, and could even have coincided with the removal of the Abbot of Croyland's influence at St. Mary's, arising on the dissolution of the Abbey in 1539, or upon the hand-over of the Chancel to the Archdeacon of Leicester, Robert Johnson in 1594, (see **Part One: 7**. The prelude to the final handover of responsibilities in 1594, and the turmoil beyond).

During the late Victorian period, the present structure supporting this immense block of limestone 'marble' was constructed. In the latter part of the 20th century, the whole arrangement for the High Altar was moved several inches forward from the rear screen, which enabled the Priest to conduct the Holy Sacrament whilst facing the congregation, instead of having to stand with his back to them.

The consecrated High Altar with *Mensa Tablet* in the Chancel (fig.72).

View of the High Altar and East window in the Chancel (fig.73).

2.

The Architectural Structure and Principal Fabric Heritage of St. Mary's

THE EARLY CONSTRUCTION OF THE 'NORMAN' FOUNDATIONS

Probably the most unusual feature of St Mary's, and it has numerous outstanding features, is the fact that it was constructed, like many Norman buildings, with the minimum of foundations. Evidence of this was proven a little over fifty years ago, when it was decided that something had to be done about both the poor condition of the south wall, and the increasing evidence of damp in the walls around the north side of the chancel. When the workmen tried to unearth the foundations, or footings, they discovered remnants of animal skins (thought to have been sheep skins). The reason for this is believed to be as follows: Given the nature of the ground beneath Whaplode arising from the area's geological formation – i.e. formerly Fenland marsh comprised of silt from the sea, and/or the river estuary, [102] which has become so well compacted over the centuries that it acts almost like base rock – it provided sufficient stability for the original builders of the church to place scores of animal skins on the ground thereby forming a permanent membrane between the silt and the quarried stone, and then to build the superstructures on that foundation.

This may provide an interesting insight into a reason why the result of surveys carried out over the years to measure the movement of the building have not, to this day, registered a deviation more than +/-5mm, with the result that the original four Norman Bays are still in the perpendicular, and provides a distinguishing feature of this part of the church as against the alterations carried out between 1470 and 1530. By comparison, there are several churches in Lincolnshire, where they have been built alongside waterways, e.g., St. Botolph's (Boston Stump) at Boston, and St. Laurence Church at Surfleet, that have developed degrees of subsidence, and as a result their buildings lean at various angles towards the water course. An insight into the early excavation work carried out in 1309 on the pre-foundations of the Boston Stump makes interesting reading. [103]

THE TIMELINE OF ARCHITECTURAL CHANGE

St Mary's Church is a Grade I Listed Building under the Historic England Listed Entry Number 1359295 – Date first listed - 30 Jun 1966, and thereunder can be seen a detailed architectural listing of the fabric of the church building,

and its many artefacts aligned with their respective century designation, to be found on the National Heritage List for England web site:-
https://www.historicengland.org.uk/listing/the-list/list-entry/1359295

Hereunder we endeavour to portray a timeline of the principal architectural developments that have occurred at St. Mary's. However, it does not purport to be a derivative chronicle of the architectural styles discussed, neither does it claim to be complete in all aspects of the Church's construction that occurred during each of the designated periods.

View of South Porch entrance and South Aisle windows (fig.74).

EARLY NORMAN – LATE 11th and 12th CENTURY ORIGINS

Probably, the early works were taking place around 1090-1100, with the clearing of the former Saxon building, and the preparation of the foundations for the Church, the extraction of quarried stone from Barnack, and the recruitment of enough local monks from Peterborough Abbey, with the knowledge of the blue-print for the building. The founding of the building of St. Mary's is generally attributed to the monks of Crowland Abbey, however, there remains a degree of uncertainty since there is the other possibility that it was indeed the monks of Peterborough Abbey who established the original foundations. Whichever Abbey provided the monks it is without question that they were of the Benedictine Order of monks given that both these Abbeys belonged to the same Order.

While all the early key features of the Church are from Norman architecture, the period from 1130 to 1190 is recognised as transitional in nature (See below: Late Norman - Early English or Transitional Period) when architectural features changed; no longer were square capitals being used along with underlying scallops and flutes, these were replaced with foliage designs.

THE SOUTH DOOR ENTRANCE

St Mary's is currently entered by the South porch door. An outer 'bird cage' door gains access to the main inner South Door. Although much of the surrounding framework of the doors was added to the church in the Tudor period, when the church was widened to incorporate both south and north nave aisles between 1470 and 1530, the inside wooden parts of the doors, together with some of the metalwork, are original 12th-13th century, and remain within the newly re-constructed doors.

South Porch Entrance – Outer 'Bird Cage' door (fig.75).

Inner door from inside (fig.76).   Inner door from outside (fig.77).

This required alterations to the hanging of both the outer and inner main doors, which not only provided much more secure fittings, but they also ensured the doors would be less prone to rotting from their base. More recently, alterations have been made to the inside of the south porch to accommodate wheel chair, and push chair/buggy access, with the removal of two successive steps descending into the nave being replaced by a sloping floor.

Once inside the church, the proportions of both the roof space together with the nave and stoutness of the supporting pillars are immediately evident. Foster expresses the following sentiment *"One is struck on entering the church with the massive Norman columns forming the easternmost portion of the nave; these were evidently originally designed to carry a far heavier and larger structure than was ever placed on them."* [104]

As if to further emphasise the impact that is felt upon entering this church, the renowned architect Sir Gilbert Scott, in 1856 on his visit to St. Mary's, recorded the following: *"The nave is of great magnificence, about one-half being in the Norman style, and the other of the early English, or Pointed period, all on a grand scale, with a high roof and clerestory, and carried out in a manor more resembling an abbey church than the church of a country village."* [105]

NORMAN PIERS (PILLARS)

As one walks down the central aisle, facing the altar, there can be seen a distinct separation from the original church and its later additions as indicated by a step down to a lower level (albeit, alleviated by a ramp). This is where the bulk of the evidence is to be found for the purposes of dating the church to its Norman origins, dominated by the magnificent array of piers and arches (figs.78 and 79), and one of the more unusual design features associated with St. Mary's is the pairing of the four symmetrical and finely proportioned Norman Arches, extending from the West End extension down the Nave, incorporating alternate circular and octagonal-shafted pillars abreast of the Nave aisle.

Looking ENE down central Nave aisle towards Chancel (fig.78).

They, along with the magnificently carved Norman arch over the Chancel, are estimated to have been built circa 1110-1120, with the church being consecrated in 1125 during the reign of Henry 1, the son of William the Conqueror.

Looking ESE down central Nave aisle towards Chancel (fig.79).

115

The extended West End, with the pillar decoration being gently more sophisticated was to be built some 30 to 40 years later (albeit some sources suggest 50-60 years), but in any event the extension was completed before 1190.

The immediate evidence of this distinctive change in pillar decoration at the time of the build of the West End extension can be seen in the following photographs (figs. 80 and 81) which show the resultant unfortunate *'mix'* of architectural timeline features appearing on the respective columns on either side of the nave that are located at the architectural divide – the step down – to the original church from the West End extension, which was built post 1130. (See fig. 67: The Architectural Timeline layout plan of St. Mary's, circa 1870, with the West End extension highlighted thereon).

North Aisle Pillar 4
West >1130: East < 1100
(fig.80).

South Aisle Pillar 4
East<1100: West>1130
(fig.81).

Notwithstanding, given that both Norman pillars at this junction would have not only been sitting at the end of the original pre 1130 Norman build, but would also have exhibited an outside 'terminal' design, it is perhaps not surprising that the integration of the resulting external/internal 'pillar' designs post 1130 lacked precision.

When one looks at the supporting pillars and walls, they are of such sturdiness that it is believed the building was, initially, intended to be an Abbey. However, it is surmised that the clergy at Croyland had a hand in depriving St. Mary's of both money and masons, as they needed their Abbey to be *the* grand building in the area. In any event, the masons, with their innate sense of symmetry and proportion gleaned from knowledge of stone-built structures across Europe, have managed to leave their own signature on the church resulting in exceptionally fine work.

The tremendous undertaking of church and castle building in William the Conqueror's time is one of the most striking episodes in the history of medieval architecture, and such was William's interest in the work of the *Comacine Guild* that he made his masons study Italian masons to build the same impressive stone structures in Normandy, and post 1066 in England, this gave rise to the building of the magnificent ecclesiastical 'Romanesque' stone structures that have since graced our landscape down the centuries.

As an example of the sturdiness of the bays and pillars of such Norman structures, see the photograph below (fig.82) from the Abbey Church of Notre-Dame de Bernay. This Abbey church is the oldest surviving Romanesque church in Normandy. Building began around 1010 and was finished at the end of the 11th century, under the supervision of St. Guillaume (William) de Volpiano, a renowned Italian cleric and architect. [106]

The 'Romanesque' bays and pillars of the Abbey Church
of Notre-Dame de Bernay (fig.82).

The clerestory windows on the north side of St. Mary's Nave aisle are also Norman in origin, whilst the clerestory windows on the south side are believed to have been re-constructed circa 1500 when the present roof was erected. It can be said therefore that, architecturally speaking, the resultant eight bays (four on each side of the Nave) constitute a significant solid load bearing formation, upon which one can readily see that the rather 'light' construction of typical Norman clerestory bays could not possibly have been within the original specification of this wonderful building.

In 1925 a group of Archaeologists who were interested in measuring the girth of the upper walls where the roof sits, confirmed the measurements as being over 1.5m (Overall the thickness of the walls do range from 1m to 1.5m +), which suggested to them that together with the enormous girth of the support pillars for the main Norman Arches, the building was meant to be a much taller construction with the intention of incorporating a third tier known architecturally as a 'Triforium.'

The North Aisle showing the original Norman clerestory and plain aisle windows (fig.83).

Outside view of North side clerestory & Aisle windows (fig.84).

This would have led to the second storey now occupied by the clerestory being a gallery linking from the southwest end of the building up to and across the Chancel Arch, then back down along the north side to end at the northwest. A visitor advised that a format not dissimilar to this can be seen in an ancient church in Corsica that not only has the structure of the same support pillars, but that these pillars are identical in position to those in St. Mary's. The exception being that the church in Corsica has double bell towers, one each on the South-East and the North-East end of the building, together with the three tiers ('Triforium') culminating in a clerestory.

There is in existence a floor plan of St. Mary's showing the additional belltower on the North-East end, which is kept in the Lincoln County Archives. This plan also positions the Pulpit within the second Norman Bay on the north side of central aisle, being alongside the supporting pillar.

The expansion in religious buildings in the 11th century was such that little pre-Conquest architecture has survived in any English Cathedral/Abbey or church. There remain a few churches displaying Anglo-Saxon-Norman architecture which pre-date the building of St. Mary's, and these include the Chapel of St. John's in London (AD 1080); The Church at St Firmins, Thurlby (nr Bourne) (AD 925-reconstructed from AD 1100); The Minster Church of St Mary, Stow in Lindsey (AD 975-reconstructed from 1034).

Therefore, when set against some of the finest architectural examples of early Norman architecture, i.e. the Cathedrals of Durham, Lincoln, Peterborough, Winchester, Westminster, and Wymondham Abbey, etc, etc, if one accepts the original plan, that St. Mary's was intended to have double bell towers, together with the third level (the inclusion of a Triforium and gallery, making the clerestory the highest level), then one can reasonably see what form the intended building would have taken, and justly conclude the level of importance that was attached to the development of St. Mary's within this part of the country during the early years of the Norman conquest.

The South Aisle showing the reconstructed clerestory, and below
the Memorial window & two windows bearing four crests (fig.85).

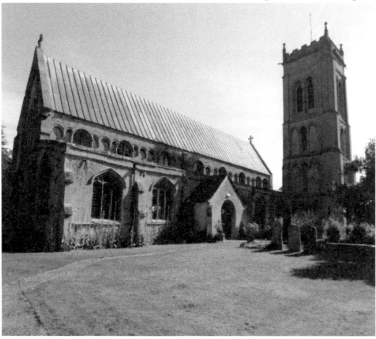

Outside view of South side clerestory and aisle windows (fig.86).

The East Nave, Chancel Arch, together with the high-pitched Chancel, now
depicted by the outline of the original roof on the exterior wall outside the

120

present Chancel, as well as the clerestory, and the small window, above the Chancel (situated just below the east finial) are the finest examples of this period of architecture within St Mary's.

It may be somewhat puzzling to architectural scholars who experience the inside of St Mary's, as to why the colossal abbey like pillars in the east nave were not complemented with a superstructure of similar proportions. As intimated earlier, it is possible that the monks who were labouring to build St Mary's had additional (and pre-eminent) commitments to their Mother Church - Croyland Abbey - and given those financial commitments there may also have been a shortage of funds available to ensure the continuous construction of the church with such planned magnificent proportions.

Foster gave full vent to his feelings on the matter of the rivalry between the Abbeys of Spalding and Crowland, and the outcome which resulted in such beautiful parish churches, during his discourse on the *"Notes on the Fabric of All Saints' Church, Moulton",* at the 1890 Annual General Meeting of The Lincoln and Nottinghamshire Architectural Society, as follows.

"The church of Moulton was the first of those under the jurisdiction of Spalding monastery, to which the monks turned their attention. A question frequently asked by strangers to this locality - How is it that there are such large churches and so few inhabitants in these places? - I do not for one moment wonder at the question, when viewing the churches of Gedney, Moulton, Whaplode and Pinchbeck, the great size of these edifices presenting so striking a contrast to the limited number of houses surrounding them. The query is easily answered – these magnificent churches owe their origin and size to the rivalry which existed between the Abbeys of Spalding and Crowland. That monasteries should try to eclipse each other in building such glorious and costly piles was not an uncommon thing in those ages, which we "the latest seed of time" are wont to call the dark ages of ignorance and superstition. Do we fenmen ever realise that but for the zeal of those despised Monasteries, this fenland of ours could not boast, as it now can, of such beautiful parish churches, beneath whose shade our forefathers rest in their long sleep, and which should rekindle within us a desire to know something of the manners and times of our ancestors who erected those glorious piles? We cannot but look upon this laudable ambition of the Monasteries, as one of the brightest characteristics, which mark the zeal of those much-abused institutions, the only seats of learning of those ages, the founders of our present colleges, the builders of our many Cathedrals, and the teachers of learning, the fruits of which we are still gathering. In church building, Crowland first set the

example by building at Whaplode; next Castle Acre erected Sutton St. Mary; then Spalding within one mile of Whaplode commenced the present Parish Church of Moulton (the old one had either fallen away, or was not large enough for the requirement, or the Priory), having grown wealthy, wished to vie with Crowland, that had recently erected the beautiful Church at Whaplode (and/or with Castle Acre viz Long Sutton), then followed Gedney built by Crowland, and Weston and Pinchbeck by Spalding." [107]

Such was the result of the development of the string of ecclesiastical buildings in this region, it was subsequently remarked that *"in no part of the kingdom, not even in the neighbouring Norfolk Marshland, can such a line of churches be found as in the twelve miles from Spalding to Long Sutton."* [108]

The Norman and Early English Parish Churches

..... Coastline in 1307

Norman and Early English parish churches across the Fens on the highest or best drained land in that period.

Norman and Early English churches in Lincolnshire (fig.87).
(Whaplode Village History Archive) 1307 (Source unknown)

Anecdotally, and by way of confirmation of the abundance of churches in the region, in terms of a similar mileage, a comparable 'line of churches' can also be seen in North Lincolnshire – Holland East Deanery, between Fishtoft and Wrangle, which were all constructed between 1100-1300, as shown by the above map of Norman and Early English churches in

Lincolnshire, with the attendant coastline as in 1307 (however, note thereon that Boston appears out of position) (fig.87).

EARLY NORMAN ARCHES

The four pairs of symmetrical and finely proportioned Norman Arches extend from the beginning of the West End extension down the nave to the Chancel are a sight to behold and are augmented by the fine alternate pairing of the supporting circular and octagonal pillars, as highlighted earlier.

Another aspect worthy of mention regarding the detail indicative of the Early Norman period arches is the finely patterned area around the Chancel Arch, as highlighted by Foster with the following 'ink drawing' (fig.88). [109]

The detail exhibited portrays the outer edges of a double colonnade, immediately followed by the lozenge or 'diamond' shapes. The next inner portion is known as the 'zig-zag' formation, which if it were laid on its side at 90^0 then attracts the designation of 'dog-tooth'. The final part of the structure is the elegantly carved roll forming the inner covering for the complete arch.

Architectural detail exhibited on the Chancel Arch
An ink drawing 1889 (fig.88).

Normally, the 'zig-zag' formation is continued right through the whole of the supporting pillars, however, sadly, these original decorated Norman pillars are no longer with us in the Church, having been replaced during the

Transitional Period. (See below: Late Norman – Early English Transitional Period. 1130 – 1190).

The richly decorated Early Norman Chancel Arch (fig.89).

A significant aspect of the design of the early pillars supporting the Norman Arches is the use of square capitals (see below, figs. 90 and 91), unlike those of Late Norman-Early English period design post 1130, pictured below (figs.93-94). [110]

Early Norman use of Scalloped 'square' Capitals
Pre 1100 eastern end of the Nave (fig.90).

East end Norman Pillar – Square capitals
with flute design (fig.91).

Knowledge of these early design techniques was probably passed on to the monks from their Lombardian architectural tutors the 'Comanici' who were consulted by the Norman French architects as they had no previous experience of building with stone.[111] Along with the flute designs at the capitals, they also incorporated designs known as scallops (virtually semi-circular in form) and completed the inner part of the arch with a round.

An 'early' Norman arch in the North Aisle displaying
sunken circles within the spandrels (fig.92).

LATE NORMAN-EARLY ENGLISH: TRANSITIONAL PERIOD (1130 - 1190)

This period is best seen in the extension to the Nave and South and North aisles at the West End of the church. The resultant Norman and Transitional Nave together form the longest and narrowest one in the area being 110 feet long and only 19 feet wide. Of significance here is the change in the level of the floor, as commented previously, and the shape and size of both the support piers (pillars) and arches which form the extra three bays (arches) on either side of the Nave aisle, with notably rounded capitals and a floriated decoration beneath; unlike the early Norman support pillars with their square capitals and scalloped or fluted decorations.

EARLY ENGLISH CAPITAL DECORATION

One distinguishing feature is the foliage on the capitals of the pillars, where the design reflects either a more one directional form (fig. 93) or a rather stiff attempt to disengage the flower and leaf from the capital out of which they are carved (fig.94).

The 'directional' foliage design - Early English (fig.93).

The 'stiff leaf' foliate design - Early English (fig.94).

Foster, in his *"Notes on the Fabric of All Saints' Church, Moulton - as read to the Members of the Lincolnshire and Nottingham Architectural and Archaeological Society at the Annual General Meeting of 1890" (page 244 AALN),* refers to Edmund Sharpe's (ES) comments in his book '*An Account of the Churches visited during the Lincoln Excursion of the Architectural Association, 1870,* on the similarity of the carved work as displayed on the pillars in All Saints' Church, Moulton with that of Whaplode, as follows;

*"In the pier capitals of the eastern part of the nave of Whaplode, and the nave
of Moulton Churches, we see the early efforts of the artists of the period to
produce relief, and to disengage the flower and the leaf from the surface to
which it was attached. The strong resemblance of the ornamentation of the
capitals in these two churches leaves no doubt that the transitional portion of
the nave of Whaplode, and the nave of Moulton, are contemporaneous works,
the same artists having probably been employed in the carved work of the
capitals of the nave."* [112]

Such doubling up of the work required from the same masons
provides, perhaps, yet another reason St Mary's did not achieve the greatness
of its intended magnificence.

The other distinguishing feature is the change from sunken circles
(fig.92) to sunken quatrefoil shapes within the spandrels of the Norman arches
in the South Aisle in the west end extension (fig.95).

The sunken quatrefoils within the spandrels above the pillars
of the South Aisle in the West End (fig.95).

However, in contrast to the South Aisle's sunken quatrefoils, there is
a complete absence of any decorative structure within the spandrels above the
pillars on the North Aisle side of the extension (fig.96), and to date no evidence
has been uncovered, whether by reason of any monetary or material
restriction, or indeed, simply a build oversight, and therefore, this architectural
'oddity' remains a mystery.

Another contrasting aspect of the West End extension, compared to
the composition of the original Norman Nave build, is that the width of the

West End arches varies from 11 feet to over 14 feet, whereas the earlier Norman arches are all constructed with a uniform width.

The spandrels above the pillars of the North Aisle in the
West End - no decoration therewithin (fig.96).

Sharpe sums up the architecture of the Transitional West End extension following his visit in 1870 in a colourful fashion as follows: *"We have the clustered piers, the semi-circular pier-arches of two orders, the sunk circles, the circular clerestory window, with its outer circular arcade and corbel-table, with a difference, however, throughout in details. One pier is a cluster of four shafts considerably more disengaged, and standing on a circular base, which carries its upper order, an early example of the water-bearing hollow, so characteristic of the following period, but introduced in this. The pier capitals display in their hollow necks' early examples of the stiff foliage of the period, that burst forth with such vigour and luxuriance a few years later; and they carry the circular round-topped abacus of a clumsy and early profile but was invented at the close of this. We have again in the capitals of the pier which marks the division of the work of the two periods on its east side the Norman form of the inserted cone, and its west side one of the uncommon forms of the same feature as it appeared in the Transitional period, and in which the cone becomes, like the neck of the plain capital, bent and hollowed, as seen in Worcester Cathedral, St. David's Cathedral, and in several of the Churches of the Welsh Marshes."*[113]

It is estimated that most of the construction completed at this time took place between 1165 and 1190, with St. Mary's likely delayed by the masons working on the church at Sutton St. Mary (controlled by Castle Acre Abbey), the greater part of the nave there being built before the resumption of the work at St. Mary's, and the underlying reason for the differing levels between the

Norman nave and the later built west end nave, is thought to be attributable to possible subsidence in the earlier construction of the much heavier and bulkier Norman pillars and arches. The west end of the nave, the south and west doorways, and the lower stage of the Bell Tower (see below – The Bell Tower) are further examples of this period, and, indeed, subsequently, between 1470 and 1530, the South doorway was removed and rebuilt in its original position (current location) using all the original materials, including the 12th century timbers.

'TRANSITIONAL' CONFLICTS WITH THE 'NORMAN' FABRIC

One aspect of this period, which left an indelible mark on the fabric of St Mary's, was that of the mutilation of the original Norman Chancel Arch with the introduction of Transitional corbels to make the opening wider. As Foster highlights, *"the smallness of the Norman arch seems to have claimed the attention of architects at a very early date, who cut away the large semi-circular shafts which carried the soffit of the arch moulding and worked in a Transitional corbel to make the opening wider."*[114]

Transitional corbels
Chancel Arch - North side   Chancel Arch – South side
(fig.97).   (fig.98).

THE WEST DOOR

To see more of the changes attributable to this period it is necessary to visit the outside of the West Door, which, historically, faced land beyond the western boundary of the churchyard known as *Hangman's* or *Hanged Man's Field,* since it was reportedly used for the burial of executed criminals, or of suicides, on un-consecrated ground. [115]

This splendid door exhibits interesting architectural features, notably, on each side of the door are apses for what might have been figures of saints or something similar. The framework of the architrave around the west entrance doorway is significant and has been recorded as dating from 1180, described as having double colonnade on the outer, followed by lozenge, then zig-zag, and finally the rounded inner. In this doorway can be seen a good example of the indicative style in use in this period reflecting five mouldings and a double row of eight detached shafts on each side. [116] Such architectural 'mouldings' evident in the construction of the West and South Doors of the church during the 'Transitional' period are reproduced below (figs.99-100) as classified in Edmund Sharpe's comprehensive book on *"The Mouldings of the Six Periods of British Architecture...."* [117]

Door arch – Nave (fig.99).   Door arch – W. Doorway (fig.100).

The West End Door (fig.101).

The Revd. Geo. Oliver provided an early concise description of the 'West End' door and window in his letter to The Gentleman's Magazine in November 1829. (See Appendix V). and while the West End structure with its doorway is of the Transitional Period, it has been commented that it perhaps *'has more of an early English than a Norman feel to it, and the West window, sadly, leaves a lot to be desired'*. One can understand this comment, since unfortunately the window was reduced by approximately one third of its original size, and probably given its present 'uninspiring' tracery, either when the hammerbeam roof was lowered in 1718,[118] or perhaps even earlier in the late 16th century, however, this remains unconfirmed. Over the west doorway is imprinted 'Henry III R 1268', although since this date is carved in modern figures, it is believed to have been a later addition.

In comparing Whaplode and Moulton churches, W.E. Foster comments that each church contains two instructive doorways of the Transitional period, of which only one, the western doorway of Whaplode, stands in its original position. He continues *"it appears to have been a common practice of the architects of the period to pull down, widen the aisles, and re-build the aisle walls, using the same doorways, and often the same buttresses; and but for that practice this locality would have lost three very good specimens of Transitional doorways."* [119]

131

The 'uninspiring' West End window atop the door (fig.102).

THE BELL TOWER

It is known that this was commenced around the same time as the extension of the west nave, together with the pointed arched west and south doorways. It is recorded in some documents as belonging to the Transitional Period, and notably its lower structure, with its arcaded five-pointed arches containing zig-zag mouldings, rising from tall and slender detached shafts (like those found on the west entrance) is typical of the Transitional period.

Originally, the Bell Tower was in fact a 'Campanile' in that it was separate to the rest of the church building. As previously mentioned, the plan held at Lincoln Records Office shows that the original design of the church would have included a second 'Campanile' situated at the North-East end of the church. Anecdotal evidence suggests that there were plans to incorporate twin towers on either side of the chancel, much in the style of the Abbey buildings at Southwell and Westminster. Although the proportions of Whaplode St Mary's would not have challenged either of these majestic buildings, they were nevertheless intended to represent a very significantly important establishment within the fens; reflecting the immense prosperity associated with the area (at one point in the middle-ages Whaplode was regarded as being among the most affluent parts of the country, unlike its earlier history highlighted by Allen (See **Part One:** 1. The Anglo-Saxon Settlement of South Holland).

It is believed that much of the additional 'dormitory' building that existed between the Nave and the Bell Tower was constructed between 1250-1350 (See below: The Decorated Gothic Period), however, this original building connecting the Bell Tower to the church was largely removed between 1470 and 1530, when the present nave aisles were introduced, and the current inter-connecting section built (fig.105). Consequently, the only indication of the original structure of this connecting building is the inverted V outline of the position its adjoining roof would have held appearing on the north side of the Bell Tower. (See below, fig.106).

This is clearly visible on the north side of the Bell Tower, being one of the two early 14th century connections, the lower being the arched entrance from the church into the Bell Tower, whilst the other highlights the presence of a gable end for a roof, which would have been the roof line for the domestic accommodation for the resident clergy, accessed via the spiral turret staircase, adjacent to the Chancel, which was subsequently used to provide access to the 'Rood Loft'. (See below – The Rood Loft).

Tower South face (fig.103).   Tower West face (fig.104).

View of *current* inter-connecting 'section' between North face
of Bell Tower and the Nave at the beginning of the
Chancel (fig.105).

View of Bell Tower East face &
North face showing inverted
V roof-lines (fig.106).

Closer view of 'trefoil head'
niche in second storey
fig.107).

134

A very detailed description of the four ornamental architectural stages of the Bell Tower is provided by Revd. George Oliver in his letter of 1829, (see Appendix V), in which he also highlights the fact that *"the lower part of the tower formerly communicated with the interior of the Church by a spacious archway, and was not used, as at present, for a belfry"*. Furthermore, he goes on *"Here, under an arch in the wall, is a piscina, and close adjoining is a square recess with mouldings for a door, evidently the depository for a pyx*. These are indications of a chantry."* {*pyx -a small round metal receptacle used to carry the Eucharist to the sick – first known use: 1200-1300}.

The square recess to which he refers could be that which can be found 'low' in the wall (fig.108) immediately behind the small door (within the ground floor area of the Bell Tower – the 'Ringing Chamber') which provides access to the spiral staircase (leading up to the Clock-room and the Bells) in the south west corner of the Bell Tower.

The 'square recess with mouldings for a door.'
Possible depository for a 'Pyx' (fig.108).

In furtherance of his supposition he adds, *"In the lower part* {of the second storey on the east face} *is a niche with a trefoil head included within a pediment, in which was doubtless placed the image of the saint to whom the chantry was dedicated"*. (See above fig.107).

This is extremely interesting, since the following extract from the magazine "The Builder" on 7th August 1909, two weeks before the subsequent appointment of Mr William Weir - Architect, to undertake the supervision of the reparations to St. Mary's (See Appendix XII: IV), confirms the existence of a former 'chapel' on the ground floor of the Bell Tower, which would have served the clergy who used to live in a dormitory above what is now seen as the inter-connecting building between the Bell-Tower and the Nave (fig.106). Extract as follows: *"The beautiful XIIIth century tower stands semi-detached to the southeast of the nave, and has a later belfry story, and **a chapel in its ground story open originally to the church by a wide arch**."* [*The Builder 1909-08-07: Vol 97 Issue. 3470 – Page 152* - Internet Archive].

Regrettably, other than the evidence of the bricked up **wide arch** - as referred above - following the subsequent reparations conducted later in 1909/10 there does not appear to be any further evidence of this chapel and/or piscina in the area, let alone within the Tower itself.

THE LANCET PERIOD – EARLY ENGLISH GOTHIC (1180 - 1250)

Extraordinarily little evidence of building work done during this period has survived at St Mary's, except for the architecture around the West Door (dated 1180-8), and the second and third stages of the Bell Tower, which are decorated with 'lancet' arches, typical of other 'Early English' towers in Lincolnshire and Rutland. These two levels, although different in their mouldings from the lower level's Transitional style, do follow the original architectural design. Particularly fine examples of this period of architecture can be seen in St. Mary's church in Weston.

THE DECORATED GOTHIC PERIOD (1250 -1350)

This period is characteristically split between the *"Geometric"* style (1250-90) and the *"Curvilinear"* style (1290-1350). The original construction of the east window in the chancel was, according to Sir Gilbert Scott on his visit to St Mary's in Whaplode on October 16th, 1856, attributable to this period. However, given that the lowering of the chancel arch together with other features in order to accommodate the lowering of the rebuilt chancel roof had clearly removed much of the fine decoration and evidence, his comments around the changes were less than complimentary as highlighted by Foster: *"The east window has been a fine one of the Decorated period, but its jambs and arch have been lowered to bring it beneath the new flat roof, its' no doubt beautiful tracery destroyed, its lights reduced from five to four, and its head filled with the basest imagery. The side-windows are wholly modern, and beneath criticism."* [120]

As indicated above, it is believed that the part of the building which housed the dormitory was added during this period, accessed by the spiral 'turret 'stairway being cut into the Norman piers of the southern nave arcade and the chancel arch. Furthermore, given that that Owen indicated that the Clergy were using this dormitory in 1376, it is likely that the staircase was constructed sometime following the destruction of the original Norman Chancel, which Foster indicates was circa 1320. [121] (Noticeably, this date appears in W.E. Foster's article "Some South Lincolnshire Churches" within EM Storey's book, *"Memorials of Old Lincolnshire" 1911*, but Foster omits to mention the date in his principal book on St. Mary's written in 1889).

Whilst the upper parts of the side aisle windows are typical of the period, however, only two on either side of the aisles at the west end survive in their original condition. The remainder are later imitations of the style.

In addition, the fourth stage of the Bell Tower depicts the architecture of this period, with beautifully recessed windows on each side, and, finally, atop incorporates the battlement parapets, whose angles are completed with pinnacles terminating in balls and vanes, which is also representative of the style. Unfortunately, while there are no records to suggest that either a pyramid or spire were part of the topmost area of the tower, what we do know about this area is that the original four corner pieces of the tower were much taller with an *extension of a spire* attached to each, until one fell down, circa early 19th century, when the decision was taken to remove the remaining three *'extensions'.* This would appear to be borne out by the early lithograph drawing of the church, circa 1810-1830 (see fig.181), which shows the 'cross' extensions atop the 'ball' pinnacles on each corner.

The complete Bell Tower, which rises to a height of 78 feet (23.77 metres), is regarded as being the finest example of a campanile in the whole of the Fens, and, to reach the top of this magnificent Bell Tower requires a climb of 108 steps via the narrow spiral staircase built into the south west corner of the tower. The last stage of the ascent, beyond the Bell Room necessitates the climb of the final 'narrowing' 41+2 steps, exiting (on hands and knees) through a very narrow doorway (23 inches x 33 inches) (see fig.109) on to the top viewing area, from which there are tremendous views of the surrounding countryside. It is believed that the roof construction of the doorway is comprised of pieces of ancient burial stonework, judging by markings thereon.

The following comments are indicative of the consensus of views surrounding its architectural importance.

i)   *"This tower, though the work of several periods, is considered by many the finest in the district."* [122]

ii)   *"The tower is one of the noblest in the county."* [123]

iii)   *"Of Early English church towers, the following are among the finest and most important in Lincolnshire, Sibsey, (spires), Sutton St Mary's, (spires) and Whaplode, and the lower part of Gedney."* [124]

iv)   *"In every particular of symmetry, construction, detail and material,
this is by far the most perfect specimen of architecture in the Deanery
of Holland."* [125]

The narrow exit doorway from the spiral staircase (fig.109).

THE PERPENDICULAR GOTHIC - RECTILINEAR PERIOD (1350-1520)

During this period, the corbel table above the clerestory was entirely removed
and was replaced at a much higher level. Around 1420[126] there were several
major changes made to the architecture of the building, with the addition of the
North transept, which involved the removal of both the existing north and south
aisle walls, and then rebuilt to accommodate a widening of the aisles.
Unfortunately, while conducting this work, the architects either lost much of
the original materials, or employed masons who were indifferent to the
requirement of the job in hand. This is evident when the replacement walls are
viewed in their present state since they no longer hold straight lines in either
the vertical or horizontal planes, although it cannot be ruled out that there may
have been subsequent subsidence caused by the earthquake that occurred in
Whaplode in 1671. (See **Part One: 8.** A chronology of pastoral/other events
occurring together with non-architectural fabric features introduced - The
Earthquake).

Further evidence of this event can be seen best from viewing the north
side of the nave from the Chancel area, where there is a distinct leaning of the
first bay in the late Norman - Early English extension on the north side. One

piece of essential masonry belonging to the original south porch has been either lost or repositioned such that the original face of the stone is not now visible. This artefact would have been a carving on a stone block detailing a mass clock, which enabled local people to know at what hour mass was being said.

This period also embraced the re-positioning of the South Porch doorway in the south aisle. Fortunately, as highlighted earlier, the original south door materials were preserved, along with the south-west windows (two adjacent to the west end of the nave) and used in the construction of this new 14th century south doorway; this evidence of retention is important since establishes the inner door panels as dating from the early part of the twelfth century and therefore constitute the earliest pieces of wood in the building.

In concert with the reconstruction of both Aisles, the Rectilinear period also saw the demolition (circa 1480-1530) of the inter-connecting dormitory building which housed the Clergy, situate between the Bell Tower and the Nave, leaving the 'turret' staircase in situ.

THE HAMMERBEAM ROOF

There is the suggestion that the Hammerbeam roof was constructed using 15th century oak, which may have originated from the trees cut down during the Whaplode Riot .(See **Part One:** The Harvesting of Trees – The Whaplode Riot 1481). Regrettably, over the centuries the roof has seen many adjustments in height, and consequently many of the finer features have been destroyed, as is demonstrated in the picture below (fig.111).

The original hammerbeam roof was once a magnificent architectural feature of the church, with splendid intricate carvings, and possibly some applications of gold-leaf or similar decoration, such as those evident in both the church at Stamford and St. Botolph's, the Boston Stump. Such carvings would have been within the brace supports, and on the terminals of the hammerbeams. Few of these carvings and decorations have survived the alterations that the roof of St. Mary's has undergone in the intervening 500 years.

Traditionally, the terminals would normally have displayed carved 'flying angels', however, sadly, in St. Mary's there remains the evidence of only three religious 'artisans' or 'Knights' and these can be seen at the eastern end near to the Chancel Arch, with two carvings on the north side of the aisle and one carving on the south side (fig.110).

Knight 1   Knight 2   Knight 3

The three remaining 'artisans - knights- angels' (fig.110).

Note the differences between Knights 1 and 2 where the tool on the centre of the shield is reversed. The image of Knight Terminal 3 does not have a shield, and there is no evidence of a cross on top of the headdress, instead the figure appears to be holding a measuring tool of some description; it resembles the shape of what was referred to as a 'spherical triangle' in medieval times and was used in the design of English Gothic church windows.

It is not known whether these 'Knights' were made with wings, and thus the association with angels, however, it is interesting to note the description attributed by Revd. George Oliver, in his letter of 1829 (see Appendix V). *"The roof is composed of carved oak, and the spandrels are filled in with quatrefoils and other tasteful devices, and the imposts were formerly decorated on either side with a row of human figures in drapery, bearing shields. Three only remain. 1.A cross. 2. A bend. 3. A hammer."*

One of the principal reasons why there has been so much deterioration and damage has been the various changes made in the height of the church roof, together with much neglect especially during the 18th and 19th centuries. Another plausible reason for a great deal of the deterioration of St. Mary's can be attributed to the puritanical eras post reformation, when religious institutions faced the removal and destruction of any form of 'Papist' imagery, including inscribed stained-glass windows.

However, what is known of the original hammerbeam roof is the artistic fretwork inserted between each of the braces (fig.112), and a section of this is preserved in a box within the robing area/office space adjacent to the Heraldic Suite meeting room.

The magnificent hammerbeam roof (fig.111).

The original roof would have also been ornately decorated with a variety of colours, and perhaps the finest example of this type of roof, built in the same period, to be found locally, can be seen at St. Mary Magdalene Church in Gedney, where the roof has survived unaltered since its construction.

View of fretwork within roof construction (fig.112).

When the north and south aisles were widened, and the walls rebuilt the roofline of the south aisle was raised for some obscure reason. However, the original roofline can be detected by observing both the old stone supports that remain in the wall, and the weather stringcourse. The workmanship in rebuilding this section of the church left much to be desired, as highlighted previously, since the walls are well out of the perpendicular, added to which any skilled carpentry displayed on the roof timbers is non-existent.

Besides the lack of sympathetic materials in restructuring the outer walls of the south and north aisles, the alterations to the roof could have resulted in the loss of the original Norman clerestory windows on the south side of the church. Such was the lack of fine workmanship as is in evidence by the finish of the archways incorporating replacement windows of such poor design and even poorer finish, with no real form or style, consequently, much of the beauty of the Norman clerestory has been destroyed in this part of the church.

Further vandalism was wrought upon the church when it was decided at some point in the late 17th century / early 18th century to lower the fine hammerbeam roof from its original elevated position. (See fig.113). As a result, for a period of time, the roof surface was thatched, which attracted birds and other mammals, including bats. (See **Part One** 8 re: General In-House Maintenance).

A 1908 picture showing the Nave roof line much lower than at
present (fig.113).

However, the subsequent repairs and renovations to the church carried out in 1909/10 ensured that, in restoring the roof-line back to its original height, the original fabric of the roof was preserved, as outlined in the June 1910 Annual Report of the Society for the Protection of Ancient Buildings (see Appendix XII - V), as follows:

"Prior to the 15th century there was a Norman roof, and when the 15th century carpenters put up that which now exists {see above: fig.111} *the high Norman gables at the east and west of the nave were not cut down to lower the pitch but left as they were. This has given an opportunity of protecting the old work effectually by constructing over the old roof a new one of the same pitch as that of the Normans. For covering this, the old lead sheets recast have been used as far as they would go, and the shortage made up with sheets cast of new virgin lead."*

THE EARLY CHANCEL

The original Norman Chancel had a high-pitched roof and was destroyed about 1320,[127] following which a new one was built; however, little remains of this since it was demolished and replaced with the present chancel in 1818. (See below - 5. The Present Chancel).

The only remaining evidence of the original chancel roof is the outline of the roof which can be clearly seen on the outside of the church at the east end, together with an original Norman window in the same wall above the roof line, and beneath this a now blocked up opening that would have provided the outpouring of sound from within the chancel as the monks performed their rites including plain chants (fig.115) (inside view fig.117).

One intriguing fact has been unearthed and that is the presence of a priests bricked up doorway on the south side of the chancel wall behind the present Reredos framework (see below - The Reredos (Altar Screen)), which leads to the supposition that the original Norman chancel was a much larger building, but it was subsequently rebuilt on a much smaller scale, a belief supported by Foster. [128]

East end chancel roof; revealing the original roofline (fig.114).

A closer view, of the original Norman chancel roofline, & top
window, below which is the 'blocked-up' opening (fig.115).

During this 'Rectilinear' period the wonderful and elaborate Norman carvings
around the top part of the Chancel Arch were chipped away to accommodate
the Rood Loft, (see below – The Rood Loft). This alteration, coupled with the
earlier mutilation of the *'large semi-circular shafts which carried the soffit of
the arch mouldings'* to accommodate 'Transitional' corbels, was to leave a
lasting mark on the aesthetic beauty of the Chancel, which was to be dealt a
final 'blow' with yet another re-build in 1818, when the patrons (the Governors
of Uppingham School) were persuaded so to do by the curate Revd. Samuel
Oliver. (See below - 5. The Present Chancel).

The North Transept was also introduced at this period and included
an access doorway into one of the side Chapels (the original entrance to this
Chapel can be seen inside the Chancel on the north wall (on which appear the
memorial plaques to two former St. Mary's Vicars) as one enters the Chancel.
However, the date when this side Chapel was built is not known, albeit it is
likely to have been prior to 1376, and it was eventually removed when the
Chancel was re-built in 1818.

THE STONE 'ROOD SCREEN'

In accordance with tradition at that time, the access to the Chancel premises
was screened behind a stone 'Rood Screen' (See below -The Rood Loft). The
only remnant of the original 'Rood Screen' is a piece of stone projecting from
behind the choir stalls on the north side of the transept (crossing) (fig.116),
which aligns with the edge of the first Norman Bay now occupied by the organ.

The screen would have exhibited a clear division between the Pius
clergy and the commoners who made up the congregation. In those days, the
congregation would probably have been standing on an earthen floor and

would only have been able see shadowy figures of the clergy through the various openings in the carved screen, but they would have been able to hear their various chants, benedictions, and hymnals, as the clergy went through their oblations of the service.

Remnant of the stone 'Rood Screen' (fig.116).

Near the top of the Chancel wall can be seen the blocked-up opening (fig.117) (outside view - fig. 115) as previously referred thereto, through which the congregation would have heard the clergy's service offerings.

'Blocked-up' opening above Chancel (fig.117).

Of note is the fact that this 'division' of the commoners from the clergy has overtones of the middle age practice of using 'incense' in churches as a means of fumigating the church against the 'foul smells' emanating from the masses of pilgrims. This practice is not altogether common today; however, it is still in use in some countries.[129]

THE TUDOR/ELIZABETHAN & JACOBEAN PERIODS (1485-1625)
THE ROOD LOFT

Besides separating the Clergy and the Laity, a Rood Screen served to support a horizontal beam - the rood-beam - which stretched across the chancel-arch, and itself supported the 'Rood.'

The 'Rood,' which, traditionally, comprised the figure of Christ crucified in the centre, with the figures of the Virgin Mary and St. John, the Evangelist, flanked on either side, was introduced early into churches, circa late 11th century. The 'rood beam' was a heavy rafter let in at both ends into the chancel walls; and serving as it did to uphold the rood, so that the priest all the while he said mass could look up to it, stood to the east of the Altar. This beam led, in time, to the formation of the 'Reredos' (see below: The Reredos) which was formed by merely filling up, with stone-work or wooden panel, the space between the ground and the beam.[130] Frequently, on this rood-beam there was a gallery - the 'Rood-Loft' – which, it is believed, came into general existence in the 14th century, and, in relation to such, the stone staircase access is often the only evidence left in many churches.

With regard to St. Mary's, it is believed that the Tudor 'Rood Loft' was built circa 1500, however, its construction impacted the top portion of the magnificent and elaborate Norman decoration around the arch, leaving the arch without a great deal of its original carvings.

The entrance to the loft was essentially already in place by reason of the 'turret' staircase ('Monks steps'), built into the stone fabric of the south side in 14th century, which in 1376 had provided the access to the dormitory for the thirteen clergy at the time, attached to the north side of the Bell tower. (See **Part One**: 5. Endowments, Tithe Returns, Offerings, etc., & Clergy Stipends: Income)

The photograph below (fig.118) would have been taken circa 1908 prior to the final renovations being carried out in 1909/10, since it is noticeable that the original organ is not situate in the archway adjacent to the curtained former Rood Loft entrance.

1908 photograph of the Rood-Loft (Singing Gallery) entrance
(behind curtained staircase-left) (FB Plate p.116) (fig.118).

At the 1909 Annual Meeting of the Royal Archaeological Institute, in their
report on Whaplode St. Mary's, it was pointed out that on a carved beam
attached to one of the pairs of hammer-beams in the nave roof the treatment of
its ornament showed the beam to have been a portion of the rood-screen or loft,
as evidenced by the traces of scarlet thereon, which proved that the screen and
loft had been decorated with painting. [131] The authenticity of this remnant of
the Tudor Rood Loft woodwork, which can be seen pinned to the east wall of
the Lady Chapel (part of the North Transept) above the small window*, was
confirmed following inspection, on a visit in 2009 by Mr Nigel Leaney, an
expert on Medieval Paint from Lincoln Diocese. (See Appendix VI).

*This small window (see fig.119) having been built within the wall in
1909/10 now occupies the space which was previously an arched opening
which formerly gave access to the known 3rd Chantry Chapel that was
accommodated alongside the Chancel North wall.

WHAPLODE'S 'GREEN MAN'

The 'Rood Loft' remnant has several images carved therein – those most
identifiable can be seen below (fig.120) - represented from left to right; a Tudor
Rose, a Royal Oak Leaf and 'The Whaplode Green Man'.

Remnant of the Tudor 'Rood Loft' ('Singing Gallery')
pinned to the wall, above the window (fig.119).

A closer view of the images on the remnant. Whaplode's 'Green
Man' can be seen on the extreme right (fig.120).

A further 'Green Man' carving can also be seen on the west tracery around the
upper parts of the Bell Tower (fig.121). Whaplode's 'Green Man' is clearly
recognisable as one of the many 'Lincoln Green Men' and bears all the
hallmarks associated with these images, and such pagan images are quite well
known in numerous churches throughout the country. (See Appendix VII).

Bell Tower-West tracery-The 'Green Man' - extreme left (fig.121)

THE 'SINGING GALLERY'

Foster and Allen, in their books, made statements as to the *erection/installation of a* 'Singing Gallery', respectively, in 1773, [132] or 1748,[133] implying that the original 'Rood Loft' would have been destroyed prior to either of their quoted dates. However, the subsequent authentication in 2009 of this piece of wooden fabric, which was the only 'artistic' remnant to have not only survived any earlier 'Reformation' destruction, but also the 1844 demolition of the 'Singing Gallery', as being of early Tudor origin, disproves their assertions, and reinforces the belief that the said 'Singing Gallery', in use as such from the early 18th century until its demise, was simply a re-utilisation/re-configuration of the basic structure of the *original* Tudor 'Rood Loft' as built circa 1500.

The Revd. Geo. Oliver in 1829 confirms its existence (albeit not its origins) when describing the Chancel, as follows*: "Over this is a wooden singing gallery, which occupies the place of the ancient rood loft, and is accessible by the old stone staircase within the south pier."* (See Appendix V).

THE 'ROOD LOFT' FRESCOES

It is thought that the east wall of the Chancel (above the Chancel arch, now adorned by the Royal Coat of Arms (See **Part One**: 9. The Royal Coat of Arms of George III - 1773) was originally decorated with a fresco of the 'Last Supper', although Foster makes the point that the paintings were of the Lord's prayer and the Nicene Creed (a statement of the orthodox faith of the early Christian church), accompanied by the names of the two churchwardens John Aistrup and Theodolphus Perkins, dated 1*722,* albeit these dates suggest this latter adornment had itself replaced an earlier painting.[134]

Alternatively, EMS suggests another adornment in that *"there were frescoes on the east wall of the nave just above the chancel-arch of Whaplode church- very probably 'The Doom' or picture of the day of judgement, as this was a favourite place for it".* [135]

There is also the belief that an earlier painting of 'Christ in Glory' - of which there exist many artistic interpretations - could also have been in situ, at some point. However, the existence of this earlier painting should not be confused with the later painting 'Christ in Glory' by Miss Mary Henrietta Dering Curtois, which was not commissioned until 1907, and thereafter sat above the Chancel Arch, until its removal in 1973. (See **Part One**: 9. 'Christ in Glory' Oil Painting on Canvas and Zinc Plate 1907).

It is difficult to imagine the colourful artwork and ornate carvings that would have adorned St. Mary's Rood Loft, and by way of example the construction of a Rood Loft can be seen below (fig.122), which is a photograph of Lincolnshire's only Rood-Loft to have survived the Reformation, and having been fully restored in 1884, is to be found at St. Edith's Church, Coates-By-Stow. St Edith's Church, Coates (wasleys.org.uk)

Note the staircase on the right gaining access to Rood-Loft. The accompanying narrative on the site indicates that "*On the back wall of the loft is the tympanum* {a semi-circular or triangular decorative wall}, *which originally had a painting of the crucifixion with Mary and St. John on either side. This was probably destroyed during the reformation when the painting of Christ was removed and replaced by newer panels of wood. The outline of Mary with a halo can just be made out.*" [136]

Restored 'Rood Loft' at St. Edith's Church, Coates-By-Stow
(fig.122). (Courtesy of Peter Grey – DMO Plate VIII p.74).

THE RESTORED 'JACOBEAN' PULPIT

Historically, post the Conquest, under the control of the bishops' the clergy were seen as the mouthpiece of the almighty God, and the pulpit, therefore, was the medium for delivering the message. As such the pulpit was ornately carved and elevated to give the congregation a sense of awe, as the clergy delivered sermons that would convey to a god-fearing community the dreadful retributions that would befall them if they strayed from a righteous path.

Little is known of the early Pulpit(s) in St. Mary's. There is evidence to point to that at one stage a pulpit was situate at the 2nd pillar in the North Aisle from the Chancel Arch, however, the current Pulpit is situated at the first pillar in the North Aisle from the Chancel Arch, a position it has held, predominantly, since its restoration post 1910. While the precise date of the current pulpit is uncertain, it is believed that its composition is Jacobean. Sadly, it underwent dismantling at some point in the 18th or early 19th century, such that its fine decorative panels were used to form a screen /cupboard framework in the 'old' Vestry, which was at that time situated in the North Transept. Foster refers *to "a new pulpit was placed in the church in 1854, the old one being removed to the vestry to make a cupboard".* [137]

However, there is a degree of confusion as to whether this 'new' pulpit was completely new, or some form of restoration, not least because while there is evidenced a record of work undertaken in 1854 by Thomas Wilkinson Wallis on the 'Pulpit' and 'Poppy Heads' within St. Mary's, (see below- Benches and Pews), the precise nature of the work on the pulpit remains uncertain.

What would appear to be clear is that in 1909 a 'pulpit' was in existence, but it did not embrace the fine 'Jacobean' decorative panels, etc, which were *still* in use forming a screen /cupboard framework in the 'old' Vestry, for such was the comment at the Annual Meeting *of "The Society for the Protection of Ancient Buildings"* in June 1910 (see Appendix XII-V) wherein the Society recognised the work that had been carried out in the church under its direction, but there still remained some work to complete, and "...*if possible, the resuscitation of the old pulpit, which some years ago was removed and utilised in fitting up a vestry in the north aisle".*

Quite when it was 'fully' restored has not been established, (possibly circa 1930), however, whilst there have been several pieces repaired over time (especially the stairway and supporting material) all the original carved panels (echoing the shape of the chancel arch), etc., *were* reclaimed and the resultant pulpit now in use embodies a sensitive restoration of its former Jacobean finery. (See below figs.123 and 124).

Subsequently, in a booklet entitled "*The Parish Church of St. Mary Whaplode – Historical Notes and a Walk Round the Church*" written by Charles Kightly (CK) in July 1991, on behalf of the Lincolnshire Diocesan Tourism Consultancy, Kightly refers to the pulpit as "*a fine example of Jacobean craftsmanship*".

The restored 'Jacobean' pulpit   A closer view of the pulpit's
and 'sounding board' (fig.123).   ornate panels (fig.124).

The unusual feature that sits directly above the pulpit, is that of the *'sounding board'* (known as the 'Tester'- see fig.123) which was designed to project the celebrant's voice to all parts of the church. However, with the onset of modern technology, radio microphones, amplified speakers, etc., this apparatus has become redundant, but for historical context, it is retained in its rightful place.

BENCHES AND PEWS

One can only ponder at the possible ornamentation and decoration that ought to have been contained within St. Mary's, given the status that the church seemed to have both in the earlier medieval times and throughout the Middle Ages, also through the Tudor and Elizabethan periods, especially since there were so many wealthy families connected to the church, and clear evidence of these facts is borne out by the family Coats of Arms on display within the Heraldic Suite.

The presence of ornately carved oak benches and pews with their elaborately carved end pieces, often dedicated to, and paid for by, such families, was a feature of many medieval churches down the years. Unfortunately, during the Reformation, and the following 'puritanical' struggles, churches were forced to destroy such 'pagan' symbolism, with the result that in later years the challenge was to seek to restore such 'lost' heritage.

In 1854 St. Mary's clergy commissioned Thomas Wilkinson Wallis ("TWW"), a Lincolnshire carpenter of some note, to restore several of the Elizabethan 'poppy heads' to the pews. TWW was a recipient of both the Gold Medal at the Crystal Palace Exhibition of 1851, and the Bronze Medal at the Paris International Exhibition of 1855, for his exhibits of wooden carvings, notably his "Golden Plover." 1855, (fig.125).

T. W. WALLIS *fecit*, 1852.
GOLDEN PLOVER.
PRIZE MEDAL, PARIS, 1855.

The Golden Plover sculpture - T.W. Wallis (fig. 125).

TWW makes specific reference to the work he completed in 1854 at St. Mary's, within his book an *"Autobiography of Thomas Wilkinson Wallis, Sculptor in Wood", and extracts from his sixty years journal".* See below, fig.126, which is the reproduction of a page therein showing that an amount of £15 8s. 0d. was charged for the work carried out in relation to the 'poppy heads' on the ends of pews, and the 'Pulpit'. (£15 spent in 1854: Comparative purchasing power in 2023 would be in excess of £1,600).

There follow some typical examples of Pew carved 'Poppy Heads' (figs 127-129), and a Pew 'End' carving (fig.130), that could otherwise have adorned such furniture.

235

APPENDIX B.

THE PRINCIPAL CARVINGS EXECUTED BY T. W. WALLIS IN LOUTH :

	Description, &c.			£	s.	d.
1844	Poppy Heads, Elkington Church	...	...	8	2	6
1846	Flowers, J. H. Tuke, York	...	...	2	0	0
1848	Cornices, Bland, Halifax	...	...	9	11	0
,,	Dead Game, G. Tomline, Esq. ...	...	...	16	0	0
,,	Drawings—Church, G. Tomline, Esq.	...	...	10	0	0
1849	Antique Chairs, J. Hardwick	...	...	12	10	0
1850	Golden Plover, G. Tomline, Esq.	...	...	25	0	0
,,	Group of Game (5), G. Tomline, Esq.	...	...	100	0	0
,,	Wedding Present, A. Tennyson ...	...	...	3	13	6
,,	Society of Arts and Silver Medal	...	...	3	0	0
,,	Punch Library, J. Brooks	...	...	14	13	6
,,	Vine Branch ...	...	...	5	0	0
1851	Golden Plover, Sir J. S. Hippesley	...	...	50	0	0
,,	Ditto J. Webb	...	...	50	0	0
,,	"Iris," Lord Carrington	...	...	5	5	0
,,	"Spring," G. Tomline, Esq.	...	...	200	0	0
1852	Golden Plover, Sir John Cathcart	...	...	55	0	0
,,	3 Trusses, Fulljaines & Co.	...	...	15	0	0
,,	Golden Plover, J Earle	...	...	30	0	0
,,	Vine Branch Ditto	...	...	28	0	0
,,	Golden Plover, W. Gott, Leeds ...	...	...	35	0	0
,,	Group of Game (3), Russell Gurney	...	...	65	0	0
1853	Autumn, H. R. Smith, Troy, America	...	...	45	0	0
,,	Oak frame, Boston, America	...	...	17	5	6
,,	Group of Game (3), S. Ashton, Manchester		...	73	10	0
,,	Golden Plover, J Earle	...	...	26	5	0
,,	Heron, etc., Lord Beauchamp	...	...	194	5	0
,,	Truss, Corn Exchange ...	...	...	5	5	0
,,	Statuette Plover, A. Vardon	...	...	63	0	0
1854	Woodcock, Marquis Ailsa	...	...	40	0	0
,,	Snipe, J. Carlton, Manchester	...	...	21	0	0
,,	Wagtail, Miss Daniels ...	...	...	12	12	0
,,	Poppy Heads and Pulpit, Whadpole Church		...	15	8	0
,,	Jewel Box, Sims Reeves	...	...	1	10	0
1855	Statuette of Birds (3), A. Vardon, London		...	120	0	0
1856	Wagtail, W. Carritt, Birmingham	...	...	10	10	0
,,	Wagtail, H. W. Eaton, London	...	...	10	10	0
,,	Woodcock, R. Napier, Glasgow	...	...	35	0	0
,,	Holly, Hon. Mrs. Grame	...	...	1	10	0
,,	Mural Monument, W. Loft, Trusthorpe Church	...	18	18	0

Pulpit & Poppy Heads – costs 1854. TWW Book (fig.126).

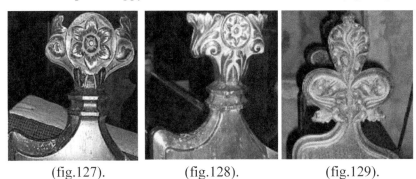

(fig.127).   (fig.128).   (fig.129).

Typical examples of Pew carved 'Poppy Heads

Courtesy of www.duddington.church.co.uk

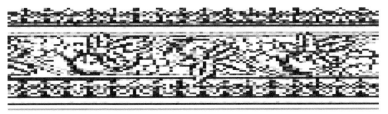

Example of a Pew End carving (fig.130).

154

Fortunately, a description of some of carvings on the 'lost' oak benches and pews that were *still* in existence in 1829 is preserved within a letter to The Gentlemen's Magazine by Revd. George Oliver on 2nd November 1829. Therein he records the remaining existence of carvings of two shields on an oaken pew in the north aisle, a further two shields in the north pew, and carved ornaments in the south pew being divided within five compartments. (See Appendix V).

However, regrettably, even those benches with ornate carvings and pews that had undergone restoration were wantonly destroyed by the late 19th and into the early 20th century when decisions were taken to replace them with the more conventional unadorned communal (family) style of pews. Understandably, Foster expresses his disappointment when describing the seating that had already been replaced when visiting St. Mary's in 1889, as *"oak benches with beautiful carved ends cleared away for family* {churchwarden ordinary} *pews of the churchwarden epoch".* [138]

It is worth noting that during 1855, in a similar vein, the subject of whether there should be doors on the ends of pews/benches had led to several 'heated' exchanges between the Vicar (supported by the Archdeacon and the Bishop), and the churchwardens/parishioners, as typified by the following extract below from the minutes of one of the Vestry Committee meetings in 1855.

"We the undersigned being a majority of the parishioners of Whaplode in Vestry assembly, do hereby require that Mr Richard Wright- Churchwarden - shall present to the venerable Archdeacon H.H. Bonney the above copy of the notice concerning the meeting with that of the resolution now passed and for the settlement of this disputed question. We humbly beseech the Archdeacon to withdraw the recommendation that "all should concede to the present arrangement according to which the doors are omitted," and at once allow the pews to be completed in accordance with the original understanding upon which the parishioners sanctioned the proposed alterations in the church."

There is still to this day a combination of those pews/benches with, and without, said doors, however, alas, no remnants of any of the ornate shield carvings, or 'poppy heads' that would otherwise have adorned them.

OTHER ELIZABETHAN/JACOBEAN FURNITURE

CHURCHWARDEN'S CHEST

A particularly prized possession of St. Mary's is that of an original late 16th century Churchwarden's chest. This can be seen inside the church next to the West Door (fig.131).

Late 16th century Churchwarden's Chest (fig.131).

ALTAR CHAIR and DRAWING TABLE

A modestly carved Altar chair of the Elizabethan/ Jacobean era (date unknown, however, it could also be a replica thereof, made circa mid-19th century) can be found in the Chancel, situate on the left-hand side of the High Altar 'Mensa Tablet' (as you view it) (fig.132).

In addition, located under the north window in the Chancel there is a small, late 19th century, Drawing table with carved inlay front (fig.132.1).

Altar chair (date uncertain)　　Small late 19th century Drawing table
(fig.132).　　　　　　　　　　(fig.132.1).

3.

Whaplode's Family Coats of Arms and Stained-Glass Windows

ST. MARY'S 'LOST' HERITAGE

COLONEL GERVASE HOLLES' REPORT

Colonel Gervase Holles (1607-1675) visited the Lincolnshire churches before and after the Parliamentary Wars (1642-1649). He was a renowned antiquarian of the period, as well as being a lawyer, statesman and a soldier. His family had property throughout the county of Lincolnshire, including in Whaplode and Moulton, hence his interest in St. Mary's Church. His manuscripts (MSS) are held in the British Museum, and the following are loose translations of his notes made on his visit in 1655 to St. Mary's, as extracted from W.E. Foster's book. [139]

It is understood that most of the windows to which he refers in his report are those that <u>were</u> found within the North Transept, the remainder being those relating to other locations which were clearly identifiable, and **all of which,** regrettably, have either disintegrated over time, and/or were, subsequently, wantonly destroyed with no regard to their heritage, at some point, thereafter, or even during various 're-builds'.

The crests identified by Colonel Holles, were, as follows:

i).   In the Bell Tower on the south side of the building is a barred window with cross pieces. The window had a stained-glass image of insignia in the form of a shield with a horizontal wavy red band between three images of a five- pointed star and six silver/ white points. It had, in addition to the above, a stripe (chevron) of silver between three crossed plants cut to a red point. {Families unidentified}

ii).   In the east window of the north Transept were insignia which belong to several Families- namely

Fitzwalter *- Represented by a shield with a horizontal band between two chevrons, the band gold and the chevrons red. Included in the design was a black ornamented fretwork with six pieces of silver.*

Littlebury *- A silver shield with two lions on the left side of the shield with paws raised and facing towards the viewer in red. The shield included two bars, one gold the other blue.*

Porter *- This shield had a blue band across from the top to the bottom, with three silver roses decorating the band.*

*iii).   In a curved recess (location not known) were figures of men laden with
goods in a supine state and clothed in robes bearing three roses.*

*iv).   In another window on the east wall of the North Transept were figures
and quotations about John de Porter and his wife, together with their insignia.*

*v).   In the north window of the North Transept, the family dedications were
to the following:*

Foster reports on page 45 of his book that the first inscriptions in this
window were as follows - *Gu. A bend betw. 6 fleur-de-lis arg. ....& Gu. Abend
ermine. .... Rye*

At first sight a translation, which combines both lines, provides us with
- *A red banded shield with the band running from the top left to the bottom
right, decorated with six fleur-de-lis and a further band in white against a red
background* – as being attributed to **Rye.** However, further heraldic crest
research points to the fact that it is only the **2ⁿᵈ line** which principally defines
the crest of the **Rye** family, i.e., *"Gu. Abend ermine".*

Whereas the **1ˢᵗ line** *"Gu. A bend betw. 6 fleur-de-lis arg."* would
appear to be the crest of **Conan fitz Elias** (otherwise known as Conan fitz
Ellis) of Holbeach & Whaplode, who died in Lincolnshire, after 1213 (see
Appendix VIII). He was one of the "Twelve Men of Holland" involved in the
dispute surrounding land ownership in South Holland, which embroiled St.
Mary's, in 1189, as mentioned in **Part One.**

vi).   Continuing, *In the north window:*

Beke - *This shield was red with a silver Moline cross (this is a cross
with a millstone rind added to both cross end pieces, making the cross ends
curve both up and down and outwards).*

Quaplod - *A quartered shield in black and gold with a band from the
top left to the bottom right in red. An adjoining shield had bars of gold and
blue, with a band across from top to bottom inscribed with silver seashells
(escallops). (See below: The Two windows with Crests).*

*On the same window were figures of men and women wearing breast
armour, with insignias inscribed. The window was in dedication to John de
Quaplod's blessed wife Mariae, and blessed daughter Edmundi Martynnis, on
bequest from him.* ¹⁴⁰

*vii).   In the main south aisle window were dedications to the following
families through their insignia:*

Littlebury - *The insignia stayed the same as those described above.*
Porter - *The same as described earlier.*
Venables - *A silver shield with two bands across in white.*

*viii).   In the west window of the north Transept were dedications to the
following families with their insignia:*

Littlebury - The same as described earlier.

*Ettys - A red shield with a horizontal band over the centre of the shield
in gold between three crescents, and the right top quarter white.*

Kyrketon - A red shield with three white bars.

*Dalyson - A red shield with three gold crescents, and the top right
quarter in white.*

*Pulvertoft - A blue shield with a stripe between three swan's heads
'erased' in silver. An adjoining silver shield had three black maces. Alongside
the Pulvertoft insignia was a dedication to Thomas Pulvertoft and his wife
Catherinae, their son, Gilberti Pulvertoft and his wife Elizabetae.*

Haultoft (Haltoft)*- A white shield with three lozenges in a creamy-
white. The Haultoft insignia was accompanied by a dedication to Willhelmi
Haultoft, his sons Gtlberti Haultoft and Willi Haultoft, Willi's wife Elizabethae
and daughters Agnetis and Alicinae.*

ix).   In a northern apse, were stone sculptures of both the **Walpole** *and*
Welby *family insignia.*

For the **Walpole** family:

Walpole: *The insignia for the* *Walpole* *family consisted of a gold
shield with a horizontal band between two black stripes with a joint shield of
three small crosses in blue, together with three lozenges.*

Walpole was one of the oldest families in the region. The family lived
principally in Houghton, Norfolk, but also held lands in Whaplode. **Thomas
Walpole of Houghton** married Joanne Cobbe Sandringham and had three
sons.(See Appendix IX).

a)   John – who died as a single person.

b)   Edward (b. circa d.1558), who lived at Houghton, and married
        Lucy Robsart, and his family lineage descended to England's
        1st Prime Minister - Sir Robert Walpole (b.1676: d.1745) and
        beyond.

c)   **Henry** (b. circa 1486: d. 1549) who lived at Harpey, Norfolk,
        married Margaret Hollofte [Haltoft] (b. circa 1486 d.
        Unknown) co-heiress of Gilbert Holtoft, Baron of the
        Exchequer (b. circa 1431: d. after 1486) who lived in
        Whaplode. Subsequently, it was their son, **Thomas. who was
        to live in Whaplode** and died prior to 15 June 1549.

For the *Welby* family:

     *Welby: The insignia for the **Welby** family had a black shield with a horizontal band between three blue fleurs-de-lis. Adorning the south wall in the place where the priests sat on a stone seat were two joint coats of arms, this also being a **Welby** connection- **Welby**: One with three lozenges, the other black with a horizontal band between three fleurs-de-lis.*

x).   *A further sculpture was set on a ledge of a criss-crossed window, dedicated to the **Ogle** family. Their insignia, also represented by two coats of arms. The first, a sliver shield with a horizontal band between three crescents overlying red fleur-de-lis, the second a chequered horizontal band between three five-petalled flowers.*

St. Mary's Church - Family Coats of Arms

Coats of Arms I (fig.133).

Coats of Arms II (fig.134).

Coats of Arms II (fig.135).

THE REMAINING WINDOWS SUFFER DEVASTATION

Unfortunately, two of the fine Norman clerestory windows on the north side have been bricked up, along with the most westerly window on the north aisle.

A window of crude decoration, described by Sir Gilbert Scott in 1856 and referred to by Foster as being *"of the barest form of churchwarden's architecture imaginable-most probably the design of a village bricklayer"* [141] is situated at the eastern end of the Norman clerestory on the north side. Its function was thought to have been the provision of added light for the musicians/ choristers housed on the rood loft.

Many of the windows within the church have been altered from their original design, and even dimensions, as described earlier with the alterations to the east window. This is probably best viewed from outside the church, where the lower elements of the window can be seen to have been blocked up to accommodate its lowered position within the east wall.

Similarly, the west window has also been lowered at some time (resulting in a loss of a third of the window's original size), perhaps, as suggested, when the nave roof was lowered in 1718. The evidence for this can be seen in the changes made to the archway of the west door, where the top of the apex has been roughly chiselled away. Only one window has anything approaching the standard of glazing that was probably common throughout the church where plain glazing was applied. This sample can be found in the diamond shaped glass in a window on the north aisle.

Following either the forceful removal of, or centuries of dilapidation, all earlier traces of stained-glass windows (see below: 4. The English Reformation) there remain only three windows reflecting any evidence of pre-20th century stained-glass ornamentation. Namely, the plain gold-coloured stained-glass window behind the altar, and the two consecutive windows situate in the South wall prior to the South Porch door.

THE TWO WINDOWS WITH CRESTS

Within these two windows can be seen, respectively, the crests of CROWLAND and LINCOLN, followed by IRBY and WHAPLODE. (See below figs.136 and 137). For more information on the Irby Family, see below - 8. The Irby Family and St. Mary's.

We have not been able to establish the date of the creation of the crests within the windows, or indeed, whether there were, at some point, other crests therewithin which are no longer present.

The crests of Crowland and Lincoln (fig.136).

The crests of Irby and Whaplode (fig.137).

The Whaplode crest as displayed (*bars of gold and blue, with a band across from top to bottom*) (right hand side, fig.137, see also fig.137.1) is incorporated within the double insignia of John de Quaplod, which having been subsequently destroyed, is only captured as the description recorded by Colonel Holles, across two shields, as mentioned earlier, as follows:

First shield: *LATIN inscription: "Quarterly sa. and or. over all a bend, gu."* Translated as: - *A quartered shield in black and gold with a band from the top left to the bottom right in red.*

Adjoining shield: *LATIN inscription: "Barry of 6, or. and az .on a bend gu.,
3 escallops arg.*

Translated as: -*"bars of gold and blue, with a band across from top to bottom
inscribed with silver seashells (escallops). – Quaplod* (See fig.137.1)

This is an intriguing insignia, since there are genealogical family references to
a **John de Quappladde** of Suffolk, whose family, apparently, is said to have
its origins in 14th century Whaplode, which would not be an unreasonable
supposition given the many earlier derivatives of 'Whaplode' that were evident
- one being 'Quappladde'. [142]

The Whaplode (Quaplod) Crest (fig.137.1)

THE 1914-18 MEMORIAL WINDOW

The only other window within the church with ornate stained glass is that of
the memorial window created in the early 20th century, which is to be found in
the South wall near to the Vestry. This memorial window, which was financed
by funds raised by public subscription, [143] is dedicated to the men and women
of Whaplode who gave their lives during the 1914-1918 World War and is now
also a focal point for commemorating those who lost their lives in the 1939-45
World War, since an additional commemoration plaque in respect of the
Second World War sits beneath the window (fig.139).

1914-18 Memorial Stained-Glass Window in South aisle wall
(fig.138).

THE 1939-45 MEMORIAL PLAQUE

1939-45 Memorial plaque beneath Stained-Glass
Commemorative Window (fig.139).

In addition, adjacent to the window, on the left-hand side of the decorative
1914-18 'poppy' banner, is a framed 'Roll of Honour' memorial cloth listing
ninety-four members of Whaplode Parish who died in the 1914-18 World War.
This memorial cloth was found under a parishioner's bed following her death
and kindly given to St Mary's by her family.

4.

The English Reformation

THE ONSET OF DESTRUCTIVE INFLUENCES

The building of churches had already slowed somewhat after the great boom in the earlier centuries; however, it was brought to an abrupt end by the onset of the English Reformation. The Dissolution of the Monasteries was a policy introduced in 1536 by King Henry VIII (r.1509-1547) to close and confiscate the lands and wealth of all monasteries in England and Wales. The plan was designed as a lucrative element of his Reformation of the Church.

During this period and the subsequent Puritan era, St. Mary's underwent many significant changes, mainly associated with the removal and destruction of anything identifiable with Roman Catholicism. This would have included the religious 'frescoes' (regardless of the precise nature-as referred to earlier) positioned within the 'Rood Loft', together with any symbolic paintings or murals elsewhere (wall above the Chancel) and many other artefacts displaying such 'catholic' adornments, etc.

Clerestory Window above North Aisle highlighting 'red'
fleur-de-lys design (fig.140).

Such has been the destruction, or disintegration, down the centuries, there remains only one clerestory window displaying its earlier 'red' fleur-de-lis design, above the North aisle (second window from the Chancel Arch), which is slowly 'fading' with time. A 'fleur-de-lis' design has long been associated with English / French heraldic usage since the royal House of Plantagenet originated from the lands of Anjou in France and held the throne of England from 1154 (with the accession of Henry II) until 1485, with the death of Richard III. The design is also symbolic of the Blessed Virgin Mary.

The destruction of all such images began in 1547, with the result that every rood in the country, with its attendant images of Mary & John, was to be fully removed, only to be interrupted by the interregnum of Queen Mary's 'catholic' reign (r.1553-1558). In 1561, the second year of Queen Elizabeth I, the rood lofts were attacked, once again, however, considerable liberty was left to the parishes as to their level of 'removal' or desecration. [144]

EMS in his paper refers to a quote attributed to Dr. Rock [Daniel Rock, an English Roman Catholic priest and antiquarian of the period] in that the churchwardens of a parish were directed to take down their rood-loft "and superstitious dome." A.D.1572. [145] He goes on to describe the remnants of the Rood Loft at Coates-By -Stow - *"There was only a skeleton of the Rood Loft, the rood-beam, some of the ribs of the coved cornice, and some uprights from the cornice to the transverse beam above, before its restoration by Mr Pearson in 1884."* [146] As mentioned earlier, the resultant beautiful restoration can be seen above in fig.122.

Subsequently, by way of a form of 'artistic' replacement, given that the chancel arch was a favourite position for the royal arms, the presence of such began even as early as Henry VIII's reign, in 1660 it was made compulsory to put up the royal arms. [147] (See **Part One -** 9. The Royal Coat of Arms of George III - 1773).

Some churches had their murals plastered over; however, it is known that in the late 19th and early 20th centuries St. Mary's church underwent a thorough cleaning, especially the removal from the walls of severe staining marks from oil lamps and candle holders. This was probably not the only time the church underwent such a thorough cleaning, possibly removing some of the plastered or lime-washed areas that had previously covered original murals. Sadly, in common with many churches throughout the land, many of the murals that would have adorned walls, etc, have been removed, and none of the original stained glass has survived, and any earlier decorations within the St. Mary's, unless removed for safety during the Reformation, were destroyed following the Civil War.

It is also believed that another cause of the disappearance within the church of those magnificent stained-glass heraldic crests, some of which may have survived the earlier destruction, was a great many years of subsequent neglect, and unrepaired dilapidation, extending up to the early 20th century, leaving St. Mary's bereft of its colourful artistic heritage.

In summation of this unforgivable period in St. Mary's history, Foster once again gives vent to his feelings:

"We can point to Whaplode; not a vestige remains of arms and monuments noted by that antiquary (Holles), many of which had been in that edifice for several centuries; one and all were swept away by the puritanical zeal of the Stuart period" and furthermore, *"It is truly lamentable to look at this church and think that the stained glass should have been destroyed and the mullions pulled out of the windows to make the church lighter, & attic windows inserted in the nave in place of transitional lights."* [148]

5.

The Present Chancel

THE MODERN CHANCEL

From St. Mary's Church records it is known that the present Chancel was rebuilt in 1818-19, at a cost of £400, following the demolition of an earlier Chancel that had replaced the original Norman Chancel. It was this original Chancel building which had a high-pitched roof, the outline of which can be seen on the exterior of the east end. (See above fig.115).

In his letter of 2nd November 1829 to The Gentleman's Magazine, the Revd. Geo. Oliver confirms: *"The nave opens into the chancel by a beautiful Norman arch, finely ornamented with a double row of zig-zag mouldings."* (See Appendix V). However, even this beautiful Norman archway had been earlier disfigured when the Chancel Arch was widened and the 'transitional corbels' introduced, in place of the lower elements of the supporting Norman pillars.

The present Chancel has a very decorative Reredos, which is probably Dutch or Flemish in design and believed to date from the early 18th century. The screen is exquisitely crafted with representations of the bread and wine, through the wheat and grape carvings. It is known that the area during this period was home to many families from Holland and Belgium, who were drafted in to help with the engineering work required on the system of dykes and sluices interlacing the fens.

In 1856, Sir Gilbert Scott describing the present chancel, as he viewed it, suggested that some of the oldest masonry dated it to the fourteenth century, which would point to the fact there would have been a partial reconstruction of the original chancel dating from the twelfth century. He further commented, as captured by Foster, *"The Chancel has, however, never so far as one can see, been proportional to the rest in size, or architectural treatment, or it is possible that it might have been rebuilt in a smaller scale."* [149]

Moreover, in conclusion, considering the history of the changes wrought on the Chancel, and yet another re-build in 1818, he was to sum up his overall assessment of the Chancel in 'damning' fashion, as follows:

"Its great defects arise from well-intended but tasteless reparations of recent times. The roof is of insipid construction, and of the most miserable insipid design; indeed, the whole Chancel is reduced to the lowest possible architectural character, and although not out of repair, appears to every person who has a particular taste or feeling a perfect blot upon the beauty of the church." [150]

Contrastingly, at the Annual General Meeting of the Society for the Protection of Ancient Buildings, in June 1904, the following 'less critical' observation was recorded: *'The chancel, which is small in comparison with the rest of the building, is modern, having been built in 1818. It retains portions of earlier work and traces of a north aisle. The chancel arch is the original Norman one, beautifully moulded on both faces and ornamented on its west face. With the exception of a slight crack on the faces of the north and south piers near the floor level, it is in excellent condition.'* (See Appendix XII. II).

The view east towards the Chancel (fig.141).

Evidence of the original Norman chancel build can firstly be seen outside by looking at the east end. In addition, while undergoing some damp-proofing, there was discovered an old doorway inside the sanctuary, where it should have been part of the chancel (see below – The Reredos), and on the south side of the Chancel is a large window, which dates from 1819-20, which, regrettably, replaced the three smaller pointed and traceried medieval windows.

It is beneath this window on the south side of the Chancel (through which provides a closer view of the inverted V roof-line of the former 14th century dormitory, as referred to earlier - see fig. 106) that sits a small, recessed cabinet in the wall (fig.142). Formerly, an open recess, which likely stored holy oils for anointing; in 1978 there was installed therein an *Ambry (Aumbry)*.

Thereafter, this cabinet was used to house the sacramental wine remaining following the Sunday Service for use during the following week.

The Ambry [Aumbry] in the Chancel (fig.142)

On the north wall of the Chancel are two commemorative plaques associated with two former Vicars of St. Mary's, namely Revd. John Fairfax Francklin, M.A. (Vicar: 1859-1883) and Revd. Lancelot H.N. Carter (Vicar: 1977-1985) (fig.144). The plaques occupy the space of the blocked-up archway that led to the former 13th century side chapel, which was demolished when the present chancel was built in 1818/19 (fig.143).

This former chapel can be seen represented on an illustration circa pre 1800 (fig.150). See below: 6. The 'lost' chapels of St. Mary's.

View of north wall of Chancel - The blocked-up archway
in the centre - to the right of the window (fig.143).

Commemorative plaques re- two former Vicars
of St. Mary's (fig. 144).

THE REREDOS (ALTAR SCREEN)

The centre piece provides us with a great deal of information about the origin
of this part of the Church, also the date when it was created. Given the history
of the various rebuilds of the Chancel this Reredos (Altar Screen) was erected
sometime at the beginning of the 18th century and is believed to be from the
'Flemish Region' of the Low Countries.

The Reredos detail (fig.145).

It has a typical centre piece directly in line with the High Altar, bearing an image of a flagon in the centre (representative of the concentrated wine) on the left are sheaves of wheat and a loaf of bread, whilst on the right is depicted the chalice and grape vines with fruit (of significance in the Low Countries - Holland, Belgium).

Considering that the area at that time was heavily populated with Dutch/Flemish families who were supplying engineers and workers for the huge changes to the drainage systems, it is more than likely that a family decided to make this their contribution to the Church. One may also detect the form of what used to be an image in the centre panel below the carvings, however, the true nature of it remains a mystery.

As mentioned previously, situate behind the present Reredos surround panelling on the right-hand side (south side of the Chancel) is the presence of a priest's bricked up doorway which led to the supposition that the original Norman Chancel was a much larger building, but it was subsequently re-built on a reduced scale. The fact that when the stone 'Rood Screen' was in situ (prior to its destruction in the 16th century) it sealed off the congregation from the Chancel, consequently, the clergy would have needed their own access to the Chancel, serves to reinforce this point.

Outside view of bricked-up doorway behind the south wall
Reredos panelling – seen to the left of the Chancel
window (fig.146).

6.

The 'lost' chapels of St. Mary's

Dorothy Owen provides evidence that, at one stage within St. Mary's, there were resident five priests or monks who each had the responsibility for a specific chapel within the building. Foster, however, acknowledged that there had been three chantry chapels within the church [151] (excluding the High Altar), and, to date, research has not discovered any concrete evidence of a fourth.

THE FOUR CHANTRY CHAPELS

Owen described the church as having four Altars.[152] These can be identified as being the known three Chantry Chapels within the main building as well as the High Altar, which is the *'Mensa Tablet.'* These additional three Chantry Chapels were dedicated to specific families (the names of which remain unknown to date) where they would pay for a Priest to administer the sacraments to them in private. It is likely that many of these were established before the end of the twelfth century, and a family would also have been responsible for the upkeep of the Chantry Chapel, and fortunately the precise location of these additional three is known:

The location of the first one, and most readily recognisable, is at the southwest corner where the present Elizabethan Irby Tomb stands. On close inspection, just to the left of, and under, the window ledge, is a piscina, distinguishable from a holy water stoop as it has a drain for the Priest to ensure the remains of the sacrament are untouched by human hands (fig.147). Also, alongside this towards the south door is a distinct notch cut into the rail where the east wall of the Chantry Chapel was originally situated extending across to the nave pillar.

This Chapel would have predated the Irby Tomb, but since both the south and north aisles were extended by several feet during the latter part of the 15th century and early part of the 16th century, originally, it was thought that the Chapel could not have existed prior to the alterations. However, it is known that much of the materials contained within the original walls were in fact transferred complete, and re-constructed, and this fits in with the reports of St. Mary's serving at least eight other Chapels within the parish.

The Chantry Chapel Piscina – adjacent Irby Tomb (fig.147).

The evidence for the second Chantry Chapel was found in tile fragments, discovered when preparations were being made for the construction of the Heraldic Suite between 2004 and 2006. The flagstones in the north-west corner of the church had to be raised and the ground thereunder excavated in readiness for a new flooring to be laid. Artefacts unearthed included several fragments of medieval floor tiles, including two individual pieces, which warranted the most attention, for they contained richly coloured decorations of various scenes.

One tile had a fleur-de-lis in a corner, together with the design of a key above it, with a further piece of another design. When these were shown to a specialist expert in Lincoln, he produced from his records a black and white copy of a much larger piece of tile, described as the 'Nottingham Tile' since it had been discovered in the village of Talbert in Nottinghamshire in 1917 at the site of a ruined monastery; the other piece, whilst exhibiting similar characteristics, remains unidentified to date. The expert did refer us to the British Museum, which held within their collection, a two volume *'Catalogue of Medieval Lead-Glazed Earthenware Tiles in the Department of Medieval and Later Antiquities, British Museum'* with 14,000 tiles listed and illustrated with more than 3000 designs, published in 1980. An extensive book which defined the remarkable research carried out by Professor Elizabeth S. Eames (1918-2008).

Examples of the 'Nottingham Tile' found therein would appear to date the St. Mary's tiles from the period 1325-1365, and, in support of a second chantry chapel in this position, there is a map of St. Mary's in the Lincolnshire Archives which provides an indication of the chapel being sited at the north-west corner of the church, as now occupied by the 'Heraldic Suite'. (Notably, distinct notches made in original plaster dado).

St. Mary's fragment of 'Nottingham Tile' style (fig.148).   Unidentified fragment of a tile (fig.149).

It is understood that these highly decorated tiles were normally reserved for the use as the elaborate floor covering inside the Chantry Chapels, in cathedrals, monasteries, or country manor houses. The tiles can now be seen in the upper part of the display cabinet nearest the west door, together with a brief explanation as to their origin, and their estimated date, which also indicates that the chapels, if that is where they belonged in the church, date from a much earlier period than that associated with the changes in the formation of both the North and South aisles.

The third Chantry Chapel was known to have been at the corner of the North Transept (see the shape of the first window on the east wall of the transept and in the Chancel proper) extending northwards, as evidenced by the bricked-up archway in the north wall side of the Chancel. The photograph below (see fig.150) would appear to be of a sketch which shows the outline of the third chapel extending east from the North Transept to align with the East end of the Chancel, as defined by the buttresses on the corner.

Pre 1800 Sketch of the east view showing the Medieval Chancel, and the side chapel in situ. (fig.150).

In conclusion, with regard to these 'lost' chapels, we do have some further fragments of the decorated terra cotta screens, which are now to be seen situate on their own display units at the base of the Irby Tomb in the West End of the church (see figs. 151-152).

It is with grateful thanks that we owe the identity of the fragments to a visit to St. Mary's by a group of historians from the Morley College Group in London, who advised that the remnants were in fact not only from Chantry Chapel Screens, but also that they would have been part of sculpture work carried out between the 15th and 16th centuries. Furthermore, they believed the style could be attributed to that of the school of Pietro Torrigiano (1472-1528) a Florentine sculptor, who, according to Vasari, was one of a group of talented youths who studied art under the patronage of Lorenzo the Magnificent in Florence. (See Appendix X - The life of Pietro Torrigiano - d. 1528).

Two Chantry Chapel screen remnants on display (figs.151-152).

Remnants of Chantry Chapel Screens and other notable artefacts on the display (fig.153).

177

THE NORTH TRANSEPT (LADY CHAPEL)

This addition to the original Norman building took place during the period when there were major changes made to the church. However, as highlighted earlier, with the chancel having succumbed to decay, by the 17th century a significant amount of its tracery and the entire north transept needed replacement.

When the school room (situate in the position of the North Transept) was initially established, circa late 18th early 19th century, it was not connected to the Church. The Revd. Geo. Oliver, in his letter to the Gentleman's Magazine in 1829 (see Appendix V), confirms its existence *'In the north front is a transept supported by diagonal buttresses, which has at present no internal communication with the church and is used as a school room'*.

Later, in the 19th century, circa 1854, the original floor of the North Transept was raised, which likely occurred when the Church floor was refitted and levelled to provide space for the reconstituted school room, which remained closed off from the rest of the church, and in the north wall a fireplace was built therewithin.

When the subsequent re-connection with the Church occurred, the original old masonry arched around the top of the north window was regrettably removed in order that the window looked more 'fitting' for a schoolroom. Fortunately, the north window did undergo restoration in an unusual way with the emphasis on preserving the fine tracery, albeit the stained-glass could not be replaced.

The re-build of the North Transept & North door (fig.154).

The re-construction of the window within the North Transept, which took place in 1909/10 is quite unique, since it is one partially made of oak and masonry. The upper half of the window is made completely of wood; whilst the lower part (from below the arched top) is masonry. The restorative work was done by Ernest Grimson on the recommendation from the Society for the Preservation of Ancient Buildings ("SPAB"). He adhered to the strict principles of the SPAB, refusing to restore missing medieval features, but 'create' masterful copies, and the new wooden tracery in the window was probably made at his workshop at Daneway House, Sapperton, Gloucestershire. The following sketch was the basis for the reconstruction of the window. (See fig.155).

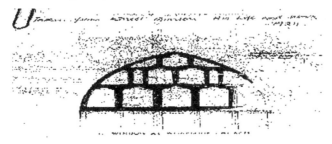

Sketch of uppermost part of the window in arch (fig.155).

The black & white picture below (fig.156) highlights how the two separate components which form the window are distinctively portrayed photographically, with the Oak replacement tracery in the archway showing much darker than the natural stone parts of the window below.

The North Transept window tracery of Oak and Masonry (fig.156).

As well as the latter part of the east wall of the North transept displaying the converted window (from an archway in the 'old' vestry area, which extends from the transept) above which is now pinned the remnant of the 'Rood-Loft,' the outer west wall also exhibits a bricked-up doorway/archway (fig.157), which would have been part of the open archway separating the former schoolroom from the church in the early 19th century.

Exterior West wall of North Transept – 'Bricked-up.'
doorway (fig.157).

In particular, it was the east and north windows that housed many of the magnificent stained-glass Coats of Arms, as recorded by Colonel Holles in his report of 1655, but, regrettably, they have since been destroyed. (See above: 3. Whaplode's Family Coats of Arms & Stained-Glass windows).

There is a one remaining 'stone' insignia embedded in the north wall of the North Transept, which, whilst the family crests of both the **Walpole** and the **Welby** families were quartered thereon, the remaining elements, until a number of years ago, were of uncertain family designation (see below fig. 158).

This situation was clarified, to a degree, following the discovery of an article '*In Search of our Lincolnshire Ancestors*' by '*Titus Rawlins*' in the July 1984 edition of *Lincolnshire Life*, wherein Titus (who points out that his great grandfather was the 7th Baron Boston – Greville Northey Irby) remarks that on a visit to Whaplode, he was shown the house which was built on the site of the former house (destroyed, however, apparently elements of the original house remain) of the Irby Family, on Millgate, just outside Whaplode, and advised that the stone arms appearing on the wall "… *are those of Welby, quartered with Walpole, Holtofte and Apreece*". (See below, fig.158.1).

Comparatively, therefore, whilst the 'Millgate' stone crest is not a copy of that to be seen in the North Transept, not least since it displays a 'doubling' of the principal crest portrayal, the symbols displayed on the Millgate crest, which are somewhat less distinct having undergone wear and tear, do appear to be similarly reflective of the heraldic symbols shown on the North Transept crest.

This similarity provides us with the reasonable supposition that the stone crest of arms displayed on the wall in the North Transept of St. Mary's **is** indeed reflective of the four families, who are all linked by marriage, and with the marriage of Anthony Irby MP. (1547-1625) to Alice Welby this completes the family connections. [153] (See below – 8: The Irby Family and St. Mary's).

The North Transept Stone Crest of Arms of Welby & Walpole, Haultoft (Holtofte) & Apreece (fig.158).

The Millgate stone 'crest' displaying Heraldic symbols, similar to those within the North Transept stone crest (fig.158.1).

7.

The Jacobean / Charles I Font

The Font was, according to the Revd. Canon Moore, in his account of St. Mary's Church within the book '*The Fen and Marshland Churches,*' *Third Series. Leach & Son. Wisbech. 1878,* (the photographs therewithin are by Edward Johnson, and the text was contributed by various authors), a creditable imitation of the original Norman font.

Notably, it has a central cylinder of black stone surrounded by octagonal panelled and fluted stonework, together with barley-twist legs, which may also suggest that it reflects a degree of Jacobean/ Charles I period influences. In the circumstances, it has been described as having been designed to be 'sympathetic' with its surroundings rather than a copy *per se.*

The Revd. Geo. Oliver in his letter to the Gentleman's Magazine comments "*The font is placed in its legitimate position in the centre of the unpewed space at the west end, and exactly between the north and south porch doors. The whole height is about seven feet.*" (See Appendix V).

The font of 'uncertain' heritage (fig.159).

8.
The Irby Family and St Mary's

THE IRBY FAMILY

The Irby family have lived in, principally, Boston and Whaplode, Lincolnshire, and at Hedsor House, in Buckinghamshire, for a great many years. Genealogically, Irby family history can be linked to William de Irby, knight, (circa 1251), with descendants to Robert Irby (b. circa 1365) born at Irby on Humber, Lincolnshire. He married Isabel Flinton, daughter of Sir Herbert Flinton of Flinton, Yorkshire.

During the reign of Henry VIII, the family had settled at Gosberton, co. Lincoln, and Anthony Irby of Gosberton, married Alice, daughter of John Bunting. Anthony was born after 1517 and died 21st June 1552, and he and his wife had five daughters and seven sons. His fourth son, Thomas Irby, whose seat was at Whapload (Whaplode) Hall, married Isabel, daughter, and co-heir of Thomas Sarjeant, of Moulton, and finally inherited the estate. Thomas Irby died in 1561 and his heir by Elizabeth was Anthony Irby (b. 1547: d. 06.10.1625, buried at Whaplode).

Anthony was the M.P. for Boston, in the reigns of Elizabeth and James I, an eminent lawyer, as well as a bencher of, and Autumn reader to, the Society of Lincoln's Inn, and he was appointed one of the Masters in Chancery, in the reign of James I. On 22 December 1575 at Whaplode, Anthony Irby married Alice Tash, widow; and daughter of Thomas Welbye (Welby), of Moulton, and he subsequently acquired the manors of Moulton, & Fitzwalter, being part of the estates of the Lords of Moulton, Barons of Egremont. The Irby residence in Whaplode, Irby Hall, was almost a mile to the south of the church, and the family exerted quite an influence on the church.

His coat of arms was deposited in the third window, towards the north, of the Lincoln's Inn Chapel, which according to Sir William Dugdale, were *argent, fretty sable*, with his name, *Anth. Irby,* over them.

THE IRBY TOMB

Sited at the west end of the South Aisle, the canopied ten poster tomb is that of Anthony's heir Sir Anthony Irby, (b. 9 January 1577: d. 1610), who was an M.P. and High Sheriff of the county of Lincoln in the reign of Charles I. Sir Anthony married Elizabeth Peyton in February 1602(3), daughter of Sir John Peyton, M.P. 1st Baronet Peyton of Isleham, co. Cambridge. Within this magnificent altar tomb can be seen the bed for the effigies of Sir Anthony, and his wife Lady Elizabeth, beneath which are held their remains.

The magnificent Irby Tomb (fig.160).

Surrounding the tomb on either side are the five children of their marriage, three boys beside their father on his left, and two girls alongside their mother, on her right. Sir Anthony and his wife have their heads resting on pillows and their feet braced against their respective family mementoes, a collared hound for him and a griffin for her, which are incorporated in their family crests.

*SIR ANTHONY IRBY, KNIGHT – THE ELDEST SON [*including extracts from *"Sir Anthony Irby 1605-1681. A Lincolnshire Knight" by John Almond. (JA) Lincolnshire Past & Present No 76. Summer 2009].*

Their eldest son, also Sir Anthony Irby (b. 17.01.1605: d. 2.01.1682), is depicted as the largest statue of the children on the north side of the tomb. He was one of Cromwell's commanders during the Civil War. (East Anglia, including Lincolnshire, was strongly anti-Royalist), having been asked by the Earl of Essex to raise and captain a troop of Parliamentary dragoons. In the process, it is believed he housed the army's cavalry horses in the west end of the Church in readiness to attack the Royalist held Crowland Abbey, and

184

subsequently, he and his troops assisted Oliver Cromwell and Sir Miles Hobart at the siege of Crowland, taking the town on 28th April 1643.

However, just prior to this, the Royalists of Newark had convened a Commission of Assize naming 85 local persons, including Sir Anthony, Thomas Welby of Boston, Thomas Ogle of Pinchbeck, and William Ellis of Holbeach, indicting them for high treason having joined with the Parliament against King Charles I.

Subsequently, later in 1643, in the pursuit of peace, the King issued a pardon. Sadly, peace was not restored, and the Civil War continued, and on 6th December 1648 Sir Anthony, who had resumed his parliamentary duties as an MP (he had been elected in 1628 as an MP for Boston), was imprisoned by the army, in what was really an army coup. However, on 20th December, he was summoned to meet with Commissary-General Henry Ireton at Whitehall, when, upon refusing to promise he would not attempt anything against the proceedings of the Parliament and army, he was dismissed without an engagement, and left at liberty to sit in the House again, if he thought proper.

Following Cromwell's victory, and the beheading of King Charles I on 30th January 1649, it was only after the death of Cromwell and the restoration of the Monarchy in 1660 with King Charles II (Reign 1660-1685) that there was passed the Indemnity and Oblivion Act of 1660 which afforded a general pardon to everyone who had committed crimes during the English Civil War, other than those who were *directly* involved in the regicide of King Charles I. Whereupon, Sir Anthony, who was in receipt of this pardon, sought re-election as MP for Boston, and held the seat until his death.

In view of his position, in 1665, 1669 and 1678, on behalf of the King Charles II, he was called upon to 'present' respectively three new Vicars, on the occasion of the deaths of the former Vicars, at our sister church, namely, All Saints' Church, Moulton. His last 'presentation' being that of Philip Tallents, clerk, M.A. who was inducted by John Thomas, Vicar of Whaplode (1662 – 1688).

Sir Anthony had inherited his father's estates at Whaplode and Moulton, and other property in Weston and Brothertoft, and his country seat was Irby Hall, Whaplode; his Boston residence, also known as Irby Hall, was situated on the opposite side of the Haven River to St. Botolph's Church. He also had a residence in the Little Almery, St. Margaret's, Westminster, London, and it was at St. Margaret's Church that he was buried in 1682.

He had four wives: Frances Wray (Daughter of Sir William Wray); Margaret Smythe (daughter of Sir Richard Smythe); Margaret Barkham (daughter of Sir Edward Barkham); and finally, Katherine Paget (daughter of

William Paget, 4th Baron Paget, of Beaudesert) with whom he had a son, Anthony Irby, who was born in 1649. Subsequently, Anthony married Mary Stringer (Daughter of John Stringer of Ashby, Kent), and died in 1684, being buried at Whaplode.

His heir was Sir Edward Irby, MP, born 31 July 1676, who married Dorothy Paget (granddaughter of Sir William Paget, 5th Baron Paget, of Beaudesert). Sir Edward was made 1st Baronet Irby of Whapload and Boston, by Queen Anne on 13th April 1704, and was buried in Whaplode on November 11, 1718.

Sir Edward was succeeded by his son, William Irby, who was raised to the Peerage by King George III in 1761 and created 1st Baron** Boston, having already succeeded his father as 2nd Baronet** Irby of Whaplode and Boston in 1718. William married Albinia Selwyn in 1746 and had three children.

** *A Baron is a peer of the realm, and sits in the House of Lords, whereas a Baronetcy is not a peerage, and therefore the holder does not sit in the House of Lords.*

THREE FACTS ASSOCIATED WITH THE TOMB

There are three interesting facts about the family that can be gleaned from viewing the tomb.

a) One of Sir Antony's daughters is depicted holding a skull, which indicates that she died early in infancy.

b) Sir Anthony (not his eldest son) died at home (or at least away from battle), since the collared hound sits at the base, instead of a rampant lion which would otherwise signify death in battle.

c) The 'Griffin' seated at the Elizabeth Irby's feet indicates that she was of Welsh stock, that of an aristocrat, which is borne out by examining her family's genealogical marital connections, determined as follows.

Elizabeth's grandfather, Sir Robert Peyton, MP. married Elizabeth Rich, daughter of Sir Richard Rich, Lord Chancellor of England, MP, and their family line can be traced back to a Robert le Rich (1310-1353) who married the daughter of Sir William Boteler, 1st Baron Boteler (1274-1335). Baron Boteler had married Angharad verch Griffith, who was the daughter of the Gruffudd Maelor II ap Madog, arglwydd Dinas Bran (Crow Castle) - the Prince of Powys, Montgomeryshire, Wales. (b. circa 1195 – d. 1269).

THE INSCRIPTION AROUND THE CANOPY OF THE TOMB READS:

HERE LYETH BURIED SR ANTHONIE IRBY KNIGHT SONNE OF ANTHONIE IRBY ESQUIRE AND ALICE HIS WIFE, DAUGHTER OF THOMAS WELBY OF MOLTON ESQUIRE, WHICH SR ANTHONIE TOOKE TO WIFE, ELIZABETH, DAUGHTER OF SR JOHN PEYTON OF ISELHAM IN THE COUNTIE OF CAMBRIDGE KNIGHTED BARONET, DESCENDED FROM THE NOBLE RACE OF UFFORDES, SOMETIMES EARLES OF SUFFOLK, BY WHOM HE HAD ISSUE, SR ANTHONIE IRBY KNIGHT, EDWARD, THOMAS, ALICE AND ELIZABETH WHO DIED AN INFANT.

SR ANTHONIE THE ELDEST MARRIED HIS FIRST WIFE FRAUNCES, DAUGHTER OF SR WILLIAM WRAY KNIGHT AND BARONET AND FRAUNCES HIS WIFE, DAUGHTER AND COHEIRE TO SR WILLIAM WRAY OF HAWSTED IN SUFFOLK, HIS SECOND, MARGARET DAUGHTER OF SR RICHARD SMITH OF THE COUNTIE OF KENT, KNIGHT.

The Irby Tomb inscription (fig.161).

Lady Elizabeth Irby (fig.162).   Sir Anthony Irby (fig.163).

SIR WILLIAM WRAY'S BURIAL MONUMENT

A further fact, one of historical coincidence, is that in the Church of St. Peter at Ashby-cum-Fenby, in the division of Lindsey (about 6 miles south of Grimsby), Lincolnshire, can be found a tomb dedicated to Sir William Wray MP, 1st Baronet of Glentworth, (1560-1617) and his wife, Lady Frances Wray

(1576-1642) which, it would appear, is a copy of the Irby Tomb in Whaplode, as evidenced by the following extract from *"Notes of Lincolnshire being an Historical and Topographical Account of Some Villages in the Division of Lindsey 1890"* by John G. Hall (JGH), as follows:

"The north aisle {of the church} *is supported by circular arches springing from clustered columns of four conjoined shafts , under which is a fine monument in Grecian style, and a copy of the one to the memory of Sir Anthony Irby in Whaplode Church near Spalding to which family the Wrays were related by marriage* {see above, fig.161 - the inscription around the canopy of the Irby Tomb viz Sir Anthony Irby}. *It is probable that the two monuments were executed by the same artist, as Sir Anthony died in 1623, and the Lady Frances Wray before 1647. The monument has been neglected, and time and dilapidation unchecked have made sad havoc with the ornamented details. The monument consists of a massive altar tomb, on which lie the figures of a knight in complete armour, and a lady in the rich dress of the period at his right. It is surmounted by a canopy supported by ten pillars of composite order and crested with a shield containing 14 quarterings."* [154]

THE IRBY & PEYTON FAMILY CRESTS

Irby: *Argent (white) fretty Sable (black), on a canton Gules (red), a wreath Or (gold) - A side facing helm, denoting a Gentleman, is the base on which a torse of cloth Argent and Sable supports the crest of a stylised hound's couped Argent maned Or gorges with a collar Argent fimbriated (lined) Gules.*

The Irby Crest (fig.164).

Peyton: *South facing is an ovoid, signifying that this represents a female. Argent, fretty Sable on a canton Gules, a wreath Or-Irby impaling (at its side) Sable, a cross engrailed (wavy edged) Or - Peyton above is a cherub head face white and wings gold. At the peak is a stylised hound's head.*

The Peyton Crest (fig.165).

WORK ON RESTORATION OF THE TOMB

In 1963 the Parochial Church Council ("PCC") approved the incumbent 8th Lord Boston's plan for the programme of restoration work for the Irby memorial, and it was noted in the minutes of a PCC meeting in 1968 that *"the Lord Boston had spent a lot of time renovating the Tomb and putting it in order."* However, sadly, Cecil Eustace Irby, 8th Baron Boston, of Boston, co. Lincoln, [G.B.,1761] and 9th Baronet of Whapload and Boston, co Lincoln, [G.B., 1704] (born 14th July 1897) died four years later, unmarried, on 12th October 1972.

Following his death, he was succeeded by his third cousin once removed, Major Gerald Howard Boteler Irby, 9th Baron Boston, and 10th Baronet of Whapload and Boston. He was the great-grandson of Rear-Admiral Frederick Paul Irby (second son of the 2nd Baron) and married Erica Hill in 1936.

Upon the death of the 9th Baron on 17th February 1978, he was succeeded by his son, Timothy George Frank Boteler Irby (b.1939), 10th Baron Boston, and 11th Baronet of Whapload and Boston, who took a great deal of interest in the upkeep of the Tomb. He had married Rhonda Anne Bate in 1967, and, following his death on 3rd February 2007, the title(s) now currently rest with his son, George William Eustace Boteler Irby, 11th Baron Boston, and 12th Baronet of Whapload and Boston (b. 1971).

THE IRBY HELMET ('Sallet') AND BANNER

To be seen on the railings surrounding the Tomb is a picture of what appears to be an 'English Civil War' Parliamentarian's helmet, however, this fine, hinged visor, ceremonial helmet, is far from being a mere Parliamentarian helmet (fig.166).

The Irby Helmet ('Sallet'), described as a popular form of head armour, is a fine and rare example of 15th century work of Flemish origin in

189

the style of North Italian (probably Milanese) knight headgear. The skull is beaten out of a single piece of steel, the whole decorated with strips of gilt copper, and the original main surfaces would have been coloured blue. The gilt brass enrichments were added in the 17th century when it is believed the helmet was reserved primarily for use at family funerals, possibly worn by family members.

There is a remarkable history behind the helmet, for it had 'languished' sited in a variety of places in the vicinity of the Tomb; hung with the 'banner' on an extended bar on the south wall adjacent the Tomb; hung on one of the railing spikes that surround the Tomb- for many years up until the mid-1950s, when on one occasion, a visitor to the church enquired of a member of the church, Mr A. Crawford (the father of June Crawford, who was Churchwarden in 2002), if he could have a look at the helmet, whereupon the visitor was advised that it was only an old replica helmet and carried no great significance. The visitor happened to be one of the curators from the Royal Armouries at Her Majesty's Tower of London, who at once informed Mr Crawford that the helmet was in fact a genuine, and rare, example of an Italian ceremonial dress helmet of 15th century vintage.

The visitor asked if he could take it away for further examination, however, he was advised that the PCC, and The Lord Boston (Greville Northey Irby, 7th Baron Boston) would have to be consulted, and in November 1957, after taking additional advice from Solicitors, and the Lincon Diocesan Board, the PCC and the Lord Boston, agreed that the helmet should be passed into the custody of Sir James Mann, the Master of the Royal Armouries at the Tower of London, on loan for exhibition.

The exquisite 'Irby' ceremonial helmet ('Sallet') (fig.166).

This position was confirmed in a letter of 1st December 1957, wherein The Royal Armouries advised the Revd. W.H Gibb that the helmet was on display there, and that a loan contract would be set up with termination at an agreed notice of six months from either side. Furthermore, in the meantime, Sir James Mann would complete his notes about the helmet, which would later be published in the *Antiquaries Journal.* (See Appendix XI - Exchange of Letters surrounding the safekeeping of the Irby ceremonial Helmet).

Subsequently, the PCC, who, earlier, had been advised as to the risks and responsibilities surrounding the safe-keeping of the helmet, not least its potential value at the time for insurance purposes, began to express the desire that the helmet be brought back to the Church for display within a special cabinet.

In May 1963, the PCC were advised that the Spalding Gentlemen's Society ("SGS") had safe storage facilities available, which would alleviate any concerns surrounding the safe display of the helmet within the church, and finally in May 1964, following agreement with the new Lord Boston (Cecil Eustace Irby, 8th Baron Boston, had succeeded to the title following the death of the 7th Baron Boston on 16th September 1958), who had visited the SGS, and was very happy with their display & secure storage facilities, arrangements were put in place to have the helmet returned from the Royal Armouries for placement and safe-keeping within the SGS, where it has remained ever since, together with the remnant of the family banner clearly displaying the family insignia.

Recent developments, following discussions with the Irby family, point to proposals to undertake photogrammetry (3D imaging) in 2024 of both the Helmet and the Banner (which will also undergo appropriate preservation) to enable the important heritage of these family heirlooms to be promoted, under strict conditions, more widely for the benefit of future generations of the public, antiquarians, and historians .

9.

The Stone Coffins

The Revd. Canon Moore further highlights that these two stone coffins, both of which have extensively decorated ledgers with a distinct English Cross, were unearthed during the re-flooring of the church in 1855, when they were found at the south side of the nave. These are fine examples of such coffin lids (more of which can be seen at Crowland Abbey), and the location of their find within the South Aisle junction at the West End of the Church is now marked by the distinguishable replacement flagstones.

THE PRINCIPAL 'ENGLISH CROSS' COFFIN LID

With regard to the most elaborate of the two complete stone coffins to be found inside the church, the beautifully carved 'English Cross,' a floriated design also known as the 'Tree of Life', that appears thereon (see fig. 167), upon examination by a lecturer of the Department of Church Archaeology at York University, Dr. Aleksandra McClain, was identified as being 13th century work, and in 2006 she described the markings as follows:

The 'English Cross' stone coffin lid, circa 1250-1300 (fig.167).

"This coffin lid is exceptionally fine work, with detailed and elaborate high-relief carving. It almost certainly originates from the major medieval quarry and sculpture workshop located at Barnack, a centre of production and innovation that exported work across the whole of the east midlands and southeast. Stylistically, the cross slab probably dates to the later part of the 13th century. The cross head is of the 'bracelet derivative' style, which first appears circa.1200. The elaborate nature of the head, the use of Fleur-de-Lis (as can be seen on the terminals of the cross, the branches coming off the shaft

of the cross, and the shape of the base), and the flowing, naturalistic nature of the foliation suggests a date of circa 1250-1300. The foliated motif of the cross may allude to the medieval concept of the cross as the "Tree of Life," referring to Jesus' death and resurrection. Foliated crosses are also found in other forms of medieval art."

The fine work displayed on the principal coffin lid would probably indicate that the priest was of some status, or else that the grave marker was provided for the parish priest by the local lord, or someone with similar wealth and access to resources.

Priests' wealth and social status could vary widely in the Middle Ages, depending on their family's status, their association with a monastic house, or the importance of their parish church and its land holdings, and this could be an example of a priest on the higher end of the social scale.

The 2nd stone coffin lid -outside the Irby Tomb (fig.168).

Equally, the fact that the coffin slab was found in conjunction with identifiable burial emblems (See below: 10. The Early English Chalices) makes it a particularly important example, as cross slabs are almost always *ex situ*, and thus we can only speculate as to the types of people that they commemorate, and therefore it is possible that they related to wealthy landowners in the 12th & 13th centuries.

THE BROKEN DECORATED 'ENGLISH CROSS' COFFIN LID

Latterly, during the excavations for the Heraldic Suite, as well as removing some fourteen tons of earth, the builders came across yet another 'decorated English Cross' stone coffin cover.

This latest example is much smaller than the first two, and was found broken in two, lying at a curious angle in the ground, giving the impression that, perhaps, it had been deliberately damaged.

The broken 'decorated English Cross' stone coffin lid (fig.169).

All three coffin lids are on display in the West End of the Church, outside the Heraldic Suite, and adjacent to the Irby Tomb. All skeletal remains discovered were given a Christian burial, accordingly.

10.

The Early English Chalices

In 1855 when the first two coffins and their lids were unearthed, complete, therein were found their respective skeletons (which were subsequently given Christian burials in consecrated ground) each together with a soft Early English pewter chalice and paten found on the breast within, which gave rise to the suggestion that the skeletons were those of either a priest, or other dignitary.

The burial of a chalice and a paten with a skeleton is particularly interesting since they are seen as common 'secondary emblems' on cross slabs. Such emblems are found most often on slabs in northern England, and are thought to stand for the rank, trade, or occupation of the commemorated person, and in this case a priest. The inclusion of these replicas within the burial suggests that secondary emblems may have represented objects that were buried with the body. Such emblems are much less frequent in more southerly areas of the country, and especially around large workshops like Barnack, where it was more likely that a centralised mode of production did not allow for much personalisation of the grave slabs.

The presence of the remnants of both the chalices and paten provided the church with a subsequent opportunity to engage with the Lincoln University Department of Conservation, by presenting them with the ideal material to use as a project for one of their graduate master's degrees. In doing this, it not only provided the University with some much sought-after material it also gave the church an opportunity to have much of the research work verified.

In her comprehensive write-up on the items, Elizabeth Welfare, who, at the time, was studying for her master's degree in Archaeological Conservation and Preservation (2004/5), confirmed that the items were indeed early English Pewter albeit that some of the metal had deteriorated through inadequate storage. She also confirmed that the age of the items placed them in the late 12th and early 13th centuries through the comparison with almost identical items preserved in the Lincoln Cathedral Museum collection (access to this museum is restricted to graduate students and academics doing relevant research).

The sketches below provide a representation of both original chalices as they would have appeared in an earlier life.

Pewter sepulchral chalices from Whaplode Church as they might have looked when whole

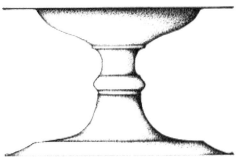

Chalice One: 9.7 cms x 11.5 cms approx.

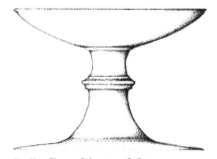

Chalice Two: 9.2 cms x 9.5 cms approx.

Liz Welfare   October 2005

Sketches of Early English Pewter Chalices (fig.170).

A copy of Elizabeth Welfare's report, together with the remnants of the chalices, can be seen in the cabinet display area within the church outside the Heraldic Suite. As well as working on the chalices and paten, Elizabeth Welfare also did some partial reconstruction work on two of the three Charity Boards. (See **Part One**: 9. Specific artistic and commemorative contributions to the fabric of St. Mary's - The Charity Boards).

11.
The Village Cross and the Robert Collins Monument

THE VILLAGE CROSS

The remains of a 14th century Village Cross can be seen on the right at the beginning of the churchyard entrance. The Revd. George Oliver, in his letter to the Gentleman's Magazine in 1829, comments on its status. (See Appendix V).

The stone cross beam from this monument is on display within the West End of the church, amongst many other items of miscellaneous masonry, etc., recovered over the years (refer earlier fig.153).

Remains of the 'Historic' Village Cross (fig.171).

HISTORIC ENGLAND LISTED DETAILS:

The Churchyard cross at St. Mary's Church, Whaplode, is a good example of a medieval cross with quadrangular base and octagonal shaft and is constructed of limestone. Limited disturbance of the area immediately surrounding the cross indicates that archaeological deposits relating to the monument's construction and use in this location are likely to survive intact. The cross has been little altered in modern times and in use as a public monument and amenity from medieval times until the present day.

The base takes the form of a socket of square section with chamfered corners and a grove running below the upper edge. It stands to a maximum height of 0.23m above the ground surface. The shaft fragment is set into the centre of the socket stone and is rectangular in section at the base rising through chamfered corners in tapering octagonal section to a height of about 0.99m. The top of the shaft fragment is flat and includes a number of holes containing the remains of iron and lead by which an upper stone was formerly fixed.

The monument was first registered under the list of buildings of special architectural or historic interest under Section 54 of the Town and Country Planning Act, 1971, on 7th December 1987, and subsequently, it was recorded in **Historic England** Listings as follows:

Heritage Category: Scheduled Monument

This monument is scheduled under the Ancient Monuments and Archaeological Areas Act 1979, as amended as it appears to the Secretary of State to be of national importance.

> *List Entry Number: 1010673*
> *Date first listed: 06 Jan. 1995*
> *Legacy System RSM – Reference No. 22686*

Churchyard cross, St Mary's churchyard, Whaplode - 1010673 | Historic England

Similarly, Lincolnshire HER has information recorded under the reference MLI22197 for both the Church and the Churchyard Cross. Heritage Gateway - Results

THE ROBERT COLLINS MONUMENT

This 12-feet-high stone pyramid monument adorned with emblems of freemasonry stands in the churchyard. It was erected by Robert Collins, as a monument to himself and his family (fig.172). In this stone pyramid he deposited a stone box within which he placed some copper and silver coins of

George III, also some garden seeds in labelled glass vials; so that when the monument falls to decay the curios may try to see if they will vegetate.

The Robert Collins Monument (fig.172).

Robert Collins, who had been a curate at St Mary's between 1802 - 1811, died 25th January 1812, aged 51. Foster records that the Revd. Samuel Oliver, who took over as Curate from Robert Collins, gives an account in the Church register not only of his view as to the bad state in which he found the vicarage on taking over from Mr Collins, but also his rather unflattering opinion thereof. [155]

12.

Architectural 'Graffiti' and other Ancient Stone/Wooden remnants

Careful examination of the various parts of the roof supports and, indeed stonework, will reveal the evidence of graffiti, with people having left their mark on the fabric of St Mary's. Some of this can be seen in the northwest corner of the new suite of rooms *'The Heraldic Suite'* where one James Tanner in 1706 etched his record.

Other such 'dateline' markings in this area are to be found on the roof support timber across the west window – a carefully recorded date of 1623, and a certain 'R. Collins' informed us that he was there in 1782.

The carved inscription - 'R. Collins 1782' (fig.173).

Interestingly, it is quite likely that this 'R. Collins' is the same Robert Collins, whose stone pyramid monument stands in the churchyard (see above fig.172). Equally, it could have been Richard Collins, a relative (?), who had been a churchwarden in 1769.

Section of Wooden cross-beam - carved 1655 (fig.174).

200

To be found at the base of the Irby Tomb, in the West End of the Church, together with other remnants of stonework is a section of a wooden crossbeam preserved with the date of 1655 carved thereon (fig.174). This wooden crossbeam sits on top of the stone Village Cross 'top' beam, now situate in front of the new units displaying the Chancel Screen Fragments at the base of the Irby Tomb (refer to fig. 153).

Also, to be seen on the masonry above the third pillar from the Chancel Arch on the South Aisle side of the Nave is the inscription '1399' presumably posted by a 'mason' working on the Church.

A further collection of other ancient stone remnants can also be seen on the windowsill directly above the piscina in the south wall alongside the Irby Tomb (see fig 175).

Collection of other ancient stone remnants (fig.175).

In July 2003 R. John Lord (Department of Conservation, Lincoln University) identified a fragment of a Saxon grave slab with carved decoration reminiscent of a Maltese cross, probably of 'Barnack' work. We were advised that similar pieces had been located in Yorkshire, and the fragment is now retained within the West End of the church.

13.
The Unknown

CHURCHYARD RECLAMATION

By the mid-20th century, a large part of the Churchyard had become considerably overgrown, with many graves therein unattended, and gravestones in a disintegrated state. Therefore, in 1963 the PCC decided that the Churchyard should be cleared of any tombstones that were either 'unknown', no longer 'maintained' or the 'ownership' was untraceable, and duly obtained a diocesan faculty to undertake the work.

Thereafter, having 'notified' the community to provide confirmation of any family ownership to allow re-siting of 'family' tombstones, the PCC appointed John H. P. Wright, a local farmer and landowner, whose family members have long been benefactors to St. Mary's (as earlier mentioned), to clear designated areas of the churchyard, and prepare it for levelling and re-seeding, and on 4th June 1963 John Wright received authority to commence the work.

WHAPLODE PARISH COUNCIL

4th June, 1963.

Dear Mr. Wright,

I write to confirm that the Parish Council have now received their faculty for removal of the tombstones and they have agreed to let you have the stones provided that you are prepared to remove them free of charge. Before work is commenced I think it would probably be advisable if we could meet the Vicar one evening and show you exactly what has to be done: possibly you could suggest an appointment and I will then come over: in the meantime I will try to mark in chalk those stones which are not to be moved.

The Parish Council are very grateful to you for undertaking this work, which should certainly provide you with a fine bottom for your road.

I think it would be helpful if work could be started on clearly at least one or two sections very soon so that the Parish Council in their turn can start dragging the land about and getting it levelled.

Yours sincerely,

J.H.P.Wright, Esq.,
Oaklands,
WHAPLODE FEN.

PCC Letter of authority for clearance (fig.176).

1963 South side of Churchyard reclamation begins (fig.177).

1963 clearance of undergrowth –'nettles, brambles & ivy'
on the North side (fig.178).

THE GRAVE BENEATH THE PULPIT:

Arthur Mee commented in his book on this gravestone as being *"a fine 13th century floorstone* {gravestone} *with leafy cross"*, [156] and Revd. David

Carney, Vicar of Whaplode (1991-2002), claimed that the odd markings visible on this grave were attributed to the Cross of Jerusalem, with reference to the Crusades.

However, following extensive enquiry, both into significant grave markings and the Crusades, it was established that, firstly, the fact that most of the markings clearly end in the form of a petal, or leaf, rather than the customary ball shape, rendered the attribution much more difficult. Secondly, the only individuals who bodies were brought back from the Crusades had to be figures of significant importance; other casualties had their hearts removed and saved in 'Heart Graves' such as those seen in Crowland Abbey.

Partial view of Gravestone beneath Pulpit (fig.179).

Considerable research was conducted by Cyril Hearn trawling through many reference books on grave markings, as well as consulting experts, examining gravestones, and visiting Jerusalem, only to conclude that the markings on this gravestone do not support the contention that they represent the cross of Jerusalem, and therefore the occupant is still unknown.

Indeed, seeking further to have the grave investigated, he sought advice and assistance by way of an approach to Lincoln Diocese, the BBC 'Time Team' and the Home Office. Unfortunately, the resulting estimated costs, and lengthy administrative requirements, proved to be too prohibitive, and the project was shelved.

THE FACE

As one walks down the north aisle towards the east end of the church, at the penultimate Norman pillar, the archway connecting the pillar to the north wall has a most unusual feature. Carved at the end of the arch is the figure of a man's face; whether this is representative of the chief mason of the day (often a tradition for the image of certain masons to be recorded within religious buildings), or whether it is an effigy of the principal monk, or even the Abbot of Crowland at that time, one can only guess. However, it is most intriguing, since these types of carvings (in wood or stone) are readily found *outside* churches, Abbeys and Minsters, not normally inside.

The mysterious stone 'face' (fig.180).

The face remains a mystery to this day.

14.

20ᵗʰ Century Preservation

LONG OVERDUE ARCHITECTURAL RESTORATION 1909/10

Over the centuries the fabric of the church had deteriorated quite considerably in numerous areas, and in the late 19ᵗʰ century there was increasing concern being shown by the clergy, and others, and action was being sought to remedy the parlous situation. The consternation as to the state of St. Mary's was epitomised by the following scathing comment made by members of 'The Builders Federation' following a visit to the church in 1890, as expressed in their publication 'The Builder'. (See Appendix XII) *"It has been reduced to a half-ruined state by long-continued neglect or barbarous usage."*

The initial target was the restoration and reconfiguration of the Church roof, which also embraced changes to the north window in the Lady Chapel, given that the roof in the North Transept was also to be raised, allowing the window to be restored to its former glory.

However, with regard to the window, after long discussions with the Society for the Protection of Ancient Buildings ("SPAB"), with whom the Church has always had a long association, being one of the first Churches to be involved with the newly formed organisation in the latter part of the 19ᵗʰ century, and being unable to find an architect willing to take on the responsibility of rebuilding the original masonry, it was decided the North Transept window should be restored by the inclusion of oak timbers in the top tracery.

Herewith, an extract from the Parish Register, which is not dated, but is most probably circa 1909-10, since the content appears to be based on articles taken from the SPAB.

*"The case of Whaplode Church opened after a press cutting was received in 1889, reporting that J L Pearson {a respected Architect} estimated the cost of restoration to the nave would be £5,000 and to the chancel, £1,500, However, restoration did not take place owing to local disagreements. The Revd. John William Rhodes seemed sympathetic to the views of the Society, and in 1903, after negotiations, **William Weir** was able to make a detailed report, whilst Ernest Grimson and George Jack took on the repair work. Weir recommended that the nave and chancel roofs should be strengthened. The north window in the north transept had been 'mutilated' by the insertion of a brick chimney, to form a flue for the fireplace beneath it. It ran upwards, cutting through the top of the arch and continued above the gable. Weir suggested that 'the brick chimney should be removed, and the defect carefully*

made good.' This was carried out and a sketch of Grimson's shows how the stone tracery was replaced in oak." (Refer to fig.155).

The above narrative is borne out by the text of various Annual General Meeting minutes of the SPAB in June 1904, 1908, and 1910 (see Appendix XII), which provide an insight into the regular discourse occurring at the SPAB, and also elsewhere – following visits by many interested parties, antiquarians, builders, etc., and observations voiced in their books, and magazines, expressing concern surrounding the serious state of disrepair into which the church had descended, and the efforts of various vicars, and others, to instigate action to repair the damage.

Ernest Grimson (b.21.12.1864:d.12.08.1919) was an English furniture designer and architect, whose reputation is secured as one of the most influential designers of the English Arts and crafts movement in the late 19th and early 20th centuries, and there are several of his notable restorative works across England, which include our very own North Transept window, as herein referred. (See above: 6. The 'lost' chapels of St. Mary's - The North Transept (Lady Chapel)).

In an effort to spur the local populace to contribute to the restoration during the period of work, the following appeal was placed in the Lincoln Diocesan Magazine in 1910, as follows:

"For more than thirty years the church of this parish has needed restoration, the walls being unsound, and the roof giving free access to the rain. The Church is one of the oldest and most interesting of the many fine edifices in South Lincolnshire, containing original Norman pillars and arches, whilst the west front reminds the visitor of a stately abbey rather than the village church. During the vicariate of the Rev J. W. Rhodes, a keen controversy centred round Whaplode church for eleven years, on the question of the obligation of the rectors, but proved barren in its results**. The present vicar the Rev E. W. Brereton++, proceeding on other lines, has {been} enabled to carry the restoration of the church. The total cost will probably amount to £1,600 towards which £1,100 has been received or promised. The vicar will be glad to receive contributions, and for the liquidation of the debt a grand bazaar will be held at the Corn Exchange Spalding on Oct 6th and 7th." William Weir concluded the work in 1910.

This episode, as covered earlier, (see **Part One: 7. The prelude to the final handover of responsibilities in 1594, and the turmoil beyond: *October 1900: The public campaign by Revd. Rhodes)* however, did ultimately result in the ceding of the responsibilities of the patronage of the Chancel by the

Governors of Uppingham School back directly to the Crown to be latterly assumed by the Diocese.

++ The Revd. E.W. Brereton (Vicar 1909-1913) recorded all the various architectural changes occurring as seen by him in 1909, as well as highlighting the varieties of designs present in the church from the Normans through to the 'churchwarden' style of the late 19th century. He also confirmed earlier important measurements of the church: Total outside length - 157 feet (Foster reported 151 feet): Height of West Gable - 46 feet: Height of Tower - 78 feet. Length of Nave - 110 feet.

15.
The Future

St. Mary's Church heritage is registered with its Grade I Listed Building status as referenced under the detailed Historic England entry which can be viewed at: CHURCH OF ST MARY, Whaplode - 1359295 | Historic England and its heritage is also recorded under Lincolnshire HER Gateway Reference MLI22187. Heritage Gateway - Results

However, what does the future hold for this noble church? Such a monumental heritage must be preserved, and each year brings yet further age degradation. The need for continual restorative work to maintain the underlying fabric of this wonderful church, both inside and outside, is a necessity to ensure that St Mary's 900-year heritage is extended for many more centuries enabling its 'magic' to be enjoyed by future generations.

Lithograph of St. Mary's - circa 1810-1830 (fig.181).

This lithograph by Alfred Newman appears as Plate No. 49 – page 102, in Johnson, J & Newman, A. (1857). *Reliques of ancient English architecture.* Published by Day & Son, London: Getty Americana. Digitised by Getty Research Institute: Internet Archive.

APPENDIX I
The Early Lineage of the Saxon Earl Ælfgar (c. 1002: c.1062)

Ælfgar was the son of Leofric, Earl of Mercia, by his well-known wife Godgifu (Lady Godiva). He succeeded to his father's title and responsibilities on the latter's death in 1057. Ælfgar gained from the exile of Earl Godwin of Wessex and his sons in 1051, when he was given the Earldom of East Anglia, which had been that of Harold, son of Godwin. Earl Godwin and King Edward were reconciled the following year, so Harold was restored to his earldom. However, this was short-lived since at Easter 1053 Godwin died, and Harold on becoming the Earl of Wessex, relinquished the earldom of East Anglia to Ælfgar.

Ælfgar seems to have learned from the tactics Godwin used to put pressure on King Edward. When he was himself exiled in 1055, he raised a fleet of 18 ships in Ireland and then turned to Wales, where King Gruffydd agreed to join forces with him against King Edward. On 24 October, two miles from Hereford, they clashed with the army of the Earl of Herefordshire, Ralph the Timid. The Earl and his men eventually took flight, and Gruffydd and Ælfgar pursued them, killing and wounding as they went, and enacting savage reprisals on Hereford. They despoiled and burnt the town, killing many of its citizens. King Edward ordered an army mustered and put Earl Harold in charge of it. This was more formidable opposition, and Ælfgar and Gruffydd fled to South Wales. However, the issue was resolved by diplomacy and Earl Ælfgar was reinstated.

Ælfgar is known to have had at least four children. One son, Burgheard, predeceased his father, expiring while returning from Rome early in 1061 and was buried at Reims. This led Ælfgar to give to Reims Abbey lands in Staffordshire and Shropshire, which became the endowment for Lapley Priory. He was survived by three children, two sons, Edwin, later Earl of Mercia, and Morcar, later Earl of Northumbria, and a daughter Ealdgyth, who was first married to Welsh king Gruffydd ap Llywelyn, and later to Harold Godwinson, King of England.

(The above text, together with associated links, is taken from the published references on the page Ælfgar, Earl of Mercia - Wikipedia)

APPENDICES

APPENDIX II
The Families of De Craon and D'Oyry

II.A. De CRAON (CREDON/CRODON or CROUN)
ROBERT de CRAON (d. 13/01/1147-49)

Robert de Craon was the youngest son of Renaud de Nevers/(Craon). Originally, betrothed to Amelie de Chabanais, the marriage was later repudiated, and he left for the Holy land in 1125, and there were no children.

He later became a Templar rising to become Grand Master upon the death of the founder of the order, Hugues de Payns, in 1136. Whilst an excellent administrator and legislator he was less successful militarily, suffering later losses in the battles with the Turks in the Crusades. During his period of governance as Grand Master it is more than likely that he had at least two serious connections with the papacy – the first being when Pope Innocent II issued a papal bull "*Comne datium optimum*" translated as "Every Best Gift" on March 29th, 1139, this was just three years after Robert de Craon had assumed the title "Grand Master Knight Templars." The second of these incidents being the papal bull declared in 1145 by Pope Eugenius, that of "*Militia Dei*" (translated as 'Knights of God').

Crest of Robert de Craon Robert de Craon

(fig.182). (fig.183).

Courtesy of: https://en.wikipedia.org/wiki/Robert_de_Craon
Robert de Craon, 2nd Templar Grand Master (b. - 1147) - Genealogy (geni.com) - Alex Moes.
Painting by Boyan Yanev-Kamakapualani Pahinui photos

He remained Grand Master of the Order of the Temple until his death, the date of which is in doubt, since the Obituary of Reims indicates his death as 13th January 1147, whereas other sources suggest 13th January 1149, which was just prior to the end of the Second Crusade.

ALAN de CRAON (1090-1155)

Alan de Craon succeeded his father, Wido (see **Part One**), and was a great steward of the household to Henry I, and together with his wife, Muriel [allegedly, *de Beauchamp*], and his son Maurice, they founded Frieston Priory as a cell of the Abbey of Croyland, and he also gifted land to the Abbey of Swineshead in Lincolnshire, and to Reading Abbey. In addition, in 1142 he accomplished one of the earliest pieces of water engineering in medieval England, helping the port of Boston by enabling a river to change its main course from Bicker Haven to the present Boston Haven. [HEH-SS, p.220].

Alan, who was related to Geoffrey d'Orleans and Robert de Prunelai, respectively the Abbots of Croyland (Crowland) and Thorney, laid the foundation stone of the Abbey Church at Crowland in 1114 (the fire in 1091 had destroyed the former building). He and his wife were also benefactors of Spalding Priory. *"He was buried on the south side of the high altar at Crowland; and a figure (in the west front of Crowland Abbey) dressed in a mantle and on its head a coronet, on the breast a fibula, the hands supporting a fringed robe, was designed for Alan."* [JL, p.163].

Alan had two daughters and three sons. Alan's second son was GUY de CRAON I – who was cited in the *"Libre Vitae"* (The Book of Life of Thorney Abbey - signifying the friends and 'benefactors' of the Abbey), alongside his father and his four siblings. *[Keats-Rohan: 'Domesday People Revisited' (May 2012), p.18 quoting Thorney Abbey Liber Vitae].* Alan's heir was Maurice de Craon II.

MAURICE de CRAON II (b. circa 1130- d. after 1188)

Maurice de Craon II was appointed keeper of the castle of Ancennis by Henry II, and governor of the provinces of Anjou and Main; he was also one of the representatives of King Henry invested with full powers in negotiations between him and Philip, King of France. He was Lord of Frieston, Lincolnshire, and a benefactor of the Templars. He married Clarice (unknown), with whom he had two sons, Raol, and Guy de Craon II

GUY de CRAON II (1148-1205)

Guy de Craon II succeeded his father Maurice, and circa 1181 married Isabella de Bassett (Widow of Albert de Gressley, the younger) daughter of Thomas Bassett. Guy accompanied Richard I in his voyage to the Holy Land in 1190, and was, allegedly, present at the peace treaty signed in 1192, between Richard I and Tancred, King of Sicily.

He was succeeded by his only child, his daughter, Petronella, who was subsequently married three times, and descendants of those marriages were inter-married amongst some of the noble families of England – i.e. de Badilsmere; de Ros; de Neville, de Stafford and de Percy to name but a few - with the properties (Manors in Frieston, Moulton, Butterwick, Spalding, Holbeach, Fleet, Whaplode etc.) having devolved to Petronella, as the only heiress, being passed down and shared out accordingly.

OTHER IMPORTANT FAMILY MEMBERS
MAURICE de CRAON I (d.1119/1120)
Maurice, eldest son of Renaud de Nevers (Craon) and a sibling of Wido, married Tiphaine (Anguilla) de Chantoce et d'Ingrandes. His son Hughes de Craon (d.1140) succeeded him, and married Marquise de Vitre, as his 2nd wife. They had two sons Guy (1110-1164) and Maurice de Craon III.

MAURICE DE CRAON III (d.10.08.1196)
With his marriage to Isabella de Beaumont-le-Roger, dame de Meulan, (dame de Mayenne by 1st marriage) (born c.1148 – 10 May 1220), a French noblewoman, daughter of Waleran IV de Beaumont, 1st Earl of Worcester, Count of Meulan, Maurice brought together two of the chief Franco-Norman families of the 12th century. He left to join the Third Crusade in 1189 and died on 10th August 1196.

Maurice and Isabella had seven children. Amongst them was Amaury I de Craon (1175-1226) who married Jeanne des Roches (daughter of Geoffrey des Roches and Marguerite de Sablé (Amaury's half-niece)). Their daughter, Isabella de Craon married Ralph de Fougères, and in so doing brought together, by blood, or marriage, six of the most powerful dynasties in the provinces of Maine, Anjou, Brittany, and Poitou in France, with subsequent links to English nobility. [DP, pp. 244-245].

II.B.   **D' OYRY (D'ORY/OYRi or D'OYRii)**
ENGLISH BRANCH
GEOFFREY (I) D'OYRY (died by 1160)
Geoffrey (I) d'Oyry was the founder of the English branch of the d'Oyry family. He was born, prior to 1100, at Oiry, Maine, Champagne-Ardenne, France, and came to England settling in Gedney, Lincolnshire, and died before 1160. His father was likely Fulk (I) who was born in France, but this is unconfirmed. Geoffrey (I) married Emecina (parentage unknown) who was born in Maine, France.

After Geoffrey's death, Emecina, in turn, married secondly Walter de Cauntelo (Cantilupe), but there were no children from this marriage. It was Emecina who had visited the Abbey of Croyland in 1114 (the year of its consecration), and it is recorded that it was she who later gifted the churches of Whaplode and Gedney to Croyland Abbey, as confirmed by Pope Hadrian IV at Nepi in June 1158. Geoffrey and Emecina had three children, Baldwin, Waleran [see **Part One**: 3. Influential Landowners in South Holland post the Norman Conquest] and Fulk (II) D'Oyry. [KM, pp.10-11].

BALDWIN D'OYRY (died 1189-90)

It is confirmed that Baldwin was the first Rector of Gedney, and it was usual for the younger sons of such families to be presented to livings in their gift of their relatives, and Baldwin held Whaplode as well as Gedney. The date at which he became rector of Gedney is uncertain, but it was certainly before 1161, and may have been as early as 1150: the year of his death is not known but since two of his nephews {Geoffrey and Fulk – see below} were joint vicars of Whaplode circa 1185-93, it is possible that he died in 1190 [KM. p.13] however, there does not appear to be any confirmed evidence that he had any offspring.

FULK (II) D'OYRY (died by 1189)

Evidently, there were certainly two English Fulks after 1150, not least because of FULK (III)'s attestation that his father was, indeed, FULK(II), who married, allegedly, Adeliza, a sister of Gilbert of Walsoken. They, in turn, had three children, two sons, FULK (III) and William, and a daughter Emecina ## who married Conan fitz-Ellis (see Appendix VIII), who became one of the 'Men of Holland' involved in property disputes with Crowland Abbey in 1189. [DP, p.514] [HEH-SS, p.25].

It is also possible that Emecina was the daughter of Waleran D'Oyry, since Fulk (III), her husband, was of the generation of Conan who seems to have reached his majority by 1174 and was dead by 1221. [KM2, p.3].

LAMBERT D'OYRY (died by 1230)

Lambert D'Oyry was a son and the heir of Waleran, however his date of birth is not known, but it is likely to have been before 1160, since in 1185 his brothers, Geoffrey and Fulk, were old enough to be the joint incumbent parsons of Whaplode St. Mary's Church. In 1208 Lambert was described as a 'knight', and it is recorded that he gave to Spalding Priory four acres of land in the new *marsh* area of Whaplode, lying between the lands of his brothers Thomas and William. Later, he also gave to Spalding additional land in Whaplode [as rented by one of his 'serfs' thereby embracing the serf's family as sitting tenants] with *free entry from the sea to the marsh.* [KM2,p.40]. The inference from these records serves to confirm that Whaplode's river/marshlands/broads fed directly into the sea in medieval times and adds credence to the view that a harbour was likely in existence at some stage in the development of the area and village, which is also supported by the belief that a house in the village was, indeed, that of the harbourmaster.

SIR ROBERT D'OYRY (died before 1261)

Lambert's son, Robert, succeeded to his father's property before 1230, following the death of his brother John. On 31 December 1237 Robert obtained a licence from Bishop Robert Grosseteste for a private chapel with its own chaplain in his house *versus Mariscum* [towards the sea] in Whaplode, without 'fonts and bell', however this was a chapel in a manorial hall, not a chapel of ease. The whereabouts of this hall is unknown, but it may have been at Whaplode St. Catherine. Thereafter, between 1244 and 1 April 1247 he gifted the buildings / chapel to brother Thomas de Cressi of the order Friars of the Holy Cross. [HEH-SS, p.37][KM2, p.41].

By his death Robert was described as a 'knight' and had married Christiana (whose parentage is unknown) by whom he had a daughter, Elizabeth. Adam of Hagbeach who resided at Hagbeach Hall in Whaplode married Robert's heiress, Elizabeth, however, there does not appear to be any record of any children by this marriage. [HEH-SS, p.37][KM2, pp.2,40-42]. (See also **Part One**: 4. Claimants to the ownership of the Parish Church of St. Mary's - Outlying Chapels).

GEOFFREY D'OYRY of WHAPLODE

Geoffrey d'Oyry, Lambert's third son, held land between Asgardyke (built in 1205) and Hassockdyke (built in 1230) in the vicinity of Whaplode. His wife Mary (of unknown parentage) also inherited land in Whaplode, and their only child was Maud. In Mary's widowhood (circa 1253-1274) she granted all lands in her possession to Spalding Priory, to Maud, her daughter, and William, son of Thomas Fleet. Maud, in turn, exchanged with Prior John (Head of Spalding Monastery) all her inherited land in Whaplode for three acres of land in Spalding. [KM2, p.42].

NORMAN BRANCH
BACKGROUND
There is speculation shown by genealogists surrounding the connections of the Norman branch of the family with the English. It is suggested that perhaps Fulk

(I) came to Normandy with the exiled Odo of Champagne, the forefather of the counts of Aumale. The first certain appearance of the surname is that of a Geoffrey d'Oyry in 1114. It is surmised that this Geoffrey could be the same person as Geoffrey (I) d'Oyry who married Emecina (See above) however, the timeline does not necessarily fit their descendants. Around the era of the early to middle 12th century, there are several other D'Oyry family members, whose lineage is not easily determined, who became involved in property assignation charters around Gedney, Boston and in South Holland.

Unfortunately, available genealogical records appear to be scant as regards their specific parentage, however, given that Fulk (III) d'Oyry's daughters were his only heirs, since his only son, Geoffrey, died a single person before 1236, this might suggest that, by reason of the timeline, the following members were descended from the NORMAN side of the Family.

NOTABLE 'NORMAN' BRANCH DESCENDANTS
HUGH D'OYRY
A Hugh (I) d'Oyry (d. by 1154) and his brother another Fulk d'Oyry (circa 1155), whose son was also called 'Geoffrey' (living 1150). It was Hugh's grandson - Hugh (II) d'Oyry, who fought in the Third Crusade, and died at the siege of Acre 1190-91.[DP, p.240].

It is also suggested that a Hugh d'Oyry was the illegitimate son of Geoffrey D'Oyry (Gedney) (see below) having been in receipt from Ida, widow of Geoffrey, some land in Lutton, which was part of her dower. [KM2, p.44].

GEOFFREY D'OYRY (Gedney)
Geoffrey D'Oyry of Gedney, whose widow Ida married Lambert de Moulton, made an agreement with William de Lungespe (Longespe) as to the ownership of all places of 'moor' between *Lesgates* (Leedsgates) and Lutton Drove, and between Lutton Dyke and Thomas Moulton's dyke in Fleet (subject to some specific limitations) in the years 1230 to 1235. He also granted a second charter to William Longespe and his wife Idonea in 1250-5 which conveyed a fifth part of all Geoffrey's land enclosure in the fen outside the outer fendyke as far *Trokenholt,* belonging to Geoffrey's manor of Gedney, to be held as part of William's manor of Sutton. [HEH-SS, p.33].

SIR JOHN D'OYRY
Sir John D'Oyry granted Sir Roger Thukilby 25 acres of land in Gedney Fen between the dyke of Sutton and Gedney during the period 1236 and 1256. [HEH-SS, p.32]. No evidence has been found that John was ever married.

APPENDIX III

The 1268 declaration of Richard de Gravesend – Bishop of Lincoln

This is an extract from his declaration made in January 1268 in respect of the ownership of the Church of Quaplode (Whaplode) given to Abbot of Croyland.

*'**To all faithfull Christians** by whom this writing may be read, Richard, by Divine permission Bishop of Lincoln, sendeth health in the Lord. We will that you should by this present writing know; that, whereas our beloved children in Christ, the religious persons, the Abbot and Convent of Croyland, have long since obtained the grateful consent and assent of our predecessor, the blessed Hugh, of famous and revered memory, as also of his Holiness Honorius, sometime chief bishop of the Roman Church, likewise confirming the same of the church of Whaplode, wherefore they were and are the patrons, to have it to their own proper use in manner as in the instrument is more fully contained.'*

'We, at their devout and frequent petitions that we would favourably, more graciously in the premises, grant them our assent and consent to the permission and favour done them by our said predecessor, the consideration of their order inducing thereto, having due regard to the special devotion of the said pious persons, and their sincere love in the Lord towards our venerable church at Lincoln, and the bishop thereof, being more readily inclined to grant their petitions and requests, as therefore the monastery at Croyland the weightiness of religion and observance of their order for the sake of sanctity and principally in favour of hospitality, and which do and ought to render it esteemed by all men, remembering that favour should not be denied to such requesting it, of the assent and grateful consent concerning of our beloved children of Christ of William Lessington, the dean and chapter of our church of Lincoln, in respect of Divine piety, and especially for enlarging the duty of Divine worship therein, have given, granted, and by this our present charter have confirmed to the monastery of Croyland, and to the monks there together serving God, the church of Quaplode (Whaplode), in which they obtain the right of patronage, to be possessed to and for their own proper uses for ever, the rent and profits of which church they may indeed convert to their own use, and without any impediment, for the future have power lawfully to convert the same, a competent portion thereof still being reserved for the vicar perpetually serving the same church , wherein we likewise ordain and establish the vicarage out of the profits of the said church for the support of him and his ministers, and the charges thereof as we have thought fit by our episcopal

authority, thus to distinguish the portions of the said abbot and convent and the vicar before mentioned by them to us and our successors to presented whenever the said vicarage shall happen to be vacant, and they, the said abbot and convent may have the whole tithe of sheaves of corn of the said church of Whaplode, with al demesne lands and its rights and appendants to the ssaid church any way belonging, and all the tithe of flax and hemp purely and absolutely.' [WEF Pages 12-14].

APPENDIX IV

The Corpus of Anglo-Saxon Stone Sculpture - Whaplode Stonework 1999

Herewith are the summaries of the important findings carried out under the auspices of Durham University. Their project published under the name of *"The Corpus of Anglo-Saxon Stone Sculpture at Durham University, 2021"* conclusively establishes that three pieces of burial stonework found at St. Mary's Church are of the pre-Norman conquest era, and, therefore, support the assertion that in all probability there existed a Saxon church in Whaplode, in one form or another. The following is extracted therefrom:

*"**The Corpus of Anglo-Saxon Stone Sculpture** identifies records, and publishes in a consistent format, English sculpture dating from the 7th to the 11th centuries. Much of this material was previously un-published and is of crucial importance in helping to identify the earliest settlements and artistic achievements of the early medieval and Pre-Norman English. The Corpus documents the earliest Christian field monuments from free-standing carved crosses, and innovative decorative elements, to grave-markers.*

Durham University, under the guidance of Professor Dame Rosemary Cramp, supported by more than thirty researchers spread throughout the country, has, since 1977, coordinated the production of a series of bound, detailed, and fully illustrated volumes that provide coverage of every early medieval Sculpture in England. In recent years, with the support of the AHRC, British Academy and the Aurelius Trust, the project has sought to release the data from all volumes online, as a searchable catalogue, accompanied by digital images.

In 2018 the project won substantial funding from the Arts and Humanities Research Council to enable the completion of the project. Across 2018 to 2022 we will complete full coverage of every early medieval sculpture in England, bringing to press all remaining published volumes. The full online release of our digital data has now been made possible by substantial funding from the Arts and Humanities Research Council."

(Reproduced from www.ascorpus.ac.uk, with their full written permission).

The following analyses are to be found in The Corpus of Anglo-Saxon Stone Sculpture: Catalogue (ascorpus.ac.uk)

"Pictorial examination of the following pieces of burial stonework found in St. Mary's church was undertaken by the researchers."

Exhibit 01-385   **Exhibit 02-386**   **Exhibit 03a-b-387**

The Corpus of Anglo-Saxon Stone Sculpture: Project Lead and Senior Editor: Professor Rosemary Cramp. **Volume 5. Lincolnshire. Paul Everson and David Stocker. 1999.** Corpus of Anglo-Saxon Stone Sculpture 5.

Extracts from 'Conclusions' – Chapter 8.
There were in the order of 650 parishes in medieval Lincolnshire and of those as many as about 100, or about 15%, have to date been found to retain pre-Conquest sculpture. The list of potential 'minsters' in Table 8 accounts for at best only half of these items and so it is quite clear that a great many monuments, perhaps some 50%, were being erected at later church sites for which the sculpture is the sole evidence of burial-church status in the pre-Conquest period. These presumably represent parochial foundations. [*Evidence of such stonework provides an indication of burials of some consequence, thereby establishing that such churches were of senior status, as churches of lower standing did not have burial rights at all*].

Settlement on the silt ridge of the Lincolnshire Fens has been evidenced by surface finds of mid-Saxon pottery (Healey 1979), and its intensification in the later pre-Conquest period has been shown by the results of the Fenland Project (Hall and Coles 1994). The presence of sculpture at Bicker (ills.41-52), Gosberton, (ill. 175) and **Whaplode (Illustrations 385-7)** indicates well-developed settlements on this silt ridge by the eleventh century, which had churches of high enough status to have burial grounds.

There follows 'Current Displays - Lincolnshire' & related information:
1. Whaplode 01, 385
2. Whaplode 02, 386
3. Whaplode 02, 386: (Fig 30) Re-construction (1:8)
4. Whaplode 03a-b, 387
5. Table 5 The Fenland group of grave-covers [featuring Whaplode 01 & 03]

CURRENT DISPLAY : WHAPLODE 01, LINCOLNSHIRE
Overview

Object type: Part of grave-cover

Measurements: L. 27 cm (10.6 in) W. 38 > 35 cm (15 > 13.8 in) D. 12 cm (4.7 in)

Stone type: Pale grey (10YR 8/1) shelly oolitic limestone, with ooliths around 0.5mm in diameter, and shell fragments and small gastropods crowded together, parallel to carved face of stone. Barnack Rag type, Upper Lincolnshire Limestone, Inferior Oolite Group

Plate numbers in printed volume: Ill. 385

Corpus volume reference: Vol 5 p. 270-271

National Grid Reference of Place of Discovery
TF323240 View findspot location on a map

Present Location
Loose at west end of south aisle

Evidence for Discovery
None. Repairs were undertaken in 1909, which might have been the occasion for discovery (Pevsner et al. 1989, 795), although the floor was apparently re-laid in 1880 (Willis 1988, 24).

Church Dedication
St Mary

Present Condition
Moderate; somewhat weathered and abraded

Description
A fragment from the foot of a flat, tapered grave-cover. The boundary of the stone is marked by a border of rectangular section, damaged at the lower end, and there is a central shaft dividing the stone into two halves longitudinally. This shaft may have developed into a cross towards the head end. To either

side of the central shaft are two registers of interlace. The strands are of squared section and have broad interstices. These form three-strand plait on both sides of the shaft and are symmetrical about it. There is a loose terminal at the base of each register.

Discussion

The grave-cover represented by this fragment is closely paralleled by that at Market Deeping (no. 2, Ill. 288) and, more generally, its layout and stone type must associate it with the large Fenland group of grave-covers which were produced in the Barnack area and distributed from Lincoln to Suffolk and beyond (Chapter V and Table 5). Whaplode is the only Lincolnshire member of this group which has only three-strand (as opposed to four-strand) plait, though examples with three-strand plait are quite common elsewhere. Butler (1963–4, 109) compares the technique used here with several of the stones from Bicker, but it appears more similar to Market Deeping 2 and Lincoln Cathedral 1 (Ill. 230). The Fenland group of grave-covers probably date from the early and middle parts of the eleventh century, and the simplicity of the interlace in this example might support a date towards the end of the series.

Date
Early or mid-eleventh century

References
Davies 1914–15, 226; Davies 1926, 20, pl. VIII; Butler 1963–4, 109; Pevsner and Harris 1964, 711; Stocker 1986a, 61; Willis 1988, 24; Pevsner et al. 1989, 796

Endnotes

CURRENT DISPLAY: WHAPLODE 02, LINCOLNSHIRE
Overview

Object type: Part of grave-cover

Measurements: L.26 cm (10.2 in) W.39 cm (15.4 in) D. 16 cm (6.3 in)

Stone type: [Barnack Rag type, Upper Lincolnshire Limestone, Inferior Oolite Group]

Plate numbers in printed volume: Fig. 30; Ill. **386**

Corpus volume reference: Vol 5 p. 271-272

National Grid Reference of Place of Discovery

TF323240 View findspot location on a map

Present Location

Loose at west end of south aisle

Evidence for Discovery

See Whaplode (St Mary) no. 1.

Church Dedication

St Mary

Present Condition

Good; somewhat abraded

Description

A (top): Although this is merely a small fragment which has been squared off for reuse as building stone, it is clear that it comes from a large grave-cover with incised decoration. The upper surface was probably flat and was bounded by a border moulding of rectangular section. The remains of two panels survive. The decoration in each consisted of an incised cross with wedge-shaped arms similar to type B8, each arm probably being of equal length and seemingly formed of multiple concentric grooves.

The reconstruction of the pattern made by Butler (1964, fig. 2A) cannot, however, be arrived at from the surviving fragment.

Discussion

This fragment represents a cover whose decoration should probably be reconstructed as in Fig. 30. There is no really close parallel in Lincolnshire, but this repeated pattern of geometrical incised lines forming lozenges is clearly related both to covers like those from Crowland Abbey (Ill. 143) and Sleaford St Denys (no. 3, Ill. 429) and to the presumed cover at North Kelsey (Ill. 419). There are, however, several closer parallels outside the county; at Adel, Yorkshire WR (Lewthwaite 1867–8, 204), Forcett, Yorkshire NR, and St Andrew Auckland and Gainford, both co. Durham (Cramp 1984, pls. 6, 18 and 66, 318).

There are also close parallels in the East Midlands at Barnack, Soke of Peterborough, and Greetham, Rutland. Both of these examples are in the gritty ragstone from the quarries in the Barnack area in the lower Welland valley, and Whaplode 2 seems to be made of this same stone type. It seems, then, that Whaplode 2 represents a widely distributed cover type, which was produced at the Barnack area quarries amongst others. This group of covers decorated with lozenges was considered by Butler (1964, 119) to be late eleventh century in date, but the Crowland Abbey cover, which belongs to this group, but which was unknown to Butler, has features which strongly suggest that it, and therefore the lozenge tradition, were also found earlier in the eleventh century.

Date
Mid or later eleventh century

References
Davies 1914–15, 226; Davies 1926, 20, pl. VIII; Butler 1957, 90; Butler 1964, 119, fig. 2A; Pevsner and Harris 1964, 711; Willis 1988, 24; Pevsner et al. 1989, 796

Endnotes

Whaplode 02, 386 – Fig.30. Re-construction.

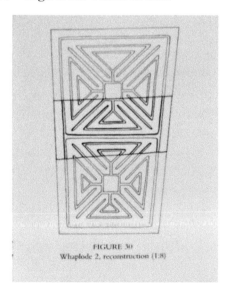

FIGURE 30
Whaplode 2, reconstruction (1:8)

CURRENT DISPLAY: WHAPLODE 03a-b, LINCOLNSHIRE
Overview

Object type: Two fragments, probably from the same grave-cover

Measurements: Dimensions of both stones as given by Davies (ibid.): L. *c.* 28 cm (11 in) W. *c.* 18 cm (7 in); D. Not recorded
Stone type: Not recorded

Plate numbers in printed volume: Ill. 387
Corpus volume reference: Vol 5 p. 272

National Grid Reference of Place of Discovery

TF323240 <u>View findspot location on a map</u>

Present Location

Now lost (1985)

Evidence for Discovery

See Whaplode (St Mary) no. 1. Both stones were on a windowsill in the south wall of the church when noted by Davies (1926, 20). They may have still been extant in the early 1960s, when Pevsner noticed 'outside the church, among architectural fragments, some Anglo-Saxon stones with interlace' (Pevsner and Harris 1964, 711). Of the surviving stones, only no. 1 above is decorated with interlace.

Church Dedication

St Mary

Present Condition

Apparently good

Description

Two fragments, perhaps from a single grave-cover, were photographed for Davies's 1926 article (ibid., pl. VIII). From the surviving illustration (see Ill. 387) it is clear that the fragments are small sections from a much larger monument with a border, probably of rectangular section – similar, perhaps, to no. 1 above, though somewhat broader. The panels themselves are filled with a simple interlace plait, although it is hard to be certain that both stones have plait work of the same type (one may have three-strand whilst the other may have four-strand).

Discussion

It is possible that these two fragments, which appear to be from the same original monument as each other, came from no. 1 above. However as far as we can judge, there are significant differences in scale and appearance and so they are catalogued separately. The monument they represent, however, is clearly of similar type to Whaplode 1 and it can therefore be suggested that it was probably another cover of the Fenland group (Chapter V), and of early or mid-eleventh-century date.

Date

Early or mid-eleventh century

References

Davies 1914–15, 226; Davies 1926, 20, pl. VIII; Pevsner and Harris 1964, 711

Endnotes

Table 5. The Fenland Group of grave covers [featuring Whaplode 01 & 03]

TABLE 5. The Fenland group of grave-covers

Lindsey
1. Lincoln Cathedral 1
2. Mavis Enderby 1

Kesteven and Holland
3. Market Deeping 2
4. Tallington 1
5. Whaplode 1
6. Whaplode 3

Soke of Peterborough
7. Barnack 11
8. Helpston 3
9. Maxey
10. Peterborough Cathedral 4
11. Peterborough Cathedral 5
12. Peterborough Cathedral 6

Cambridgeshire
13. Balsham 1
14. Cambridge Castle 8
15. Cambridge Castle 9
16. Cambridge Castle 10
17. Cambridge Castle 11
18. Cambridge Castle 12
19. Cambridge Castle 13
20. Cambridge Castle 14
21. Cambridge Little St Mary 1

22. Cambridge Little St Mary 2
23. Caxton
24. Conington
25. Grantchester 1
26. Grantchester 2
27. Little Shelford 1
28. Little Shelford 2
29. Little Shelford 3
30. Little Shelford 4
31. Orwell
32. Rampton 1
33. Rampton 2
34. Rampton 3
35. Rampton 4
36. Rampton 5
37. Rampton 6
38. Stretham
39. Whittlesford
40. Willingham 2
41. Willingham 3

Huntingdonshire
42. Alconbury
43. Keyston

Leicestershire
44. Halloton
45. Redmile

Northamptonshire
46. Oundle
47. Raunds 2
48. Raunds 3

Bedfordshire
49. Cardington
50. Milton Bryan

Norfolk
51. Bodney
52. Cringleford 1
53. Cringleford 2
54. Cringleford 3
55. Cringleford 4
56. Cringleford 5
57. North Pickenham
58. Rockland
59. Thetford

Suffolk
60. Huntingfield
61. Ixworth 1
62. Ixworth 2

Essex
63. ?Great Maplestead

London
64. St Benet Fink

BIBLIOGRAPHY

Butler, L.A.S., 1963-4. 'Some unrecorded examples of pre-Conquest carved stones in Lincolnshire,' *Lincolnshire Architectural and Archaeological Society Reports and Papers,* new series, X, pt.2, 105-14

Butler, L.A.S., 1957. 'Medieval gravestones of Cambridgeshire, Huntingdonshire and the Soke of Peterborough,' *Proceedings of the Cambridge Antiquarian Society*, L,89-100

Butler, L.A.S., 1964. 'Minor medieval monumental sculpture in the East Midland,' *Archaeological Journal,* CXXI, 111-53

Cramp, R., 1984. *Corpus of Anglo-Saxon Stone Sculpture, I, County Durham and Northumberland* (2 parts, Oxford)

Davies, D.S., 1914-15. 'Ancient stone crosses in Lindsey and Holland divisions of Lincolnshire,' *Lincolnshire Notes and Queries*, XIII, 129-57, 161-80, 212-23, 225-9

Davies, D.S., 1926. 'Pre-Conquest carved stones in Lincolnshire,' *Archaeological Journal*, LXXXIII, 1-20

Pevsner, N., and Harris, J., 1964. *The Buildings of England. Lincolnshire* (Harmondsworth)

Pevsner, N., and Harris, J. (rev. N. Antram), 1989.[1] *The Buildings of England, Lincolnshire* (2nd Edition. Harmondsworth)

Stocker, D.A., 1986a. 'The excavated stonework,' in B.J.J. Gilmour and D.A. Stocker, *St Mark's Church and Cemetery,* The Archaeology of Lincoln, XIII-1 (London), 44-82

Willia, N.T., 1988. *Fenland Churches between Spalding and Long Sutton, South Lincolnshire* (Long Sutton)

Footnote; **1**. All the entries on early sculpture in the revised edition were contributed by David Stocker (see p.18), including new discoveries made as a result of fieldwork by both authors for the present volume.

The Corpus of Anglo-Saxon Stone Sculpture: Catalogue (ascorpus.ac.uk)

APPENDIX V
Reverend Geo. Oliver – Letter 2nd November 1829 et al

The letter, elements of which are reproduced below, under Part One, was written by The Revd. George Oliver on **2nd November 1829** to the Editor of the Gentleman's Magazine. Therein he supplied some interesting insights into the architectural state of St. Mary's in the early 19th century, following Colonel Holles' defining record of his visit to St. Mary's in 1655 (*"MSS (British Museum),"* and the letter sits betwixt William Stukeley's observations in 1756, and Sir Gilbert Scott's *"Visit to St. Mary's"* in 1856. In so doing, Oliver throws light upon various aspects/areas of St. Mary's which historians have not necessarily focused on in any detail hitherto.

The Reverend George Oliver (b.1782 - d.1867) was also a dedicated antiquarian. He was the brother of Frances Oliver (d. 10.11.1811) and Mary Watkins (neé Oliver; d. 16.10.1818), both of whom have burial slabs within the alter rails at St. Mary's. He was the son of Reverend Samuel Oliver – Curate of St. Mary's 1801-1843, and W.E. Foster on page 57 of his book, refers to Dr Oliver being one of the Reverend Samuel Oliver's sons as *"having made his mark on the sands of time as a writer on Freemasonry and also as an antiquary"*.

Part Two below sets out an interesting and revealing discourse centred on the meaning of the hieroglyphics on some ancient headstones that Revd. Geo. Oliver came across in the Church grounds. Unfortunately, today, these are no longer identifiable.

PART ONE
The Gentleman's Magazine 1829-12: Vol 99. Pages 586-590.
Publication date:1829-12, Publisher: Open Court Publishing Co. Digitising sponsor: Kahle/Austin Foundation. Contributor: Internet Archive.

Extracts from George Oliver's letter to the editor of the Gentleman's magazine November 2, 1829
Page 586.
Ownership of St. Mary's
"The advowson of the church was presented to the abbot, as an offering, at the rebuilding of the abbey in 1113, by Alan, the son of Wido de Credun; and Hugh, Bishop of Lincoln, increased its value by the grant of certain tithes in Whaplode in the same century, which was confirmed by Pope Honorius." [This is interesting, since this earlier offering of the benefice, by Alan de Craon, was to be subsequently superseded by the later advowson given by Emecina D'Oyry, whose family were later in possession of the church, as confirmed by

Pope Hadrian IV in 1158, (see 4. Claimants to the Ownership of the Parish Church of St. Mary's).

Page 587 - 588.

Vicarage house

"The present vicarage house is a building in the style of Charles I. although it was not erected till the year 1683. It is furnished with a low porch in front; the old windows have massive stone frames and mullions; and the whole is thatched with reeds. An inscription on a beam in the kitchen shows its age and the name of the Vicar. I. Thomas, by whom it was erected in 1683."

Church Architecture – The Bell Tower

i)   *"The church is an eccentric though an admirable composition, and consists of a nave with aisles, transept, and a chancel, with an elegant tower at the end of the south transept; all of very considerable magnitude. The abbot of Croyland had an occasional residence within the parish - at Aswick, a farm about four miles from Croyland upon Weland water. It was the Abbates place (Leleand, vol iv. Append. P.162,163.). It appears highly probable that he intended to furnish this church with more towers than one, but the design was never executed. The present tower was erected about the latter end of the12th century, and is still in good preservation, to display the taste and science of the architect by whom it was designed and executed. It has four ornamental stages. The first is paneled with an arcade of arches slightly pointed, supported on slender cylinders, and ornamented with zigzag mouldings. The second story has a range of pointed arches above, and in each face a tall lancet window, but on the east side the window has been made up with masonry, and in the lower part a niche with a trefoil head inclosed within a pediment. has been inserted. The third story is panelled with a tier or arches, and the fourth has a pair of pointed bell windows, the arches decorated with the toothed ornament, and springing from elegant clusters of small cylinders. At the south-east angle of the tower is an octagonal staircase rising to a parapet, all of plain masonry, except that portion which adjoins the bell story, and here we have the effect relieved by a torus moulding at each angle. The whole is crowned by an embattled parapet over a cornice of heads. and furnished with pinnacles at the angles."*

ii)   *"The lower part of the tower, formerly communicated with the interior of the church by a spacious archway, and was not used, as at present, for a belfry. Here, under an arch in the wall, is a piscina, and close adjoining is a square recess with mouldings for a door, evidently the depository for pyx. These are indications of a chantry, and I cannot entertain a doubt, but an altar was established here before the Reformation, though the precise period would be difficult to determine; for I know of no place that would afford a greater facility for the celebration of private masses. Within the belfry door are two slender cylindrical columns with Ionic capitals; and over it on the outside, within a pediment and finial, is the trefoil recess already mentioned, which is of a date considerably posterior to the erection of the tower, and was evidently inserted by closing up one of the lancet- windows which originally gave light to the ringing chamber, and formed a portion of tile primitive clerestory of this detached fabric. In the niche was doubtless placed the image of the saint to whom the chantry was dedicated."*

Page 588.
North Transept
"In the north front is a transept supported by diagonal buttresses, which has at present no internal communication with the church and is used as a school room."

Wood carvings and stone shield in North Aisle
a)   *"On an oaken pew in the north aisle, carved in relief, are these two shields: 1. A cross. 2. Three passion nails in pile"*

b)   *"In the floor of the same aisle is a blue slab. with the figures of a man and woman deeply indented, and at their feet a shield. These have been filled in with massive brass-work, but not a vestige remains at this day to indicate the persons in whose honour the monument was constructed."*

Page 589
The Font
"The font is placed in its legitimate situation in the centre of the unpewed space at the west end. and exactly between the north and south porch door. It is elevated on a circular basement of three steps. and supported on a square plinth of black stone rounded at the angles. Upon this is a central cylinder of black stone surrounded with ·four- twisted columns. The font itself is square at the base, and higher up the corners are cut away so as to form a hexagon. each face being panelled and fluted The whole height is about seven feet."

The Nave and ornate wooden carvings
"The nave opens into the chancel by a beautiful Norman arch, finely ornamented with a double row of zigzag mouldings. Over this is a wooden singing gallery, which occupies the place of the ancient rood loft, and is accessible by the old stone staircase within the south pier. The chancel screen is gone, but the beauty of the lower part, which is incorporated into the pews that stand at the entrance of the chancel. extorts the sigh of regret that the

remainder has been consigned to oblivion. The designs have been tastefully carved in oak and polished. In the north pew are two shields flanked by pointed arches cinquefoil, the spandrels decorated with flowers."

1.   *"On a fess between two chevronels voided three cross crosslets; on the angle of the upper chevronel a crescent for difference; impaled with, Ermine, three fusils in triangle Ermines."*

2.   *"Quarterly, 1 and 4, as the last shield, 2 and 3, as the impaling of ditto. Impaled with a fess between three fleurs de lies."*

"The ornaments in the south pew are divided into five compartments."

1. *"A rectangle intersected by diagonal lines and decorated with balls and flowers."*

2. *"A ribbon or fillet flowing and inscribed, with these letters, cut in relief, R, O, E, TO, G, N."*

3.   *"An uncouth figure of a beast with a collar and wings tasseled."*

4.   *"A shield, charged with a fess between three fleurs de lies springing out of crescents, impaled with a fess check between three roses."*

5.   *"A ribbon or fillet, as before, part cut away, but the remainder bearing the letters M. B. O."*

Page 589 - 590
The Churchyard - Coffin shaped stones

"The churchyard is spacious, and on two short fragments of wall adjoining the public gates, are some coffin shaped stones, which bear the impress of an antiquity, though they are now applied to the unworthy purpose of a common coping to the wall {see below}. One of them, which I consider the oldest, is purified round the edges, and though it has undergone the silent operation of time for many centuries, yet the broad end may be distinctly traced a saltire indented in a circle in relief. In the centre is a device, which I confess my inability to elucidate."

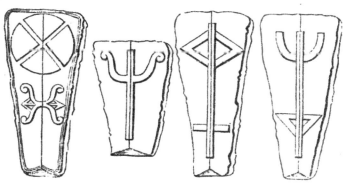

The Stone Cross

"A stump cross stands on a basement in the north-east, under which a few patches of tessellated work have been recently discovered by the Rev. S. Oliver, the present curate."

PART TWO

Also within **The Gentleman's Magazine VOL. 100: Jan – June 1830** a correspondent, E.I.C., replied to the above letter on 10 March 1830 – as follows:

"Mr. Urban

March 10.

PERMIT me to offer a few observations which occurred to me in reading some of your recent numbers.

Yours, &c

Letter to the Editor:

E. I. C:"

March 10, 1830. *Page 204*

WHAPLODE CHURCH.

"The device mentioned by the Rev. Oliver, (p. 590) as existing on a stone coffin in Whaplode Church, is a thunderbolt, a device evidently borrowed from the Romans (vide Gough, Intron to Sepul. Monuments in Great Britain, vol. I, plate 3). The devices inscribed on the other stones are probably incipient heraldic ordinaries, which, with the various crosses found on the gravestones of ecclesiastics, (the Whaplode specimens appertaining, l consider, to 'laymen') were matured into a science by the heralds, at a subsequent period."

George Oliver responded to this observation, as follows:

Sculptured Gravestone at Whaplode- Page 594

Letter to Editor

G.O. **June 26. 1830**

WITH respect to the prismatic stones in the Whaplode Church yard (engraved in your last Supplement, p. 590), I have met with a passage in Kellett's Tricoenium Christi, which induces me to think, that the circle and saltire at the head of the stone containing the compound figure, (pronounced by your correspondent E.I.C. p. 204, to be a thunderbolt,) was intended to represent the 'patiis decussatus', or consecrated wafer of the Romish Church. The passage is as follows:

"The form of the panis decussatus or bread made in likenesse to a crosse or an X, was in this wise, as Baronins hath it, from the old monuments yet to be seen. [Here the cross and saltire are drawn exactly similar to the figure under our consideration.] That the good Christians made a religious

use of this forme, because it did in some sort resemble a crosse, Gregory proveth, Dialogorum, i.11. Yea, even the unleavened bread, of which they made the Eucharist, was by the ancients framed to such a quadrangular forme in a circle, whose parts being divided by breaking, were called morsels; and the crosse not only stood upon the altar, which Chrysostom avoucheth, but was also drawn upon the Eucharist: and afterward, on the same mysticall bread, Christ crucified was formed. p. 621."

APPENDIX VI

Preservation report: The medieval Rood Screen remnant -June 2009

The following is the text of a report by Nigel Leaney an expert on '*Medieval Paint*' from Lincoln Diocesan Advisory Committee:

WHAPLODE St Mary's - Visit Report 16th June 2009

Section of Painted Rood Screen

Present:

Mr. Roy Willingham - Churchwarden

Mr. Cyril Hearn - Churchwarden

Revd. Clifford Knowles - D.A.C.

Nigel Leaney - D.A.C.

The parish wishes to reinstate a section of a medieval rood screen that has been hanging in its present position in a side chapel since just after 1844.

They would like to display it in a more prominent position to be seen more easily by the congregation and visitors.

Lincoln University has been approached to clean and repaint and to give a full analysis conservation report. Our inspection showed:

a)   The screen is 7 to 8 feet in length supported by cast iron stays at either end.

b)   There is much woodworm infestation.

c)   The painted decoration is in various states of deterioration and loss but survives enough to enable a clear impression of its original composition and colour. What remains shows a high degree of painted quality. The colors are mainly green and red. Two greens are interlaced into a floral pattern on a white background. On a green moulding a very small daisy design with a dainty central core is visible. The red is most likely to be iron oxide and the white, white lead. There is also clear evidence of gilding on the floral headed pattresses. From the section of screen that remains the impression is given that much of the screen remained unpainted.

Observations –

It has been suggested that the screen is taken to Lincoln University for treatment. Careful consideration should be given before allowing its removal from the church because of its delicate and friable condition and the extensive infestation of woodworm weakening its structure. A cradle with proper support along its length might be considered. A more satisfactory solution may be to create a small working space in St Mary's to allow cleaning and consolidation work to be carried out and eliminate the worry of damage during transportation.

I would recommend that a copy be made of the section, painted, and gilded in the original livery, to be displayed alongside the original or an artist's impression produced together with a description of the history and conservation treatment for the screen.

Nigel Leaney - Consultant to Lincoln Diocesan Advisory Committee.

APPENDIX VII
The Green Man Carvings

Glance upwards as you approach or enter many of Britain's great cathedrals and churches, and it is more than likely you will catch sight of the Green Man gazing looking down at you. But who is this strange green figure, surrounded by foliage, often with leaves spilling forth from his mouth? The name 'Green Man' was first used by Lady Raglan in March 1939 in an article she wrote for the 'Folklore' journal; before this, they had been known just as 'foliate heads' and no-one had paid them any particular attention. (Ellen Castelow. www.historic-uk-com).

The GREEN MAN is found quite extensively all-around Britain, yet some areas have far more in abundance than others. The following list, which is not exhaustive, will hopefully get you started in your quest to find a GREEN MAN yourself.

LINCOLN CATHEDRAL: Supposedly contains over 100 Green Men, yet I have only ever been able to find about 21, mostly around the cloisters. Best example at Lincoln is on the north quire aisle doorway amongst foliage.

SOUTHWELL MINSTER: Mostly around the chapter house and vestibule but a fine wooden misericord (wooden lift-up seat found in the choir stall) in the quire has a very leafy Green Man.

OTTERY ST. MARY: Several corbels (stone block projecting from a wall to support vault or roof) and bosses have Green Men carvings, the best is on a corbel in the lady chapel showing foliage spewing from mouth, nose, and eyes!!!

KILPECK: Norman carving around south door has two Green Men and much zodiac ornamentation.

SUTTON BENGER: a rather unexceptional church with a quite exceptional Green Man corbel, possible a statue base.

WIDECOMBE ON THE MOOR: Three carved wooden Green Man roof bosses (interlocking pieces of stone or wood in roof) vividly coloured and full of character. (Mirror trollies or binoculars are helpful)

OXFORD: Christchurch Cathedral has a tiny cloister which is quite literally crammed full of Green Men roof bosses, as many as 27 were counted by me, and there may have been more at one time before Cardinal Wolsey started demolishing parts of the old Benedictine priory.

NORWICH CATHEDRAL: Again, it is the cloisters, that quite space where monks could go to meditate or read, that provides us with a number of very fine foliate-face Green Men.

BAKEWELL: A fine example of a carved wooden misericord with a Green Man

EXETER CATHEDRAL: Another Green Man haven.... it seems like you cannot walk but a few yards without seeing one. Best one to look for is the unique and unusual double-headed Green Man in the quire.

WINCHESTER CATHEDRAL: A huge, towering Green Man with a sword carved in wood in the quire.

WORCESTER CATHEDRAL: Two particularly good Green Men in the cloister.

Cyril Hearn. 2016

A collection of Green Man images to be found on the site www.greenman.eastanglia.co.uk (figs.184 -190).

APPENDIX VIII

Conan Fitz *(Son of)* Ellis of Holbeach and Whaplode

"Conan son of Ellis, an Early Inhabitant of Holbeach" – by Miss Kathleen Major, M.A., B. LITT. (*The Associated Architectural and Archaeological Societies Reports and Papers, VOL. 41. Pt. II 1933*, pp.149-154). (KM – AS4).

I).   Conan son of Ellis, the most influential inhabitant of Holbeach in the late 12th and early 13th centuries, was one of the most important tenants of the Honour of Richmond. He was the holder of five knight's fees of which two and a half were in Yorkshire, and other two and a half fees were in Lincolnshire divided as to one fee in Holbeach and Whaplode (in parts of Holland) and one and half in Welton-le-World and Killingholme (in Lindsey). (KM-AS4. p.1)

II).   Conan was married four times, the names of his wives being, Emecina, Sybil, Ada, and Avice, but by none of these did he have any children, or at least none who survived him, as he was succeeded by his cousins. There is a degree of confusion surrounding Conan's first wife, Emecina. The timeline suggests that it is possible that she was a daughter of the older Emecina (wife of Geoffrey D'Oyry), however, she does not in any grant refer to a daughter, and therefore it more likely that she was a daughter of Fulk II, or Waleran (of Whaplode) his brother (both being sons of Geoffrey and Emecina). (KM-AS4. pp. 4-5)(KM2. P.3).

The Family crest of Elias (Ellis)
The confirmation that the family crest *"Gu. A bend betw. 6 fleur-de-lis arg."* (as recorded in Foster's book – WEF, p.45) is in fact that of Conan Fitz Elias (Ellis) is not only to be found in the **'*Dictionary of British Arms -Medieval - Ordinary-Vol. One. 1992'***. *Page.386.* (Edited by D.H.B. Cheshire, LVO.MA.FSA. & T. Woodcock, BA.LL.B, FSA, published by The Society of Antiquaries of London), but, more specifically, in the following extract from:
"Notices of the Ellipses of England, Scotland, and Ireland, from the Conquest to the present time, including the families of Alis, Fitz-Elys, Helles, etc." Page 194 and Fitz-Elys Lineage page 292. (By William Smith Ellis, 1817- 1890, published in London 1857-66. Source, University of Wisconsin-Madison. Digitized by Google).

"That Conan was brother of William fitz Elias, there can be little doubt. They were both minors in 1166, and their families bore the same arms, with the tinctures reversed "Argent a bend between six fleurs de lies gules" was the coat borne by William's descendants. "Gules a bend between six fleurs

*de lis argent" was **formerly in stained glass in the north window of Whaplode church.** (Harl. MSS. 2044 p.235) These could scarcely be any other than the arms of Conan fitz Elias, who according to the 'Testa de Nevill' had one knight's fee in Holbeach and Quapplade……..If the objection be raised that the 12th century is too early for the display of arms in stained glass, it may be answered by the remark that the arms in question were probably put up some time after the death of Conan, which did not take place till after 1213."*

Of further interest is that the crest of Fitz Elias AND that of the D'Oyry family – viz, *"Barry of 6 or and gules a canton ermine"* are conjoined in a window in Gedney Church.

Fulke III D'Oyry (See **Part One:** 3. Influential landowners in South Holland post the Norman Conquest- Fulk III d'Oyry) owned the manor of Gedney for a period during the reign of Henry III (r. 1216-1272), and the family members probably 'matched' at some point.

Furthermore, given that evidence was discovered in 1997 of a medieval stone cross - designated as *'Possible site of Ellis Cross' [Grid Reference: TF 3363 2478: Lincolnshire Heritage Explorer: Monument Ref: ML120542]* - near the junction of Stockwell Gate and Bush Meadow Lane in Whaplode, the above would appear to lend credence to the view that the location of the 'Ellis Cross'- where a Chapel was once sited – is probably connected with this family.

APPENDIX IX

The immediate family lineage of Thomas Walpole of Houghton (d.1512-13) as extracted from W.E. Foster's book. [WEF, p.89].

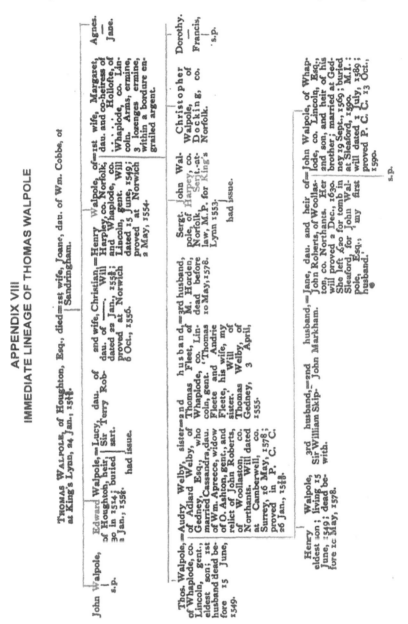

Thomas Walpole - immediate lineage - (fig.191).

APPENDICES

APPENDIX X

The life of Pietro Torrigiano (d.1528)

A history courtesy of Wikipedia [Last updated 28.01.22]. Published by Creative Commons Attribution-ShareAlike license 3.0: Wikimedia Foundation Inc.

"Pietro Torrigiano was born in Florence. According to Giorgio Vasari, he was one of the group of talented youths who studied art under the patronage of Lorenzo de' Medici in Florence. Benvenuto Cellini, reporting a conversation with Torrigiano, relates that he and Michelangelo, while both young men, were copying Masaccio's frescoes in the Carmine chapel, when some slighting remark made by Michelangelo so enraged Torrigiano that he struck him on the nose, breaking it, such that the disfigurement is conspicuous in all the portraits of Michelangelo, thereafter As a result, Torrigiano was banished from Florence. Vasari goes on to say that the assault was reported to Lorenzo de' Medici who was *"so greatly incensed against the offender, that if Torrigiano had not fled from Florence he would without doubt have inflicted some very heavy punishment on him."* Whether or not he was "banished", soon after this Pietro Torrigiano visited Rome, and helped Pinturicchio in modelling the elaborate stucco decorations in the Apartamenti Borgia for Pope Alexander VI.

After some time spent as a hired soldier in the service of different states, Torrigiano was invited to England, possibly by the young Henry VIII immediately after the death of his father, Henry VII. He produced terracotta sculptures depicting Henry VII, Henry VIII and the ecclesiastic John Fisher. He also probably made the intensely realistic funeral effigy of Henry VII. He was commissioned to create the tomb monument of Lady Margaret Beaufort, mother of Henry VII, in 1510, working to "patrones" or pattern drawings by Meynnart Wewyck. After the success of this work, he was given the commission for the magnificent effigial monument for Henry VII and his queen, which still exists in the Henry VII Lady Chapel of Westminster Abbey. This appears to have been begun in 1512 but was not finished till 1517. The two effigies are well modelled, and there can be no doubt the head of the king is a fine posthumous portrait. John Pope Hennessy called it "the finest Renaissance tomb north of the Alps". After this Torrigiano received the commission for the altar, retable and baldacchino, which stood at the west, outside the screen of Henry VII's monument. The altar had marble pilasters at the angles, two of which still exist, and below the mensa was a life-sized figure of the dead Christ in painted terra cotta. The retable consisted of a large relief of the Resurrection. The baldacchino was of marble, with enrichments of gilt bronze; part of its frieze still exists, as do also a large number of fragments of the terra-cotta angels which surmounted the baldacchino

241

and parts of the large figure of Christ. The whole of this work was destroyed by the Puritans in the 17th century. Henry VIII also commissioned Torrigiano to make him a magnificent funerary monument, somewhat similar to that of Henry VII, but one-fourth larger, to be placed in a chapel at Windsor; it was, however, never completed, and its rich bronze was melted by the Commonwealth, together with that of Wolsey's tomb.

The indentures for these various works still exist, and are printed by Neale, Westminster Abbey, (London, 1818). These interesting documents are written in English, and in them the Florentine is called "Peter Torrysany". For Henry VII's monument he contracted to receive £1500, for the altar and its fittings £1000, and £2000 for Henry VIII's monument. Torrigiano was also commissioned to work on the monument of Dr John Yonge (d.1516), Master of the Rolls during the time of Henry VIII, who was entombed in the Rolls Chapel of the now Maughan Library.

While these royal works were going on, Torrigiano visited Florence to get skilled assistants. He tried to induce Benvenuto Cellini to come to England to help him, but Cellini refused partly from his dislike to the brutal and swaggering manners of Torrigiano, and, Cellini wrote, "*This man had a splendid person and a most arrogant spirit, with the air of a great soldier more than a sculptor, especially in regard to his vehement gestures and his resonant voice, together with a habit he had of knitting his brows, enough to frighten any man of courage. He kept talking every day about his gallant feats among those beasts of Englishmen.*" When he heard the story of what Torrigiano did to Michelangelo, Cellini says he could no longer *"bear the sight of him"*.

According to Vasari, Torrigiano was swindled of his payment by the Duke of Arcos for a sculpture of the Virgin and Child. As an act of vengeance for being fooled as such he mutilated the work with his chisel, whereupon the Duke, considering himself affronted, denounced Torrigiano as a heretic. In other stories, he was carving the Virgin and made a mistake, at which point he defaced the statue in his annoyance and was seen by clerics and charged as a result.

The latter part of Torrigiano's life was spent in Spain, especially at Seville, where, besides the painted figure of St. Hieronymus in the museum, some terracotta sculpture by him still exists. His violent temper got him into difficulties with the Spanish Inquisition, and he died in 1528 in prison. (Vasari mis-dates his death to 1522)."

APPENDIX XI

Exchange of letters surrounding the safe keeping of the Irby ceremonial helmet. [From the Church archives].

a) *HM Armouries to Rev. W.H. Gibb – 9.12.57 (fig.192).*

Royal 2195

THE ARMOURIES,

H.M. TOWER OF LONDON,

E.C.

9th December 1957

Dear Mr. Gibb,

Thank you for your letter. I must apologise to you, but you did not tell me that it was Lord Boston's suggestion that the helmet should go to the Victoria and Albert Museum after all our trouble.

I am in full sympathy with the Church Council. The helmet belongs to the tomb, and if you will let me know as soon as the case is made, I will send you the helmet for display in your church.

In the meantime the public can continue to enjoy it here.

Yours sincerely,

James Mann

The Rev. W. H. Gibb,
Whaplode Vicarage,
Spalding,
Lincolnshire.

APPENDICES

b)   HM Armouries to Rev. W. H. Gibb – 1.12.58 (fig.193).

Royal 2195

THE ARMOURIES,

H.M. TOWER OF LONDON,

E.C.

1st December 1958

Dear Mr. Gibb,

Thank you very much for your letter of 27th November, in which you report the decision of your Church Council to deposit the helmet from your Church in the Armouries of the Tower of London on indefinite loan.   We have precedent for accepting loans from Churches of this kind, and I accept your offer most gratefully.   I would suggest that the loan should be subject to termination by either side on six months' notice.

You may be assured that we shall look after it very carefully and be proud to show it.   Will you please transmit my thanks to your Church Council?

I hope to put my notes into final form before long, and publish them in the Antiquaries *Journal*.

Yours sincerely,

James Mann

Sir James Mann,
Master of the Armouries.

The Rev. W. H. Gibb,
Whaplode Vicarage,
Spalding,
Lincolnshire.

APPENDIX XII

Extracts from professional contributors concerning the fabric of St. Mary's Church, and the need for its urgent restoration, and action taken (1890-1910)

Herewith a selection of observations, comments/views – analytical, complimentary and/or critical – extracted from professional periodicals, by contributors thereto, in the late 19th and early 20th century, regarding the status of the church building, and its artefacts, which served to highlight the necessary restorative work that should be undertaken to preserve the important architectural legacy of the church, the impact of which acted as a catalyst for the subsequent work that finally began in 1909.

I.   THE BUILDER – 1890-07-26: Vol. 59 Iss. 2477

Publisher: Building (Publishers) Ltd.

Digitising sponsor: Kahle/Austin Foundation. Contributor: Internet Archive.

*"**Whaplode**, the church next visited, proved one of the most interesting of the whole two days' excursion. It has been reduced to a half- ruined state by long-continued neglect or barbarous usage. The roofs have been lowered throughout leaving the gables gaunt and bare, protesting against their mutilation. Nearly all the windows have been robbed of their tracery, and otherwise disfigured, while the mean repairs of the chancel and north transept (the latter being converted into a schoolroom with a red brick chimney run up through the centre of the great window) have 'robbed' them of almost every trace of antiquity.*

The church is to be restored be Mr. Pearson*** as soon as funds can be raised; it is to be hoped this will not be carried to the length of making a new church of it. The earliest part: of the church, which is 150ft. in length, is of Late Norman. Of this date we have the enriched chancel arch and the first four bays of the nave. The piers are partly short, stout cylinders, partly compound piers, bearing arches of disproportionate width and slightness, leaving too much of the upper surface of the capital unoccupied. The clearstory externally shows a continuous circular-headed arcade, pierced at intervals for windows, with, originally, a corbel-table above. The three western bays of the nave are of Late Transitional date, on the same general plan as the Norman part, but with very instructive points of contrast. The west front, in which the Early English style reigns uncontrolled, must have been a very vigorous composition. The west doorway is a fine specimen of the style in its greatest purity. The 'richly-moulded' soffits rise from a double row of height detached *shafts on each side, set one behind the other, with capitals of foliage. The tower, four stages in height, occupies an unusual position, "as a kind of "southern transept. It is a very striking design, the three lower stages. Early English, with attached arcades; the fourth story Decorated, with a battlemented parapet."*

*** NB. This reference could refer to either John Loughborough Pearson, or his son Frank Loughborough Pearson, who continued his father's work following his father's death in 1892.

II. ANNUAL REPORTS OF THE SOCIETY FOR THE PROTECTION OF ANCIENT BUILDINGS 1903-1907

Published in 1907: London.

Digitising Sponsor: Digital Library India; JaiGyan. Contributor: Internet Archive.

Annual Report JUNE 1904 pages 66-68
Whaplode Church

"This church - one of the famous Lincolnshire churches - which was visited at the request of the Vicar, is a large and magnificent building consisting of chancel, nave, north and south aisles, north and south transepts, and a lofty and imposing tower. The chancel, which is small in comparison with the rest of the building, is modern, having been built in 1818. It retains portions of earlier work and traces of a north aisle. The chancel arch is the original Norman one, beautifully moulded on both faces and ornamented on its west face. With the exception of a slight crack on the faces of the north and south piers near the floor level, it is in excellent condition. The north transept has been considerably altered, probably when the chancel was rebuilt. A portion is walled off to form the village schoolroom. The north window is mutilated by the insertion of a brick chimney to form a flue for a fireplace beneath it, which cuts through the top of the arch and continues up above the gable. A large square-headed window has also been inserted, and an arched opening which formerly gave access to the chancel aisle has been built up, and a window formed in the arch. The south transept forms the base of the tower and has a beautiful-pointed arch filled in with masonry. The lower portion of the tower, up to the belfry, is built in three stages, beautifully arcaded and somewhat earlier in date than the belfry stage, which is of pure Early English work. There are five bells, restored to the tower in 1718, The walls are strong and well built.

The nave arcade consists of seven bays, of which the easternmost four are of Norman work, and the westernmost three, Transitional. The north clerestory retains its Norman and Transitional windows, but with the exception of two of them they have been widened by cutting away the splay of the jambs. The easternmost window has been built up and a square headed window inserted close to the east wall. The south clerestory has had its Norman windows removed and two-light Perpendicular windows substituted, probably when the present aisles were built.

The nave roof is of Perpendicular date, richly constructed, but in a most dilapidated condition. The greater portion of its enrichments have perished. The roof is of, pyramid form, and covered with stone slates, with a lead gutter, formed at the back of the parapet. The roof timbers are of oak, but the slates are badly displaced and allow the wet getting through.

The north aisle is of late Perpendicular work, its west window being blocked up, and a wood lintel takes the place of the outer order of the arch of the easternmost window. Nearly the whole of the original mullions and tracery have been replaced by modern mullions, carried up to the underside of the arches. The south aisle is also of late Perpendicular work and the windows have been treated in a similar manner. The south doorway is of fine Transitional work, with a beautiful moulded pointed arch, enclosed by a modern porch.

Although the condition of the building, with the exception of the roofs of the nave, aisles, north transept, and tower, is generally sound, there is urgent need that the necessary repairs should be undertaken without delay. The whole building has sunk into the soft soil in a most wonderful way. It is recorded that about fifty years ago two feet six inches of soil were excavated from the surface inside the building. The seven-inch step at the junction of the Norman and Transition work shews that a considerable settlement occurred in the short interval between the two periods. The general level of the ground at the present time is about two feet six inches higher than the floor of the church.

The Society's report fully explained the repairs needed but the Committee understands that nothing can be decided until after the next meeting of the rectors—the Governors of the Estates of the Foundation of Robert Johnson, Archdeacon of Leicester."

III.   31st ANNUAL REPORT OF THE SOCIETY FOR THE PROTECTION OF ANCIENT BUILDINGS 1908

Published in 1908: John Stirling-London.
Digitising Sponsor: Digital Library India; JaiGyan. Contributor: Internet Archive.

Annual Report JUNE 1908 page 94
Whaplode Church, Lincolnshire.
"A description of this building was given in the report for 1904 (pages 66-68). The Committee is glad to be able to state that there is a probability of those works of repair recommended by the Society being undertaken at an early date, under its auspices. The new Vicar is anxious to commence the work as soon as possible, and the Committee hopes that the money needed will be forthcoming without delay.

The church is much larger than is needed for the requirements of the parish, and it is reasonable to appeal for liberal assistance from outside towards the expense of repairing such an exceptionally fine example of mediaeval architecture.

The Society has promised to subscribe toward the cost of the work £10
*** from its Building Fund."**

IV.   **Extract from THE BUILDER magazine - 21.08.1909- page 221.**

Published by Building (Publishers) Ltd.
Digitising Sponsor: Kahle/Austin Foundation. Contributor: Internet Archive
General Building News.

St. Mary's Church – Whaplode
"Mr. W. Weir has been appointed to carry out the reparation of the parish church, Whaplode, Lincolnshire, whereof the Norman nave was extended, westwards, in the XIIIth century, and has an open roof. To the south-east stands the XIIIth century tower having a chapel at the ground level which formerly opened into the nave"

V.   **33rd ANNUAL REPORT OF THE SOCIETY FOR THE PROTECTION OF ANCIENT BUILDINGS 1910**

Published in 1910: John Stirling-London.
Digitising Sponsor: Digital Library India; JaiGyan. Contributor: Internet Archive.

Annual Report JUNE 1910 page 57
Church of St. Mary, Whaplode, Lincolnshire.
"In the report for 1909 (P-94) it was stated that there was a likelihood that this beautiful Church would be repaired under the Society's guidance; and the Committee is now able to state that the works thought by it to be necessary, have for the last six months been m progress by local workmen under the direction of an Architect in consultation with the Society.

What has been done is as follows:

The fifteenth-century roof over the nave has been repaired and strengthened, without taking it down. Where rotted, by wet soaking through the defective guttering, the wall slats have been renewed and the old timbers pieced-up with English oak, carefully spliced-in and bolted to the sound work. There are no tie-beams, and the thrust of the roof had disturbed and cracked the clerestory walls; so, the feet of each pair of principal rafters have been tied off together with a wrought iron tie-rod, and the walls repaired in the Society's usual way.

Prior to the fifteenth century there was a Norman roof, and when the fifteenth-century carpenters put up that which now exists, the high Norman gables at the east and west of the nave were not cut down to the lower pitch but left as they were. This has given an opportunity of protecting the old work effectually by constructing over the old roof a new one of the same- pitch as that of the Normans. For covering this, the old lead sheets recast have been used as far as they would go, and the shortage made up with sheets cast of new virgin lead.

The roof of the north aisle appears to have been a good deal renewed in the eighteenth century. The timber work has been repaired, and the lead covering made sound without recasting. The walls had been pushed outwards by the roof; they were found to have poor foundations, and to consist of an inner and an outer facing filled in with loose rubble. A new foundation of concrete has been put in, the walls underpinned from it, and the loose core taken out and good concrete substituted. The walls of the south aisle have been dealt with similarly; and the roof timbers, which are of deal, are being repaired preparatory to recasting and relaying the lead covering. In the south porch the roof timbering has been made sound and the stone slates refixed on new oak battens.

In the north transept, the walls have been repaired and strengthened, and the floor lowered to the level of that of the nave. The modern deal roof, which was indifferently constructed, is being replaced by a new one of English oak covered with the old lead recast.

Around the building the ground has been sloped away back from below the floor level, and the old drains have been repaired and connected to gullies at the feet of the rainwater pipes.

With the repair of the tower roof the work as regards the exterior of the Church will be finished. The works remaining to be done will be the repair of the leaded glazing of the windows; the lime-whiting of the plastering of the chancel and aisles walls; the installation of a Gurney stove; the enclosing of a *space to form a vestry at the west end of the north aisle; and, if possible, the resuscitation of the old pulpit, which some years ago was removed and utilised in fitting up a vestry in the north aisle.*

Towards the cost of the works the sum of £10** has been voted from the Society's Building Fund."

** NB. £10 in 1910, is equivalent in purchasing power to about £1,220 today (2023).

APPENDIX XIII

Crown Lands and Estates documentation June 1909 Contribution towards the costs of repairing fabric of St. Mary's Church, Whaplode.

1. Charles Wynn-Carrington KG. GCMG. PC.JP.DL. (Earl Carrington) Letter to the Treasury advocating a contribution of £50. (Pt I & II).

E No. 3338

●

TREASURY
11956

5 JUN 1909

OFFICE OF WOODS, &c.,

TEMPORARY OFFICES, 83 PALL MALL,

S.W.

My Lords,   4th June 1909.

Whaplode - File 7.

    I beg to report to your Lordships an application which I have received from the Rector of St. Marys Parish Church, Whaplode, near Holbeach, Co. Lincoln, (in which Parish the Crown is a land-owner), for a contribution towards the cost of restoring the Church.

    This church is said to be one of the finest and most interesting of the Fen churches. The eastern part of the nave dates from the year 1125, and is said to be the earliest specimen of Norman work in this district of Lincolnshire. The West doorway and West front also date from the 12th century, while other portions are stated to have been built in the 14th century. The church is now greatly in need of repair and restoration, the roof especially being regarded as unsafe.

    The works which it is proposed to carry out include the repair of the entire roof, and the repair of settlements in the main walls of the building, besides a number of other minor works of repair to the fabric. The estimated cost of the purely structural works,(which alone are usually considered on an application for a contribution by the Crown) is about £900, but the total estimated expenditure now required, including necessary renewals to furniture and decoration, is £1500.

    The rateable value of the Parish is about £13800, of which about £760 represents the rateable value of Crown property under my charge therein.

    There are said to be six other places of worship in the District, but the attendance at them appears to be comparatively small, and is stated by the Vicar not to amount altogether to more than three-fourths of the attendance at the Parish Church.

In

The Lords Commissioners of

Earl Carrington -Office of Woods – Pt. I. 05.06.1909 (fig.194).

11956
5 JUN 1909

In the circumstances, and having regard to the Crown property in the Parish, I am of opinion that a contribution towards the cost of repairing and restoring the fabric of the Church should be made by this Department out of Land Revenues, and I consider that £50 would be a suitable amount to contribute.

I beg therefore to request your Lordships' authority to contribute that amount towards the cost of repairing and restoring the fabric of St. Mary's Church, Whaplode, Co. Lincoln.

I have the honour to be,
My Lord,
Your obedient servant,

Earl Carrington -Office of Woods – Pt. II. 05.06.1909 (fig.195).

2. Counter proposal & signatories to £35. (Pt. I & II) 12.06.1909.

W. to The Rt Hon
The Earl Carrington KG

My Lord

In the circs explained in your R. (?) of the 4th inst, the L.C.T. are prepared to authorise a contribution from the Land Revenues towards the cost of repairing and restoring the fabric of St Mary's Parish Church, Whaplode, Co. Lincoln. They think, however, that such contribution shall not exceed £35

I am &c
N.B.
12/6/9

Counter proposal - Pt. I. (fig.196).

The cost of the structural repairs to this Church will be £900.

Crown Revenue from the parish represents 1/18th of the total rateable value.

The Woods propose a contribution of £50, or 1/18th, which would be justified if the Church were the only place of worship in the district.

But, there are 6 other places of worship in the district: & though the attendances at each singly are small, they represent together a total = 3/4 the attendance at the Parish Church.

We cannot give a contribution equal to the whole amount of the Crown's interest in the parish without treating unfairly the requirements of the other denominations.

If we kept to the correct proportions between the Church & the denominations, the Crown contribution in respect of the parish would be assignable, as to £28.10 to the Church, and £21.10 to the denominations.

That is, we shall give say £30 in the present instance.

But the grant need hardly be so strictly 'proportional' as this.

I would suggest a Grant of £35.

J.B.
17/6/9

Mr Mobbrica will probably think this quite enough.

RFW

Counter proposal. Pt. II. (fig.197).

3. HM Treasury decision - Letter in reply – 18.06.1909

TREASURY CHAMBERS,

11956
09

18 June 1909.

My Lord,

In the circumstances explained in your Report
(E.No.3538. File 7) of the 4th instant, the Lords Commissioners of His Majesty's Treasury are prepared to authorise
a contribution from the Land Revenues towards the cost of
repairing and restoring the fabric of St. Mary's Parish
Church, Whaplode, County Lincoln. They think, however,
that such contribution should not exceed £35.

I am,

My Lord,

Your obedient Servant,

C Hobhouse

The Rt.Hon.
The Earl Carrington K.G.,
Office of Woods.

Treasury decision – 18.06.1909 (fig.198).

Comparatively, £35, in 1909, is worth in excess of £4,300 at 2023 monetary values.

APPENDIX XIV

A list of pre-restoration inscriptions, monuments and memorial slabs remaining within the church in 1888, as identified by T.N. Morton *[Whaplode - page. 10]* **and W.E. Foster** *[Pages. 48-50]* **in their respective books.**

Part I – All the following memorial artefacts were identified as being present in the Church by T.N. Morton in **1843** within his book *"An Account of the Churches of the division of Holland in the County of Lincoln"* and subsequently confirmed by Foster *(italics WEF)* on his visit in **1888. All** can still be seen within St. Mary's Church.

i. *John Thomas, vicar, died October 7, 1688.*
    A slab robbed of brass on the north side of the Chancel near the Altar rails.

ii. *Alice Bullin daughter of Robert Bullin died May 2, 1700.*
    A small tablet - on the east wall in that part of the church used as a school. [NB: on east wall in North Transept].

iii. *Sarah, wife of D. Miller died January 4, 1701.*
    A small stone in the nave near the font. [NB: This inscription is almost obliterated – 'Sarah' remains visible].

iv. *Benjamin Grant died February 24, 1716, aged 52. (On wall of South aisle).* [NB: See Part One: 9. Commemorative Plaques].

v. *Ann, widow of B. Grant, died April 6, 1734, aged 62. (On wall of South aisle).* [NB: See Part One: 9. Commemorative Plaques].

vi. *Ellenor, second wife of John Aistrup, died October 17, 1758, aged 63.*

vii. *Elizabeth, wife of Jo. Aistrup, died November 3, 1719.*

viii. *Susannah Aistrup died May 17, 1170, aged 44.*

ix. *Sarah Aistrup died August 1778, aged 52.*
    (vi, vii, viii and ix are inscribed on two black marble slabs, between the east end of the South aisle and the first column close to the reading desk. [NB: In the floor leading to the Chancel, in front of the Monks' Steps and the adjacent 'Compton' Church Organ].

x. *Edward Savage died May 4, 1791, aged 59.*

xi. *Sarah, his widow, died May 15, 1802, aged 72*
    (x and xi in the west corner of the north aisle). [NB: However, today, these are now only visible in the floor from **within** the HERALDIC SUITE].

xii. *Susannah, wife of John Oliver died October 22, 1804, aged 33. (A black marble slab in the Chancel on the South side near the Altar rail).*

xiii. *Thomas Sooley Blackith died January 8. 1807, aged 49.*

xiv. *Robert Tunnard Blackith died November 20, 1811, aged 26.*

(xiii & xiv are two large slabs at the north-west corner of the Chancel). [NB: Beneath the north wall on which appear the memorial plaques to the two former Vicars of Whaplode].

The gravestones of J Frances Oliver (d. 10.11.1811) and Mary Watkins (neé Oliver; d. 16.10.1818), daughters of the Revd. Samuel Oliver (Rector of St. Mary's, 1801-1843) can also be seen within the Altar rails at St. Mary's.

Part II

Unfortunately, whilst the following memorial stone works were identified as being present in **1843** by T.N. Morton, owing to further degradation and/or removal, Foster was unable to confirm their respective locations within the Church in **1888.**

a)   *Anthony Johnson died May 8, 1700, aged 46.*

b)   *George Harrison died 1702.*

c)   *John Elkin, vicar, died July 31, 1707.*

d)   *James Harrison died October 22, 1710, aged 47.*

e)   *Tobias March died September 28, 1714.*

f)   *Elizabeth March died October 28, 17 **.*

g)   *Ann Huckbody died August 12, 1717, aged 3.*

h)   *Nathan Huckbody died April 18, 1729, aged 33.*

i)   *John March died March 10, 1728, aged 60.*

j)   *Thomas Freeman died June 11, 1720, aged 61.* [NB. The gravestone is partially visible in the floor outside the Heraldic Suite toilet area].

k)   *William Seels died 1744.*

l)   *Sophy Aistrup died December 2, 1754, aged 71.*

m)   *Susanna Maria, wife of John Wheldale died February 25, 1781, aged 28.*

n)   *William Aistrup died December 27, 1787, aged 30.*

o)   *John Cooke died April 5, 1790, aged 37.* [NB: This gravestone is faint, but visible in line with the Font at the West End of the church].

p)   *James Briggs, died 1725.* [NB: This gravestone is barely discernible in the floor of the North Aisle leading to the North Transept].

In addition, Foster highlighted the presence of the following slabs, however the inscriptions were illegible:

i).   Three slabs at the east end of the South aisle.

ii).   A large slab on which there were formerly brasses a with effigies at the east end of the North Aisle near the first Nave column.

iii).   Two slabs in the Nave near the font – which had evidently been removed.

APPENDIX XV

A list of Vicars and Churchwardens of St. Mary's Church who have served the community over the centuries (1238 -2024)

VICARS

This list is as complete as it has been practical to determine. Gaps in years arise from an absence of confirmatory records. The information comprises detail extracted from:

a) St. Mary's Church Vestry Records.
b) The Clergy of the Church of England Database [CCEd]1540 -1835.
c) Lambeth Palace Church of England Registry.
d) W.E. Foster's Book [WEF, pages 63-67].
e) Lincolnshire Archives – Lincolnshire CC.

EARLY HISTORY OF THE VICARS OF ST. MARY'S

Following the gift of St. Mary's Church to the Abbey of Crowland by Emecina D'Oyry, circa 1148-58, which was formally confirmed in 1158 by Pope Hadrian IV, the early history of the Clergy of St. Mary's, prior to 1238, is somewhat sparse, other than to acknowledge that at various times between 1150-1238 the following members of the D'Oyry family were fulfilling roles as Clergymen, either jointly, or singularly: Geoffrey D'Oyry: Fulk II D'Oyry: Baldwin D'Oyry: Hugh D'Oyry

William Ragleye: Rector	1238
Robert de Sexynton: Rector	1239
Alexander de Whappelode : Rector	1242
Simon de Sulvell: Chaplain	1246
Simon de Sulvell: Chaplain	1250
Dus Robert de Lexington: Rector	1250
Nicholas de Wendlengeburg: Rector	1251
Magister Thomas de Cotum	1290 - 1310
Robert de Radeclif, Capellanus (Chaplain)	1310
Richard de Corby, Capellanus (Chaplain)	1310
William de Luffenham, Capellanus (Chaplain)	1312
Richard de Wroxebrigg, Dus - resigned	1348
William Rossell: Presbyter (Priest)	1348
Dus Andrew Brown - resigned	1376
John Ingram: Presbyter (Priest)	1376 - 1390
John Tylney: Rector	1390 - 1392
William Angoulde: Presbyter (Priest)	1392 - 1416

William de la Lounde: Clerk	1416 - 1417
John Estoft: Presbyter (Priest)	1417
Magister John Spenser: Vicar exchange	1433
John Duffield: Mgnr - resigned	1433
John Pynder: Presbyter (Priest)	1433 - 1466
Dom Simon Gudwyn: Presbyter	1466 - 1477
Dom John Rumney: Presbyter (Priest)	1477 - 1479
Magister Richard Keele, B.D.	1479 - 1501
Magister Thomas Everard – resigned	1502 - 1505
Dom Henry Dawson - resigned	1505 - 1524

The Abbey of Crowland was dissolved in 1539. Thereafter, successive Bishops of Lincoln acted in their stead – until 1551.

Magister Roger Baynthorpe - resigned	1544
Magister Robert Watson, MA	1544 - 1546
Dom Robert Browne	1546 - 1551
John Blades:* Vicar	1551 - 1570

*(* 1st 'Perpetual' Vicar appointed in 1554 by the Monarch - Queen Mary)*

Clement Freckingham: Vicar	1570 - 1597
William Holden, MA: Vicar #	1613 - 1634

(# 'Perpetual' - appointed King James I)

Amiwell Logan: Preacher	1634
John Thomas: Vicar +	1662 – 1688

(+'Perpetual' - appointed by King Charles II)

John Ekins: Vicar $	1688 – 1698

($ 'Perpetual' - appointed by King James II)

William Speight: Curate	1698
Johannes Rustat: Vicar **	1707 – 1723

*(** 'Perpetual' - appointed by Queen Anne)*

Jacobus (James) Rustat: Curate	1723
Rev. John Chapman: Curate - *Temp*	1723 - 1725
Rev. John Tatam: Vicar [Death 1768] +++	1726 - 1768

(+++ 'Perpetual' - appointed by King George I)

Thomas Bateman: Vicar [Death 1801] ##	1768 - 1801

(## 'Perpetual' - appointed by King George III)

Rev. John Northon: Curate - *Temp.*	1769
Rev. William Betham: Curate - *Temp.*	1771
Rev. Robert Benson: Curate - *Temp.*	1776
Rev. Levold Thomas Howell: Curate - *Temp.*	1784
Rev. James Gifford: Curate - *Temp.*	1792

Rev. John Grundy Thompson -*Temp.*	1798
Rev. Robert Collins: Curate	1802 - 1811
Rev. Samuel Oliver: Curate ***	1811 - 1843
(*** '*Perpetual*' – appointed by King George III)	
Rev. Philip Fisher B.D. - resigned	1843
Rev. T. Tunstall Smith. M.A.	1843 - 1851
Rev. John Harwood	1851 - 1859
Rev. J. Fairfax Francklin, M.A.	1859 - 1883
Rev. John Collin, M.A.	1883 - 1898
Rev. John William Rhodes	1898 - 1908
Rev. Edward William Brereton. M.A.	1908 - 1913
Rev. Henry Basil McNeil-Smith. B.Sc.	1913
Rev. Emlyn Hugh James. B.A.	1913 - 1920
Rev. Harold Grasspoole Woods	1920 - 1926
Rev. Montague James Case B.A.	1926 - 1929
Rev. Herbert Conway Holland	1929 - 1944
Rev. Leslie Ronald Swingler	1944 - 1949
Rev. Wilfred Theodore Armstrong	1949 - 1953
Rev. William Henry Gibb	1953 - 1960
Rev. Cyril Newton Ogden	1960 - 1977
Rev. Lancelot Carter	1977 - 1985
No Resident Vicar	1985 - 1987
Rev. Michael Kirkham	1987 - 1991
Fr. David Carney	1991 - 2002

NB. In the interregnum, after David Carney, Revd. Richard Morrison commenced a ministry for pastoral care of the Parish from 9th October 2005, until he was made a Priest in Charge 1st August 2010. Prior to his official appointment in Aug 2010, he was the incumbent Vicar at Whaplode Drove and Gedney Hill - but covered St. Mary's at his own volition for which parishioners were grateful.

Rev. Richard Morrison	2010 - 2014
Rev. Julie Timings	2014 - 2016

There was an interregnum between 2016 and 2021, following which

Rev. Alistair Ward - became Priest in Charge	Dec 2021 -

CHURCHWARDENS

W. Kerbe & G. Dowsome	1561
W Thakere & E Scolthorpe	1576
J Martayne & W Skarlet	1577

Robert Martin & Adam Edridge	1587
Thomas Groome & Mr Browne	1589
Thomas Grimould & A. N. other	1590
Edward Lawson & Richd. Cuthbert	1603
Thomas Wright & Hugh Page	1606
Chris Blaydes & Thomas Hapley	1608
Steven Chapman & Richd Blades	1616 - 1617
Thomas Bartle & Robert Smyth	1618
John Belton & Nicholas (?)	1620
Robert Johnson & John Kelvin	1621 - 1622
William Kyrby & Rob Pinchbeck	1623
ffrancys Stonwell & Thomas Medows	1624
Thomas Medows & Thomas Bennett	1625
Thomas Smith & William Ingram	1627
Andrew Bawtrie & John Couling	1628
Robert Smith & Thom Pinchbeck	1630
John Rigdon & Thomas Pinchbeck	1631
John Rigdon & Robert Hutchin	1632
John Rigdon & Anthony Johnson	1633
James Dawson & William Ingram	1634 - 1635
Salomon Waters & Robert Hinman (Inman)	1638 - 1639
Salomon Waters & Tom Pinchbeck	1640
Not signed	1641 - 1660
William Prior & John (?)	1663
Robert Pasey & (Unknown)	1664
Richard Herroy & William Upton	1665
Richard Corby & John Bickles	1667
William Ingram & Robert Wright	1670 - 1675
Antony Johnson & Robert ffisher	1678
John Singletory & Geo Hunnings	1679
John Donger & William Freeman	1680
Millicent Hutchin & John Singletory	1681 - 1682
John Chamberlain & John Howler	1683
John ffowler & John Clark	1684 - 1686
William Ingram & Edward Nutt	1687 - 1690
Thomas Martin & Benjamin Grant	1691
William Parnham & John Grove	1692
William Wheler & Thos Bradford	1693
John Drewery & William Wilson	1702

Zachariah Nixson	1703
Enoch Harrison & John Winter	1705
Walter Johnson & William Gregory	1706
Theodolphus Grant & William Hipworth	1707
James Bolton & William Owen	1708
John Cock & Edward ? / James Bolton	1710
John Stennett & Richard Coulson	1711
Robert Lond & William Davenport	1712
Thomas Freeman & Robert Smith	1713
John Cramp & Thomas Harrison	1714
Robert Steele & Edward Stubbs	1715**
Robert Steele & Thomas Witterton	1716
John March & James Bolton	1717
James Bolton & William Owen	1718
James Bolton & Dymock Candron	1719
James Bolton & Theodolphus Perkins	1720
John Aistrup & Theodolphus Perkins	1721 - 1722
John Hunnings & John Harrison	1723
Robert Baille & Thomas Briggs	1724
Thomas Harrison & Francis Moule	1725**
Richard Coulson & John Barnaby	1726
William Orme & George Savage	1727
Thoms Harrison & John Bevill	1728
Thomas Harrison & John Moule	1729
William Seals & John Coulson	1730 - 1731
Thomas Bough & Thomas Briggs	1732 - 1733
Thomas Briggs & Thos Chamberlain	1734
Theodolphus Perkins & Thomas Briggs	1735 - 1737
John Proctor & Robert Chamberlain	1738
John Pares & Thomas Copeland	1739
James Watson & Thomas Jackson	1740
David Watson & Thomas Farding	1741
John Bates & Valentine Bullard	1742 - 1743

**Prior to 1715, it was customary for both the churchwardens to be nominated by the Vestry (the congregation) Committee. However, in 1715 the Vicar began to nominate one churchwarden, and following 1725 the process was formally adopted with the appointment of a 'Vicar's warden and a 'Peoples' Warden. The above list has been extracted from the book produced in 1889 by W.E. Foster [WEF, pp, 67-70] and/or direct from the Vestry minute books.

APPENDICES

The following list has been extracted entirely from the Vestry/Parochial Church Council Minute books:

Robert Marchant & Thomas Savage	1744
Samuel Gilbert & John Pottinger	1745
David Watson & Henry Brown	1746
David Watson & John Speechley	1747
John Biggadike & John Speechley	1748
John Biggadike & William Watson	1749
John Gibbons & John Bough	1750 - 1751
Thomas Sharp & Edward Tunnard	1752 - 1753
Joseph Hempsall & Jacob Pears	1754
Joseph Hempsall & Charles Bates	1755
Edward Savage & Charles Bates	1756
John Jackson & John Pell	1757
John Jackson & Harry Bing	1758
John Jackson & Thos. Debonough	1759
Thomas Bough & Samuel Aistrup	1760
William Seels & William Johnson	1761 - 1762
William Brown & Francis Wilson	1763
William Lown & Francis Wilson	1764
Robert Collins & Robert Watson	1765
Robert Perkins & William Money	1766
John Watson & Henry Mason	1767
John West & Thomas Jackson	1768
Richard Collins & Robert Wade	1769
Robert Goulding & William Burton	1770 - 1771
John Gibbons & Thomas Moulsworth	1772
John Moslin & Thomas Pears	1773
John Moslin & John Smith	1774
John Moslin & George Hempsall	1775
William Worrell & John Buffham	1776
William Delahey & Robert Marchant	1777
William Delahey & Hugh Worrell	1778
Richard Holdenough & John Black	1779
John Harrison & Bennett Swain	1780 - 1785
John Moslin & Richard Thompson	1786 - 1787
John Smith & Charles Biggadike	1788 - 1789
Alan Congreve & John Greaves	1790

James Measure & William Lown	1791 - 1792
John Cook & James Watson	1793
Jacob Davey & Edward Palmer	1794
Jacob Davey & Joseph Greathead	1795
Jacob Davey & Thomas Cook	1796
Thomas Cook & John Worrell	1797
James Measure & Thomas Watson	1798 - 1799
Henry Winkley & John Rose	1800 - 1801
Henry Winkley & John Burton	1802
Richard Thompson & Edward Palmer	1803 - 1813
Edward Palmer & Thomas Allen	1814
Edward Palmer & William Hanson	1815 - 1816
Ashley Palmer & Sam Congreve	1817
Ashley Palmer & James Ullett	1818
Ashley Palmer & Wm. Thomas Molesworth	1819
Ashley Palmer & John West	1820
Ashley Palmer & Robert Tomlinson	1821
Ashley Palmer & William Hatar	1822 - 1824
Ashley Palmer & John Depear	1825
Ashley Palmer & Willam Wade	1826
Ashley Palmer & Joseph Fletcher	1827
Ashley Palmer & William Rogerson	1828
Ashley Palmer & William Hitherson	1829
Ashley Palmer & Stanley Blacksmith	1830
Ashley Palmer & Thomas Harrison	1831
Ashley Palmer & John Longstaff	1832
Ashley Palmer & John Molesworth	1833 - 1834
Ashley Palmer & William Hanson	1835
Thomas Harrison & William Harrison	1836
Thomas Harrison & James Watson	1837
Thomas Harrison & Arthur Harrison	1838
Thomas Harrison & John Dixon Shepherd	1839
Thomas Harrison & Thomas Ashby	1840 - 1843
Thomas Harrison & John Faulkner	1844
Thomas Ashby & John Faulkner	1845 - 1848
Thomas Ashby & John Codling	1849 - 1852
Thomas Ashby & Richard Wright	1853 - 1854
Thomas Ashby & Richard Wright	1855 - 1873
Charles Ashby & Wright Copping	1874 - 1879

James Osborne & Charles Ashby	1880
James Osborne & Richard Harrison	1881 - 1883
Richard Harrison & Carden Wright	1884 - 1894
Richard Harrison & Richard Porter	1895 - 1898
Christopher & Fred Coates	1899
J. Benton & Mr Bourne	1900 - 1903
J. Benton & William Kilham Wright	1904 - 1909
William K. Wright & Mr F. Dring	1910 - 1943

NB. In 1940 William K. Wright and F. Dring completed respectively the 35th and 30th year in the role of a Churchwarden of Whaplode St. Mary's Church.

F Dring & S Whittaker	1944 - 1963

NB. In 1963 F. Dring completed his final year as a Churchwarden – a total of 53 years. A plaque was placed in the Church, adjacent to the Chancel Arch, in recognition of his services.

S. Whittaker & B. Dring	1964 - 1974

NB. In 1974 S. Whittaker completed his 30th year as a Churchwarden.

F. Folley & L Hawkins	1975
L. Hawkins & J. Manton	1976 - 1986
L. Hawkins & R. Clare	1987 - 1988
R. Clare & Mrs V Beba	1989 - 1995
Mrs V Beba & June Crawford	1996 - 1998
June Crawford	1999 - 2001
June Crawford & Peter Dawson	2002 - 2004
June Crawford & Roy Willingham	2005 - 2008
Roy Willingham & Cyril Hearn	2009 - 2012
Roy Willingham & Clare Christie	2013 - 2016
Clare Christie & Mariola Pisarkiewicz	2017
Mariola Pisarkiewicz & Angela White	2018
Angela White	2019 - 2024

APPENDIX XVI
A record of significant books held by St. Mary's Church

The following books held by St. Mary's were identified by **R. John Lord** of the Department of Conservation, Lincoln University, in July 2003.

a) Leather faced Prayer Book, measuring 12" x 10" x 2¼" dated **1859**, with Revd. J. F. Francklin, together with Thom. Ashby and Wright Copping – Churchwardens.

b) Leather / Pig tooled Bible, measuring 12½" x 10" x 4¼" dated Easter **1921**, with an inscription on the cover - Presented by Mr A Harpham (broken locking mechanism).*[In a display cabinet in the West End]*

c) Book of Common Prayer, printed by Thos. Kelly, Paternoster Row, **1811,** measuring 9" x 5¼" x 2¼".

d) Book of Altar Services as proposed in **1928**, measuring 13" x 9¼" x 3" – Printed by Cambridge University Press, with amendments by Revd. Leslie R. Swingler – Vicar 9th June 1946, and to the nomenclature made by W.T. Armstrong – Vicar 1952.

e) Cassell's Illustrated Family Bible of **1870,** measuring 12¾ " x 9¾" x 4". Inscribed S. Ashby. *[In a display cabinet in the West End]*

f) Book of Common Prayer, printed by Clarendon Oxford Press Paternoster Row **1822,** measuring 17¼ x 10½ x 1¾ inscribed by John Negus – Churchwarden **1826.**

g) Altar Services, measuring 12" x 8" x 2", printed by HM printers **1980,** copyright. Printer Eyre and Spotteswoode, London.

h) King James I Bible 1611, printed by Oxford Press **1890,** inscribed twice by Edith Bennison, together with a Hebrew inscription.

i) Soldiers Bible, printed by Collins **1943,** incorporating a quote by Queen Victoria in 1839, authorising the issuing of Bibles to soldiers.

j) Prayer Book **1928,** printed by Oxford University Press, and inscribed by all the Vicars from 1944 (Revd. L.R. Swingler to Fr, David Carney 1991).

APPENDIX XVII

Copy of Churchwardens' Accounts for 1908-09;1909-10

Churchwardens' Accounts 1908-09: 1909-10 (fig.199).

APPENDIX XVIII

Copy of Churchwardens' and Vicar's Fund Accounts for 1911-12

Churchwardens' & Vicar's Fund Accounts, 1911-12 (fig.200).

APPENDIX XIX

Copy of Lincoln Diocesan Trust & Board of Finance 'Tribute' letter - Feb 1958

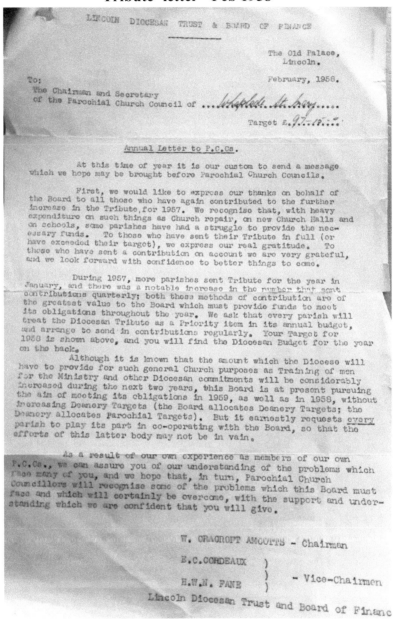

LINCOLN DIOCESAN TRUST & BOARD OF FINANCE

The Old Palace,
Lincoln.

February, 1958.

To:
The Chairman and Secretary
of the Parochial Church Council of ...Ashfield. St. Mary.....

Target £.97-15-0...

Annual Letter to P.C.Cs.

At this time of year it is our custom to send a message which we hope may be brought before Parochial Church Councils.

First, we would like to express our thanks on behalf of the Board to all those who have again contributed to the further increase in the Tribute, for 1957. We recognise that, with heavy expenditure on such things as Church repair, on new Church Halls and on schools, some parishes have had a struggle to provide the necessary funds. To those who have sent their Tribute in full (or have exceeded their target), we express our real gratitude. To those who have sent a contribution on account we are very grateful, and we look forward with confidence to better things to come.

During 1957, more parishes sent Tribute for the year in January, and there was a notable increase in the number that sent contributions quarterly; both these methods of contribution are of the greatest value to the Board which must provide funds to meet its obligations throughout the year. We ask that every parish will treat the Diocesan Tribute as a Priority item in its annual budget, and arrange to send in contributions regularly. Your Target for 1958 is shown above, and you will find the Diocesan Budget for the year on the back.

Although it is known that the amount which the Diocese will have to provide for such general Church purposes as Training of men for the Ministry and other Diocesan commitments will be considerably increased during the next two years, this Board is at present pursuing the aim of meeting its obligations in 1959, as well as in 1958, without increasing Deanery Targets (the Board allocates Deanery Targets; the Deanery allocates Parochial Targets). But it earnestly requests every parish to play its part in co-operating with the Board, so that the efforts of this latter body may not be in vain.

As a result of our own experience as members of our own P.C.Cs., we can assure you of our understanding of the problems which face many of you, and we hope that, in turn, Parochial Church Councillors will recognise some of the problems which this Board must face and which will certainly be overcome, with the support and understanding which we are confident that you will give.

W. CRACROFT AMCOTTS - Chairman

E.C.CORDEAUX)
) - Vice-Chairmen
H.W.N. FANE)

Lincoln Diocesan Trust and Board of Financ

Lincoln Diocesan Trust - Letter to St. Mary's - 1958,
showing 'tribute' target of £97-15s 0d (fig.201)

APPENDIX XX

A. Copy of St. Mary's Income & Expenditure Account 31st December 1991

Year Ending 31st December 1991

	Income				Expenditure		
2184	Collections	2095	02	1018	Fees	1069	80
2801	Envelopes	3105	15	247	Altar	146	73
2035	Fees	1680	90	299	EMEB/Gas	345	20
605	LDT & BofF	942.69		749	Magazine	380	35
380	Magazine	385	00		Quota	12932	00
2440	Spec. Collections	1525	67	1358	Sundries	2278	97
1603	Others/Donations	2448	50	19034	Repairs	4652	72
13457	Eng Herit⁹/Mary Bass	2186	44	2375	Spec. Collections	1850	05
760	Dividends	781.24		833	Srat⁹/Books	76	50
25000	FROM Dep a/c ✱	12376	14	2093	General	1862	70
				34	Choir/SS	58	09
					To Dep A/c	9000	00
	Excess Expendt.	7126	36				
		£34653·11				£ 34653·11	

£18483   C. B of F qC E Invest.   4133 @ 520.5 = £21,512·27

Current A/c			Dep A/c		
Bal br/fwd.	£7951.60		Bal br fwd.	£13284	72
Excess Exp	£7126.36		Deposit	9000	00
	£825.24			£22284	72
Bal at bank	£880.74		Withdrawn	10400.00	
less uncash chqs	55.50			11884.72	
	£825.24		Interest	1982.09	
			Bal on b/fc	£13866.81	

✱ P.O. Bank closed = £1971.14
    Don.   5.00
         £1976.14
Withdrawn P0400.00
         £12376.14

St. Mary's Accounts – 1991 - showing Diocesan 'Quota' of £12,932.00 (fig.202).

APPENDIX XX

B. Copy of Churchwardens' Statement of Accounts
April 1771

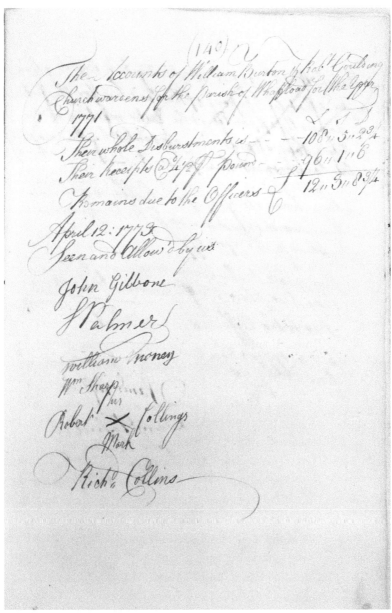

Churchwardens' Statement of Accounts – April 1771
showing an amount due to the Officers of £12. 3s. 8¾p
(fig.203).

ABBREVIATIONS AND BIBLIOGRAPHY

(JA)   **Almond, John**, *Sir Anthony Irby 1605-1681. A Lincolnshire Knight. Lincolnshire Past & Present. No. 76. 2009*

(TA)   **Allen, Thomas,** *The History of the County of Lincoln from the Earliest Period to Present Time, Vol. 1. (1833).* Digitised by Google 01.02.2007. Published by John Saunders.

(RWA)   **Ambler, R.W,** *Churches, chapels, and the parish communities of Lincolnshire, 1660-1900, (2000):* Published by The Society for Lincolnshire History and Archaeology Society. Digitised by Kahle/Austin Foundation: Internet Archive

(PFA)   **Anson, Peter** F, *Churches Their Plan and Furnishings,1948.* Published by The Bruce Publishing Co. Milwaukee. USA. Digitised by Digital Library of India: Internet Archive.

(SB)   **Baxter, Stephen** & C.P. Lewis, *Domesday Book, and the transformation of English landed society 1066-86, 26.04.2019, Publication; Anglo-Saxon England. Vol. 46.* Published by Cambridge University Press. Licensed Content Pages 343-403. License Number 5378930619156. License date. Aug. 30, 2022.

(DB)   *Domesday Book (1086)* – King William.

(FB)   **Bond, Francis**, *Screens and Galleries in English Churches, Vol 1 & 2: 1908.* Published in London. Digitised by Public Domain Mark 1.0. Internet Archive.

(TB)   **Bumpus, Thomas Francis,** *A guide to Gothic architecture, 1914*, Published by Dodd, Mead & co. New York. Digitised by MSN: University of California Libraries.

(DCAC) **Department for Constitutional Affairs Committee -** *Evidence submitted in response to Questions from the Committee re: Reform of the Office of the Lord Chancellor; Ecclesiastical Patronage Jan 2004* Published by the Department for Constitutional Affairs. Parliamentary Copyright. www.parliament.uk

(CC-MW) **Chouler, Chris, and Waters, Mary,** *The Story of Saracen's Head - A Fenland Village.* https://www.heritagesouthholland.co.uk/location/saracens-head/

(CWCC) **Carr-Calthrop, Colonel Christopher William,** *Notes on the Families of Calthorpe & Calthrop in the Counties of Norfolk, Lincolnshire and Elsewhere. 3rd Edition 1933.* Published in London for private circulation. Digitised by Google Books - Internet Archive. 2018.

(PC) **Clery, Peter**, *Green Gold- A Thousand Years of English Land, 2012.* Published by Phillimore & Co. Hampshire, England.

(WC-m) **Cole, William**, *Manuscripts [MSS]* held at the British Museum.

(FND) **Davis, Rev. F. N,** *Rotuli Roberti Grosseteste, Episcopi Lincolniensis- 1235-1253, as transcribed & edited. 1913.* Published by the Canterbury and York Society, London.

(MJE) **Elsden, Michael J.** *Aspects of Spalding Villages, 2000.* Published by Bookmark, The Crescent, Spalding. Produced by Elsam Cross & Co.

(BE) **English, Barbara**, *The Lords of Holderness. 1086-1260. A study in Feudal Society. 1979.* Published by University of Hull.

(EE-I) *English Episcopal acta, 1067-1185 VOL. I. Lincoln (1980)* Published for the British Academy by Oxford University Press. Digitised by The Arcadia Fund: Internet Archive.

(EE-IV) *English Episcopal acta, 1186-1206 VOL. IV*. Lincoln. (1980). Published for the British Academy by Oxford University Press. Digitised by The Arcadia Fund: Internet Archive.

(FNQ) *Fenland Notes & Queries-A Quarterly Antiquarian Journal for the Fenland. Vol VI-Jan 1904 – Oct 1906.* Published by Open Court Publishing. Digitised by Kahle/Austin Foundation: Internet Archive.

(WF) **Fiorentino, Wesley**, *"Guthlac of Crowland." World History Encyclopedia*. Last modified January 14, 2021. https://www.worldhistory.org/Guthlac_of_Crowland/.

(WEF) **Foster, William Edward**, *The Parish Church of Saint Mary, Whaplode in the County of Lincolnshire. (1889).* Published by Elliot & Stock, London.

(FAG) **Gasquet, Francis Aidan**, *Henry VIII and The English Monastries, VOL II, 1889.* Published by J. Hodges, London. The Catholic Std. Library. Public Domain Mark. (PDM). Digitised by the Wellcome Collection.

(AH)   **Heales, Alfred Major**, *The Archaeology of the Christian Altar in Western Europe, 1881,* Published by Roworth & Co. Ltd. London. Digitised by Google books. Oxford University Books.

(CH)   **Hearn, Cyril,** *St. Mary's Whaplode, 2006, Official Guidebook.*

(LAH)   ***Lincolnshire Archaeology and Heritage*** *Reports – Series 7, (2005) Anglo-Saxon Settlement on the Siltland of Eastern England.* Andy Crowson, Tom Lane, Kenneth Penn, and David Trimble. Published by Hodder & Stoughton, London.

(VCH)   **Victoria County History** - *A History of the County of Lincoln: Volume 2, (1906) 'Houses of Benedictine Monks: 6. The Abbey of Crowland'* Ed. William Page. Published by Victoria County History, London. British History Online.

(VCH-2)   **Victoria County History** - *A History of the County of Lincoln: Volume 2, (1906) ' Houses of Knights Hospitallers: Maltby by Louth, Skirbeck and Lincoln.'* Ed. William Page. Published by Victoria County History, London. British History Online.

(HEH)   **Hallam, H.E,** *The New Lands of Elloe. 1954 Occasional Papers. No. 6. Department of English Local History.* Published by The Broadwater Press for the Publications Board, University College, Leicester.

(HEH-SS)   **Hallam, H.E, *Settlement and Society*** *– A Study of The Early Agrarian History of South Lincolnshire. 1965.* Published by Cambridge University Press. Digitised by Kahle/Austin Foundation -Trent University Libraries. Collection. Internet Archive.

(JGH)   **Hall, John George**, *Notes of Lincolnshire being an Historical and Topographical Account of Some Villages in the Division of Lindsey. 1890.* Digitised by Duke Universities Libraries. Frank Baker Collection. Internet Archive.

(TAJ)   ***The Archaeological Journal-*** *Annual Reports- Vol. LXVI. No. 261, Second Series, Vol. XVI. No.1. March 1909.* Published by The Royal Archaeological Institute. Digitised by University of California. Internet Archive.

(HJ)   ***History Journal***, *1949-10 Vol 34. Iss 122. Re: Crossed Friars.* Published by Blackwell Publishing Ltd. Digitised by Kahle/Austin Foundation: Internet Archive.

(JJ)   **Johnson, John,** *Collection of The Laws, and Canons of the Church of England, 1850, Vol. I and II.* Published by John Henry Parker. Oxford. Digitised by University of Toronto: Internet Archive.

(AK)   **Kreider, Alan**, *English Chantries-The Road to Dissolution. 1979.* Published by Harvard University Press. London.

(CK)   **Kightly, Charles**, 'The Parish Church of St. Mary Whaplode – 'Historical Notes and A Walk round the Church' July 1991. Published by Lincoln Diocesan Tourism Consultancy.

(JL-II)   **Latham, Julia**; Douglas Edwards and Anne Daniels, *South of the Wash: Tydd St. Mary to Spalding, 1995.* Published by Battleford Books. Printed by Alpine Press .ISBN.0 9526932 0 8.

(JL)   **Leland, John,** *The Itinerary, 1506-1552 Vol. 2.* Published 1770 by Sheldonian Theatre for J Fletcher, Oxford. Digitised by The Welcome Library.

(SL)   **Letters, Samantha,** *Online Gazetteer of Markets and Fairs in England and Wales to 1516* Gazetteer of Markets and Fairs in England and Wales to 1516 (history.ac.uk) Lincolnshire / Last Update 17.11.2006. *Sub – references included therein: [N. Bennett, 'Religious Houses', in S. Bennett and N. Bennett eds, An Historical Atlas of Lincolnshire (Hull, 1993), p. 48; P. Sawyer, 'Anglo-Saxon Lincolnshire', History of Lincolnshire iii (Lincoln, 1998), p.145). Market town c.1600 (Everitt, p. 474). Fair 1587, 10 Aug (Harrison, p. 395)].*

(KM)   **Major, Kathleen,** MA., B.Litt., F.S.A. *The Story of Gedney Parish Church. 1945.* Published by The British publishing Company Limited. Gloucester. https://www.heritagesouthholland.co.uk/wp-content/uploads/2018/12/Story-of-Gedney-Church-1-2.pdf

(KM2)   **Major, Kathleen**, MA., B.Litt., F.S.A. *The D'Oyrys of South Lincolnshire, Norfolk, and Holderness. 1130-1275. 1984.* Published Privately. K. Major. Lincoln.

(KM-AS3)   **Major, Kathleen**, MA., B.Litt., F.S.A. *An Unknown House of Crutched Friars at Whaplode.* Reprinted from the Associated Architectural and Archaeological Societies Reports and Papers, VOL. 41. Pt. II. 1933, pp.149-154.

(KM-AS4)   **Major, Kathleen**, MA., B.Litt., F.S.A. *Conan Son of Ellis, an Early Inhabitant of Holbeach.* Reprinted from the Associated Architectural and Archaeological Societies Reports and Papers, VOL. 42. Pt. I. 1934. pp.1-28.

(AM)   **Mee, Arthur**, *Lincolnshire, A County of Infinite Charm – The King's County. 1949.* Published by Hodder & Stoughton.

(SHM)   **Miller, Samuel Henry**, *The Handbook to the Fenland, 1890.* Published by Simpkin, Marshall & Hamilton, Kent: London. Digitised by University of California. Internet Archive.

(TNM)   **Morton, T.N.**, *Lincolnshire Churches. An Account of The Churches in the Division of Holland, in the County of Lincoln. 1843.* Printed and published by T.N. Morton

(AALN)   ***The Architectural and Archaeological Societies of the counties of Lincoln and Northampton*** *– Annual Reports and Papers VOL 11 1871-1872.* Published by: Lincoln History. Digitised by Wellesley College Library. Contributor: Wellesley College Library. Google Books-Internet Archive.

(AALN2)   ***The Architectural and Archaeological Societies of the counties of Lincoln and Northampton*** *– Annual Reports and Papers VOL 20 1889-1890.* Published by: Lincoln History. Digitised by Wellesley College Library. Contributor: Wellesley College Library – Google Books –Internet Archive.

(TDN)   *'Testa de Neville' –"The Book of Fees" Pt. I. AD 1198-1242.* Great Britain Public Record Office. 1st published 1921. University of Michigan. Digitised by Google books.

(TDN2)   *'Testa de Neville' – "The Book of Fees" Pt.2. AD 1242-1293.* Great Britain Public Record Office.1st published 1923. Family History Library. Digitised by Family Search International.

(TN)   **North, Thomas**, *The Church Bells of the County and City of Lincoln, 1882.* Published by Samuel Clarke, Leicester.

(JBO)   **O'Connell, J.B**, *Church Building and Furnishing – The Church's Way – A study in Liturgical Law. 1955.* Published by University of Notre Dame Press. Digitised by The Library of Congress. Internet Archive.

(GO)   **Oliver, Geo.** *A Letter to the Gentleman's Magazine:1829-12 Vol. 99.* Published by Open Court Publishing Co. Digitised by Kahle/Austin Foundation: Internet Archive.

(DMO)   **Owen, Dorothy M,** *Church, and Society in Medieval Lincolnshire-Vol. 5. (1971).* Published by History of

Lincolnshire Committee. Digitised by Kahle/Austin Foundation: Internet Archive.

(NP) **Pevsner, N., and Harris, J (rev. N. Antram), 1989** *The Buildings of England, Lincolnshire. (2nd Edition),* Published by Harmondsworth.

(DP) **Power, Daniel,** *The Norman Frontier in the Twelfth and early Thirteenth Centuries. 2004.* Cambridge Studies in Medieval Life and Thought. Published by Cambridge University Press.

(WP) **Page, William, F.S.A.** *The Victoria History of the County of Lincoln. 1906.* Published by James Street, Haymarket. London. Cornell University Library. Digitised by Cornell University. Internet Archive.

(WFR) **Rawnsley, Willingham Franklin** & Alexander F. Farquharson. *Highways and Byways in Lincolnshire (1914)* Published by London, Macmillan. Digitised by University of Toronto: Internet Archive.

(CPR-A) *Calendar of entries in the Papal Registers relating to Great Britain and Ireland: Papal Letters Alexander VI. 1431-1503. Part I.* Published in 1994 by The Irish Manuscripts Commission. Digitised by Kahle/Austin Foundation: Internet archive

(CPR) *Calendar of entries in the Papal Registers relating to Great Britain and Ireland: Papal Letters 1198-1304.* Published in 1893 by Great Britain Public Record Office. London. Collection: Americana – University of Michigan. Digitised by Google.

(CPR2) *Calendar of entries in the Papal Registers relating to Great Britain and Ireland: Papal Letters 1362-1404.* Published in 1893 by Great Britain Public Record Office. London. Collection: Americana – University of Michigan. Digitised by Google.

(TQR) *The Quarterly Review, July – Oct 1891: Vol. 173, Lincolnshire, p,100-130.* Published by John Murray, London. 1892. Digitised by Kahle/Austin Foundation: Internet Archive.

(PHS) **Sawyer, P.H.** *Anglo-Saxon Lincolnshire (1998).* Published by History of Lincolnshire Committee for the Society of Lincolnshire History and Archaeology. Digitised by Kahle/Austin: Internet Archive.

(GS)   **Sir Gilbert Scott,** *"Visit to St. Mary's," 1856.*

(ES)   **Sharpe, Edmund,** *An Account of the Churches visited during the Lincoln Excursion of the Architectural Association, 1870:* Published by Spon, Charing Cross.

(ES-m)   **Sharpe, Edmund,** *The Mouldings of the Six Periods of British Architecture* London. Digitised by Getty Research Institute: Internet Archive.

(APS)   **Powell-Smith, Anna**, *Open Domesday, First on-line copy of Domesday book - 2011.* Licence: CC By-SA 4.0 Deed: Attribution-ShareAlike 4.0 International.
          Home | Domesday Book (opendomesday.org)
          Data compilation by Professor J.J.N. Palmer and team.

(AAS)   ***Associated Architectural Societies.*** *(various) Reports and Papers 1889-1890.* Digitised by Wellesley College Library. Published by Lincoln. Internet Archive.

(JS)   **Stokes, James,** *Lincolnshire. 2009.* Published by Toronto Press. CRSS Library. Digitised by University of Toronto

(EDS)   **Storey, Edward**, *In Fen Country Heaven, 1997*: Published by Robert Hale & Co.

(WS)   **Stukeley, William, M.D.** *Itinerary: 2nd Edition 1776:*

(WS2)   **Stukeley, William, M.D.** *An Account of Richard of Cirencester - Monk of Westminster, and of his work: Read at the Antiquarian Society March 18, 1756.* Published by Richard Hett. London. 1757.Internet Archive.

(EMS)   **Sympson, E. Mansel,** *"On Lincolnshire Rood-Screens and Lofts," 1890:* A paper presented to the AALN in June 1890.

(EMS2)   **Sympson, E. Mansel,** *"Memorials of Old Lincolnshire" 1911.* Published by George Allen & Sons, Rathbone Place, London. Collection: Robarts – University of Toronto. Digitised by MSN. Internet Archive.

(WHW)   **Wheeler, William Henry,** *A History of the Fens in South Lincolnshire (1990).* Published by Paul Watkins, Stamford. Digitised by Kahle/Austin Foundation: Internet Archive.

Other acknowledgments (not included in above), or not already included within the text, and those that were embedded within Cyril Hearn's St. Mary's Church, Whaplode - Official Guidebook: 2006, the referred text of which has been reproduced herein.

Cecil Adkins, (2001*). 'The Double Reed' Vol. 24. No. 3.* Denton, Texas. USA.

J.W. Belsham, (2002). 'President Spalding Gentlemen's Society,' Spalding. Lincolnshire.

Fr. D. Carney, (2002). Vicar of St. Mary's Whaplode.

R. Clare, (2001/02). Former Headmaster St. Mary's Junior School, Whaplode, Lincolnshire.

R. John Lord, Chris Robinson, Elizabeth Welfare, (2004/05), Department of Conservation, Lincoln University.

Dr. Aleksandra McClain, (2005/06), Department of Archaeology, York University.

June Crawford, (2011) 'Whaplode- Interesting Facts and Stories'.

John H.P. Wright, (2023) Landowner, and former Farmer.

NOTES TO PAGES

1.   HEH, pp. 3-5
2.   WS2, pp. 25,28
3.   T.A. pp.6-7. Allen provides an insight into the origins of the 'Car-Dyke' and its purpose. The discussion centres on features that could be interpreted as boundaries all-round the Fens which are either of Roman date or natural. Archaeological remains suggest that in some parts at least it was used by cargo-carrying vessels, whilst the finding of Roman colonisation remains across the area lends weight to the alternative reason of that being a means of creating more productive farmland through improved drainage and flood control. The fact that both these interpretations could be correct is supported by the suggestion proffered by *S. Macaulay & T Reynolds: Car Dyke a Roman canal at Waterbeach (1994)* that the effect of both deliberate recuts in the late Roman period to improve land drainage, and natural flows of surface water along some sections of the route resulted in the change of use from transport to agricultural improvement.
4.   WS2, p.26-27. Stukeley provides his assessment of the position:
     "*The Romans, when they made the artificial canal, the Carsdike, from Peterborough along the edge of the Lincolnshire fens, they introduced it into the river at Witham, three miles below Lincoln. The purpose of this artificial cut was to convey corn in boats, from the southern parts of England, to the northern Praetentura's* {Roman Fortress Encampments} *in Scotland; for the maintenance of the forces kept there. therefore, the canal entering the Witham passed through Lincoln, and then was continued by another artificial cut called the Fossdike.*" Thereafter, he considers the Roman usage of a pattern of such waterways being northern transport links via the River Trent, the Humber, and the Ouse up to York, "*by the force of the tide*" hence the reason for the city being built there.
5.   T.N. pp. 521-522. North highlights that the tradition probably stems from the fact that Henry Penn, the Peterborough Bellfounder, allegedly, in the early 18th century constructed a canal known as "Bell-Dyke" from the back of his foundry, of sufficient size to carry large boats into the river with which it connected.
6.   PHS, p.44
7.   EDS, p.132
8.   Joan Blaeu (1596-1673). The Blaeu workshop was based in

Amsterdam and produced the most magnificent atlases and maps of the period, the time in which the Netherlands was experiencing its 'Golden Age' in art, science, and commerce. A true perfectionist, Blaeu used only the best engravers, printers, and colourists and only the finest materials, including paper, to produce his atlases. In 1645 he published a county atlas of England & Wales as part of his *'Theatre Orbis Terrarum'* series. Each map epitomised the craftsmanship and artistry of the Blaeu workshop being finely detailed with ornate cartouches, cherubs, heraldic shields, and calligraphy. Later in 1662, the maps reappeared in volume five of his *'Atlas Maior'* which is perhaps the finest cartographic work ever produced in the history of map making. Extracts from *Welland Antique Maps & Prints – Richard and Amber Welland - www.wellandantiquemaps.co.uk.*

9.   WHW, p.100-Chapter IV- South Holland.
10.   TA, p.330
11.   WFR, pp. 466-467
12.   TA, pp. 331
      TA clearly implies that there was a 'wooden' Whaplode pre-Norman church which was the forerunner to a 'stone' one, and in so doing he also alludes to the one in Spalding, which relates the chapel of St. Mary which was ultimately combined with the chapel of St. Nicholas, and then evolved into the Abbey of Crowland. It is possible that he may have confused one with the other, but nevertheless, that there could still have been a Saxon pre-conquest church in Whaplode remains a possibility – not least because this is supported by the existence of Saxon settlements in the area, and the burial stonework found in and around Whaplode St Mary's (see Part **Two: 1.** Early Monastic Estates and St. Mary's Anglo-Saxon Heritage, and Appendix IV).
13.   WF, "Guthlac of Crowland"
14.   WEF, p.3
15.   WEF, p.4
16.   PHS, pp.28-30: pp.134-136
17.   Ibid, 16
18.   LAH, pp.264-88
19.   Ibid, 18
20.   SB, pp.343-403 (p.24 of the original 'Paper')
21.   PC, p.9
22.   TDN2, p.650
23.   TDN2, p.1007
24.   WS, p.25

25. APS, Search – Person; Guy of Craon.
26. KM, p.10
27. HEH-SS, p.25
28. WP, p.108
29. KM2, p.39
30. DMO, p.4
31. EE-I, p.68
32. EE-I, p.187
33. EE-IV, pp.34-35
34. CC-MW, pp.1-4
35. DMO, pp.10-12
36. VCH-2, pp.209-210
37. DMO, p.12
38. SL, County- Lincolnshire; Town-Whaplode
39. Ibid, 37
40. DMO, p.85
41. KM-AS3, p.1
42. HJ, pp.211.219
43. FND, pp.25-26
44. WEF, p.8. Within his translation of Grosseteste, Foster transcribes Robert de Ory, inadvertently, as Robert de Cry.
45. WEF, pp.12-15
46. WEF, pp.15-16
47 CWCC, pp.10 & 30-31
Sir William Calthorpe (a descendant Abbot Godric II of Croyland who shortly after the Norman Conquest was appointed by King William as Steward for all the Royal Manors in the Eastern Counties, such as Beeston, Halvergate, Henlington, Moulton, and others) was Lord of Gedney in 1321. He was the son of Sir Walter de Calthorpe of Burnham, who had married Ela de Stanhoe, heiress to the manor of Stanhoe from her father Sir Henry de Stanhoe by marriage to Ela de Bellomont. Ela was the daughter, and co-heir of Sir William Bellomont and Ela de Strange. Ela de Strange was the second daughter of Sir Ralph de Stange, Lord of Stanhoe, whose other co-heir Maud (Matilda) had married Sir Fulk III d'Oyry ('Fulso de Oiry') Lord of Gedney, Lincolnshire, in the early 13th century.
48 SL, County-Lincolnshire; Town-Crowland
49. CPR, p.196
50. CPR2, p.33
51. DMO, pp.74-75
52. JL-II, p.10
53. DMO, Appendix I, p.143

54. TA, p.332
55. WEF, p.21
56. Maurice Johnson Esq., F.A.A. Barrister-at-Law, (b.19.06.1688 - d. 06.02.1755) of Ayscoughfee Hall was the Deputy Recorder of Stamford, and Founder of The Spalding Gentlemen's Society (1710 – 1770). He started the Society in 1710 to conserve Spalding's parish and grammar school libraries and to communicate learned matters in the style of the 'coffee- house' conversations he had enjoyed in London while reading for the Bar. He recorded that *"This Society was instituted for supporting mutual Benevolence, raising, and preserving and rendring of general Use a Publick Lending Library pursuant to the statute of the 7th of Queen Anne chapt. 14th. And the Improvement of the Members in All Arts and Sciences."* He was also the benefactor of the present-day Chapel of St James, Moulton Chapel. It is reported that one Sunday in 1722 he went riding through the village and noticing a number of men congregated together in idle chat, he enquired of them why they were not at church, to which they replied that their church was four miles off and that was too far to go. He then decided to build them a chapel, which he did, and endowed it with a rent charge of £16 per year upon his estate. [MJE, p,155].
57. WEF, p.111
58. WEF, pp.109-111
59. DMO, pp.135-136
60. AK, pp.24-25
61. CPR, p.515
62. CPR-A, p.447
63. VCH, pp.105-118
64. Ibid, 63
65. Ibid, 63
66. Ibid, 63
67. WEF, pp.17-20
68. WEF, pp.90-107
69. Ibid, 56
70. The extracts are taken from a copy of Revd. John Rhodes public statement of October 1900 - *"The Tithe Payers of Whaplode versus (The Johnson Foundation) Uppingham School"* - courtesy of The Spalding Gentlemen's Society.
71. A Royal Peculiar is a church that belongs directly to the monarch and not any diocese and does not come under the jurisdiction of a bishop. The concept originated in Anglo-Saxon times and developed as a result of the relationship between the Norman and Plantagenet Kings

and the English church. Henry VIII retained Royal Peculiars following the Reformation: The Ecclesiastical Licences Act of 1533, as confirmed by the Act of Supremacy of 1559, transferred to the Sovereign the jurisdiction which had previously been exercised by the Pope. The Ecclesiastical Household is administered in the Lord Chamberlain's Office at Buckingham Palace. *[Courtesy of the Association of English Cathedrals, London].*

72.   DCAC paper on Ecclesiastical Patronage
73.   Ibid, 72
74.   JS, p.452
75.   DMO, p.119
76.   TN, pp.331-332
77.   TN, pp.264,265,268,271,273
78.   RWA, p.65
79.   Ibid, 78
80.   RWA, p.187
81.   RWA, p.197
82.   A muffle is simply a pad of resilient material attached to the ball of the clapper in such a such a way that the impact of the clapper against the sound bow is greatly reduced. This has the effect that, instead of hearing the 'strike-note' of the bell, all that is heard is the 'hum note' instead. Muffles are traditionally made of leather, which has always been a widely available material. Leather is easily worked with, and it will survive repeated impacts that it receives and provides a suitable degree of damping to make an appropriate sound.
83.   The Lincolnshire Chronicle - 13th October 1928. The full article is reproduced in a frame on the South wall of the Chancel, alongside the painting.
84.   TAJ, p.390 (See fig.68 – Part one)

PART TWO

85.   PHS, p.144
86.   PHS, pp.145-147
87.   PHS, p.148
88.   PHS, p.165
89.   PHS, pp.158-159
90.   Ibid, 89
91.   WEF, p.7
92.   TNM, p.528
93.   JBO, p.145
94.   JJ, p.195-Vol.2 *"The typical early Christian altar consisted of mensa, or a table formed of a broad, rather thick wooden plank, resting on*

four legs, which was in general use during the first four or five centuries. However, in AD 517 the Council of Epone, in France, decreed that no altar be consecrated unless it was made of stone (AD 517: Canon No. 26), and thereafter such stone mensas began to be used. This decree was reinforced in 1071 by Archbishop Lefranc under his 5th Canon."

95.   PFA, p.65: "*About the thirteenth century the custom arose of marking four crosses on the upper surface of the mensa where the anointing with the holy oils was made at the consecration. Since the publication of the Roman Pontifical of 1597 five incised or painted crosses on the mensa are obligatory.*"

96.   FAG, pp.41-43: "*By the feast of St. Michael, 1536, or in six months from the passing of the dissolution, John Freeman, the royal receiver for the district, was able to account for a large sum to the treasurer of the court of augmentation. His receipts from sales of the religious houses, including buildings, furniture, lead, bells, with stocks and moveables of all kinds, had reached a high total of £7,484 0s. 4¾d, or, in round figures, some £75,000 of our present money* {As expressed by FAG in 1890} *to which a further sum of nearly £200 was to be added for* "*pictures, clocks,*" *and other precious articles sold subsequently. Altogether, with rents and other items of receipts, John Freeman admitted having obtained for the king in the first six months no less a sum than £8,756 11s 9¾d* {the relative purchasing power at 2023 prices – over £6 million} *of which about one fourth had been paid away in the process of dissolution.*"

97.   FAG, pp.435-436

98.   AH, p.8

99.   AH, p.22

100.   AH, p.23

101.   JJ, p.214: Primarily, under Ecgbriht AD 740, Canon 139 (141). (Previously dealt with under Pope Vigilious (AD 538-555). Also see AH, p.21 "*An altar is canonically held to be desecrated by the removal of the mensa or its grave fracture, or by a change of form of the altar; and a desecration of the high altar had the effect of desecrating the church, so that both needed a reconsecration, though in some cases, as where the fracture was slight, the minor right reconciliation would suffice.(Ecgbriht AD 740). In a modern case decided by Dr. Lushington, he said: 'If the altar (of the church) has been taken down,*

there must be a reconsecration' (ref: Notes of Cases I, p.368. In the Consistory Court of London)."

102. CH, 2016. The naming of Moulton Seas End and Surfleet Seas End provides an indication of just how close the sea encroached on this area, and in the past, a tidal river came as far as the Whaplode Church. Anecdotal evidence of this in more recent times was discovered when additional properties were being built in the Cross Street area of Whaplode; the builders omitted to factor in that just beneath the surface would be found the contained River Whaplode. As they broke though the casing, the pressure of the river caused a serious flood for several of the properties.

103. FNQ, p. 377, as follows: Boston Church and Steeple in Lincolnshire – written on the fly-leaf on old book in the possession of a Mr C.J. Ridge *"Anno 1309 in the 3rd year of Edward II. On Monday after Psalm Sunday in the same year. The Miners began to break ground for the foundation of Boston Steeple continuing till Midsumer following at which time they were deeper than the Haven by 5 foot, and there they found a bed of stone, upon a Spring of Sand, and laid upon a bed of Clay, whose thickness could not have been known. The Altitude of the Steeple, and length of the Church are equal, each 94 yards, the Steps of the Steeple are 365, Windows 52, Pillars 12, as equal to the dayes, weekes, and months in the year." "Collected by Matt Humberston. Taken 10th April 1699."*

104. WEF, p.27

105. GS, Visit to St. Mary's

106. The provenance of the 'Romanesque' style of architecture is derived from the development of the craft of stonemasonry in the 'Lombardian' region of Northern Italy.

One such 'master' craftsman was St. Guillaume (William) de Volpiano, Abbot of St. Benigne in Dijon – (b. 962 – d. 1031). He was the fourth son of Robert, Count of Volpiano. William was an ardent proponent of the Cluniac reform (focused on restoring the traditional life in the monasteries, with the encouragement of art, and caring for the poor) and was ordained in 990, and became a venerated Italian monastic reformer and architect, who founded (1001-1003) the Abbey of Fruttuaria nr Volpiano in the Piedmont, Italy, to the west of the Lombardy region, together with his uncle Count Arduim of Ivrea. He subsequently went to France where he built a monastery, replacing the previous basilica, to St. Benigne in Dijon, from his own design for which he consulted many people from his own country; men of letters; masters of diverse arts, and others full of scientific knowledge. Amongst whom were the Comacine masters *(magistri comacini),* who, being united into a guild, or perhaps several guilds, were early medieval Lombard stonemasons working in this region of excellent building stone, who gave to Lombardy its pre-eminence in such craft. Having built the monastery of St. Benigne, William was invited by Richard II, Duke of Normandy, to complete similar works in that region of France, and as a result he went on to promote the Romanesque architecture in the region, founding, and erecting a number of new monasteries, including Bernay, Mont Saint-Michel and the reconstruction of the Abbey of Saint Germain-des-Prés, as well as repairing and transforming old buildings. [Compiled from a variety of Architectural/Historical sources on the Romanesque style of Architecture, and the life of Guillaume (William) Volpiano, (including with reference to pp. 57, 58, 65, 84-5, 240, 279, 286, *"Carolingian and Romanesque Architecture, 200 - 1200" Kenneth John Conant, 1959,* published by Penguin Books, Internet Archive, and *"William Volpiano in Normandy - Current Position" Véronique Gazeau, 2002.* http://journals.openedition.org/tabularia/1756)].

Such was the success of the stone building in Normandy, that William the Conqueror, following his conquest of England, brought these same principles of consecration and construction with him. These included the predominant rounded arches, so typical of the early Norman built Cathedrals and churches in England, which can now be properly attributed to the Lombard architects of Northern Italy. They also included a degree of pointed arches too, but since these are now more readily attributed to the Gothic style, which succeeded the early Norman period in England, we can readily identify the interior bays and support pillars of St. Mary's to the Lombard or 'Romanesque' style.

107. AALN, pp.252-253
108. TQR, p.112
109. WEF, p.30
110. AALN – Lincoln Diocesan Architectural Society, p.211
111. Ibid, 106
112. AALN, p.244
113. Ibid, 107 (Includes ref ES, pp.95-96)
114. WEF, p.27
115. CK, "A walk around the Church"-p.2

116. WEF, p.37
117. ES-m, pp.54-55
118. Ibid, 115
119. Ibid, 116
120. WEF, p.41
121. EMS2, p.104 refers to W.E. Foster's article "Some South Lincolnshire Churches.
122. WEF, p.39
123. Ibid, 104. WEF, p.40
124. TB, p.183
125. SHM, p.157
126. Ibid, 121
127. Ibid, 121
128. WEF, p.40
129. CH.2016.

During a visit to the Cathedral of Santiago de Compostela, in Galicia, northwestern Spain, we were introduced into the real world of the usage of incense, which although not quite as common in today's churches as it was in the Middle Ages, had the specific purpose of fumigating the church against the foul smells emanating from the masses of pilgrims. Here they have the largest incense burner known in the world, weighing 80kg and measuring 1.60m in height. It forms a huge cradle measuring 5 foot high and is hauled by a group of 8 men, which once it is loaded with charcoal and incense to produce the necessary clouds of smoke, is then swung throughout the transept from south to north and back. It is hauled up into the centre of the Nave in front of the Chancel to a height of around 40 feet it is then swung in a pendulum fashion from transept to transept. Once it is in operation, there are clear warnings to remain away from the area of the arc as there is the danger of being struck by the heavy cradle (it was said that some unfortunate who didn't heed the warning was struck dead by the action).

The day we were in the Cathedral was a celebration for world Catholic Youth and they were holding a special service which required the incense burner. A dome above the crossing contains the pulley mechanism to swing the Botafumeiro, which is a famous thurible found in this church. This thurible was created by the goldsmith José Losada in 1851. The Santiago de Compostela Botafumeiro is normally on exhibition in the library of the cathedral, but during certain important religious high days it is attached to the pulley mechanism, filled with 40 kg of charcoal and incense. In the Jubilee Years, whenever St James's Day falls on a Sunday, the Botafumeiro is also attached for all the pilgrim's mass. Eight red-robed *tiraboleiros* pull the ropes and bring it into a swinging motion almost to the roof of the transept, reaching speeds of 60 km/h and dispensing thick clouds of incense.

130. EMS, AALN2,p.186
131. TAJ, p.391
132. WEF, p.43
133. RWA, p.65
134. Ibid, 132
135. EMS, AALN2,p.191
136. As per St Edith's Church, Coates (wasleys.org.uk)
137. Ibid, 132
138. WEF, p.47
139. WEF, pp.45-47
140. The inscription attributed by Foster, as per Colonel Holles' 1655 Manuscript, reads '*Johes de Quaplod fecit fieras fenestras in honorem beatae Mariae et beati Edmundi Martyris'*. An interesting alternative translation could suggest that the window was made simply in honour of '*blessed Mary and the blessed Edmund the Martyr.*' Edmund the Martyr, King of East Anglia in the 9th Century, was the first Patron Saint of England - prior to Edward III founding a new order of chivalry in 1348 - "The Most Noble Order of The Garter". Whereupon Edward III placed St. George as Patron of the Order, and also declared him as the Patron Saint of England, thereby replacing St. Edmund.
141. WEF, p.42
142. It is just possible that John de Quaplod – was simply a name 'handle' and that his full name was John Thorpe de Quaplod – whose mother was a Margaret Quappladde - heiress of a John Quappladde (allegedly from Sussex, but whose ancestors, it is surmised, came from Lincolnshire viz – Whaplode). If this is the case, then John de Quaplod's' s coat of arms / insignia was to be merged with that of the 'Bacon' family, following the subsequent marriage of his daughter Margery to John Bacon. Since which this branch of the Bacon family [which are lineally descended from Grimbaldus, a leader of William the Conqueror's army] quarter the arms of Quaplod with their own, viz, *Barrs of six, or and azure and Bend Gules.* However, given that there is no definitive date associated with the record of these insignia, etc, it is also possible that this John de Quaplod is either the father of,

or indeed **the** John de Quappladde,(b. circa 1340), the ancestor of this family, later to live in Sussex. [Courtesy of *Bacon Family Profile - Geni & Wikitree – and Bacon Family Genealogical sources*].

143. Extract from "Boston Spalding Free Press - 8th June 1920 recording the occasion: *"It is proposed to place a stained-glass window in Whaplode Church, as a memorial to those men of the place who laid down their lives in the Great War. Designs submitted by Mr. Temple Moore in connection therewith have been approved by the Committee. It is proposed to rebuild the stonework in what is believed to be in accordance with the original plans of the church, and at the bottom the names of the fallen heroes will be carved in the stone. Judging from the designs the memorial promises to be beautiful in character, and a fitting way of perpetuating the memory of those gallant lads who made the great sacrifice in defence of their country and friends. Subscription lists for the fund are now open and it is to be hoped that the fund will meet with the success it richly deserves."*

144. FB, p.137
145. Ibid, 135
146. EMS, AALN, p.206
147. FB, p.135
148. Ibid, 138
149. Ibid, 138
150. Ibid, 138
151. WEF, p.45
152. DMO, p.12
153. *The Family links between Welby, Walpole, Haultoft, Apreece and Irby are as follows:*

Audrey **Welby** (A great, great, granddaughter of Thomas **Welby** (1458-1498) was the brother of Adlard **Welby**, who married Cassandra **Apreece.** Audrey **Welby** married Thomas **Walpole,** whose father, Henry Walpole, had married Margaret **Haultoft.** (Her father was Gilbert Haultoft [Holtofte] – Baron of the Exchequer in England). Subsequently, Anthony **Irby,** MP (1547-1625) married Alice **Welby,** who was also a great, great, granddaughter of Thomas **Welby.**

154. JGH, pp.84-86
155. WEF, pp.57-58
156. AM, p.415

BV - #0081 - 300524 - C160 - 234/156/15 - PB - 9781804678077 - Matt Lamination